THE MORAL WITNESS

CORPUS

The Humanities in Politics and Law

JURIS

Series editor: Elizabeth S. Anker, Cornell University

CORPUS JURIS: THE HUMANITIES IN POLITICS AND LAW PUBLISHES BOOKS AT THE INTERSECTIONS BETWEEN LAW, POLITICS, AND THE HUMANITIES—INCLUDING HISTORY, LITERARY CRITICISM, ANTHROPOLOGY, PHILOSOPHY, RELIGIOUS STUDIES, AND POLITICAL THEORY. BOOKS IN THIS SERIES TACKLE NEW OR UNDERANALYZED ISSUES IN POLITICS AND LAW AND DEVELOP INNOVATIVE METHODS TO UNDERTAKE THOSE INQUIRIES. THE GOAL OF THE SERIES IS TO MULTIPLY THE INTERDISCIPLINARY JUNCTURES AND CONVERSATIONS THAT SHAPE THE STUDY OF LAW.

THE MORAL WITNESS

WITNESS

Trials and Testimony
after Genocide

Carolyn J. Dean

CORNELL UNIVERSITY PRESS   ITHACA AND LONDON

First published 2019 by Cornell University Press

Library of Congress Cataloging-in-Publication Data

Names: Dean, Carolyn J. (Carolyn Janice), 1960– author.
Title: The moral witness : trials and testimony after genocide / Carolyn J. Dean.
Description: Ithaca [New York] : Cornell University Press, 2019. | Series: Corpus juris : the humanities in politics and law | Includes bibliographical references and index.
Identifiers: LCCN 2018042975 (print) | LCCN 2018047925 (ebook) | ISBN 9781501735080 (e-book pdf) | ISBN 9781501735097 (e-book epub/mobi) | ISBN 9781501735066 | ISBN 9781501735066 (cloth) | ISBN 9781501735073 (pbk.)

Subjects: LCSH: Genocide—Historiography. | Genocide—Moral and ethical aspects. | Witnesses. | Genocide survivors. | Trials (Genocide)
Classification: LCC HV6322.7 (ebook) | LCC HV6322.7 .D425 2019 (print) | DDC 345/.0251—dc23
LC record available at https://lccn.loc.gov/2018042975

CONTENTS

ILLUSTRATIONS

THE MORAL WITNESS

INTRODUCTION

If the Greeks invented tragedy, the Romans the epistle, and the Renaissance
the sonnet, our generation invented a new literature, that of testimony. We
have all been witnesses and we all feel we have to bear testimony for the
future.

—Elie Wiesel, *The Holocaust as Literary Inspiration* (1977)

By the end of the twentieth century, the "witness to genocide" had become a
pervasive icon of suffering humanity. The term initially referred to the survivors
of the Holocaust of European Jewry, but is now also the title of books, conferences, articles, and museum events about the Cambodian, Rwandan, and other
genocides. "Bearing witness to genocide" has become an increasingly common
expression of social solidarity and a protest against the pain of others, character-
izing activities as diverse as the work of journalists covering ethnic cleansing in
Bosnia and the visits of spectators to exhibits on genocidal violence.[1] How did
the witness to genocide become a central trope of contemporary moral culture?

    Like witnesses from earlier periods, including abolitionists fighting slavery, Jews
condemning pogroms, and humanitarians denouncing mass atrocities in the nineteenth and early twentieth centuries, the witness to genocide is a "moral witness" for
whom false testimony is a sacrilege.[2] Over the last two hundred years, moral witnesses

---

    1. For a small sample (the list could go on): Roy Gutman, *A Witness to Genocide* (New York: Mac-
millan, 1993); Richard A. Salem, ed., *Witness to Genocide: The Children of Rwanda; Drawings by Child
Survivors of the Rwandan Genocide of 1994*, with a foreword by Hillary Rodham Clinton (New York:
Friendship Press, National Council of Churches in the USA, 2000); "Bearing Witness to Genocide and
the Plight of the Minorities in Iraq" (panel presented by NGO leaders in Washington, DC, April 16,
2016); "Never Too Late for Justice: A Bearing Witness Trip to Cambodia," United States Holocaust
Memorial Museum, accessed May 20, 2017, https://www.ushmm.org/confront-genocide/about/
initiatives/bearing-witness-trips/never-too-late-for-justice-a-bearing-witness-trip-to-cambodia. The
expression "bearing witness" is used for the same purposes in Spanish, Italian, French, and German.
    2. The prohibition against false witness is the ninth commandment of the Hebrew Bible. The
Byzantine Greek word for martyr (*martys*) meant "witness," and described Christians who chose to
die for their beliefs. On witnessing in both the Christian and Jewish traditions in the fourth century,

embodied the Western imagination of collective violence and determined whose injuries should compel our attention, whose testimony was most credible, and whose deaths
we should grieve.[3] In the nineteenth and early twentieth centuries, they were dismayed
spectators more often than victims because distance afforded them credibility that victims' accounts did not possess.[4] Witnesses sympathized with the victims of slavery, war,
and humanitarian disasters, testified on their behalf, and spoke movingly about their
plight. They were sometimes aligned with radical political movements and sometimes
not. They appealed to audiences' sympathy for suffering humanity, on whose behalf
publics were presumed to feel aggrieved and wish to act.

The witness to genocide emerged in the interwar period (1919–39) and made
the crime of genocide legible. He or she represented the authority of the victim's experience and marked a significant shift in the Western imagination of
mass violence away from unspeakable "outrages" committed regrettably against
innocents to "genocide" perpetrated against peoples whose persecution endowed
them with moral authority. This moral witness tracks the history of how Western
Europeans and North Americans' understanding of genocide changed over time,
from an unconscionable, reparable, and at worst regrettable form of barbarism
to a permanent feature of modern political formations. Witnesses to genocide
now warn of impending catastrophe if no action is taken by those in a position to
prevent mass murder. As genocide has become a seemingly intractable phenomenon, witnesses' authority has, paradoxically, waned, and their warnings often
encounter indifferent audiences who need convincing.[5]

---

see Daniel Boyarin, *Dying for God: Martyrdom and the Making of Christianity and Judaism* (Stanford,
CA: Stanford University Press, 1999). For an analysis of links between witnessing and the rhetoric of
sympathy, see Ian Baucom, *Specters of the Atlantic: Finance Capital, Slavery, and the Philosophy of History* (Durham, NC: Duke University Press, 2005), 300. On abolitionism and the question of audience,
see Dwight A. McBride, *Impossible Witnesses: Truth, Abolitionism, and Slave Testimony* (New York:
NYU Press, 2001), 85–172. On Jewish and Armenian testimonials during the Great War and interwar
period, see Alexandra Garbarini, "Document Volumes and the Status of Victim Testimony in the Era
of the First World War and Its Aftermath," *Études arméniennes contemporaines*, no. 5 (2015): 113–36.
On the literature of denunciation and the emergence of "humanitarian rights" (which focused on
collectives rather than individuals) in the interwar period, see Bruno Cabanes, *The Great War and the
Origins of Humanitarianism* (Cambridge: Cambridge University Press, 2014).

   3. Avishai Margalit, *The Ethics of Memory* (Cambridge, MA: Harvard University Press, 2002),
163–68, used the term "moral witness" in reference to the Holocaust survivor.

   4. On this point, see Garbarini, "Document Volumes," 114–16; Robert Burroughs, *African Testimony in the Movement for Congo Reform: The Burden of Proof* (New York: Routledge, 2019); Jeremy
Silvester and Jan-Bart Gewald, eds., *Words Cannot Be Found: German Colonial Rule in Namibia*, an
annotated reprint of 1918 Blue Book (Leiden and Boston: Brill, 2003).

   5. The witness in this context is above all a moral witness, though registers of witnessing—juridical
and moral, for example—often overlap. I focus on witnesses who testify to how they or others suffered, and who, by testifying, become a conduit of victims' suffering. Margalit, *Ethics of Memory*,
163–68; Jay Winter, "The Moral Witness and the Two World Wars," *Ethnologie française* 3, no. 37

How did the witness to genocide take shape? How did this figure, now a ubiquitous and self-evident reference to the Western moral imagination, first appear and develop? Why has its moral power diminished? In this book I trace this witness icon over the course of the last century up to the emergence of its current form in the late 1990s, after genocide became a pervasive term for state-sponsored murder.

Although there are many possible approaches to the subject, including a synoptic intellectual history of the concept of witnessing, I focus on how the witness to genocide developed in the course of five courtroom battles spanning the 1920s to the 1960s. All of these trials struggled to understand, recognize, and redeem victims' suffering and survival in conditions of radical powerlessness that were distinct from conquest and war. They include the trial of Soghomon Tehlirian, an Armenian acquitted in Berlin in 1921 of murdering Talaat Pasha, an architect of the Armenian genocide, and the trial of Jewish avenger Scholem Schwarzbard, acquitted by a jury in Paris in 1927 for having murdered the alleged leader of Ukrainian pogroms against Jews (chapter 1). Two others were libel cases that paraded victims of the Soviet Gulag before the courts: the Paris trials initiated by Victor A. Kravchenko and David Rousset in 1949 and 1950–51, respectively (chapter 2). The best known is the trial of Adolf Eichmann, held in Jerusalem in 1961–62, which fashioned yet another witness figure, the Jewish Holocaust survivor (chapter 3). The last chapter assesses how the moral witness changed in the 1990s, when human rights institutions and activists—the International Criminal Court, aid workers, and spectators of atrocity photography—invoked the survivor of mass atrocities to justify their mission.[6]

(2007): 467–74; and Froma Zeitlin, "The Vicarious Witness: Belated Memory and Authorial Presence in Recent Holocaust Literature," *History and Memory* 10, no. 2 (1998): 5–42. For a discussion of different registers of witnessing—juridical, religious, historical, and moral—specifically Margalit's concept of the "moral witness," see Aleida Assman, "Vier Grundtypen von Zeugenschaft," in *Zeugenschaft des Holocaust: Zwischen Trauma, Tradierung, und Ermittlung*, ed. Michael Elm and Gottfried Kössler (Frankfurt: Campus Verlag, 2007), 33–51. For a philosophical approach to current literature, see Sybille Krämer and Sigrid Weigel, eds., *Testimony / Bearing Witness: Epistemology, Ethics, History and Culture* (London: Rowman & Littlefield International, 2017).

6. To avoid anachronism and confusion as much as possible—and because "genocide" does not simply designate mass killing—from now on when I discuss historical moments in which there was no clear designation for particular crimes, I refer to "mass atrocities," sometimes "mass violence" or "mass murder," and, where appropriate, "genocide" (as in the Armenian genocide or the genocide of European Jewry). I use "witness to genocide" consistently because that is now the prevalent term and invokes the culmination of the hundred-year history I have sought to reconstruct. Genocide designates crimes against a particular ethnic or racial group. Events now understood to be genocides were not called "genocide" at the time, not even after the 1948 Genocide Convention was ratified. After 1945, some referred to "crimes against humanity" to mean genocide because the term "crimes against humanity" was used at Nuremberg (though it

How does a victim of mass atrocities or genocide become a witness? The trials on which I focus dignified victims' lives and deaths not only because they offered victims an opportunity to testify, but also because the proceedings cleansed them rhetorically of blame and rendered them worthy of recognition. These legal forums developed narratives about the experience of mass murder that eventually replaced an older humanitarian language of horror, pity, and sympathy. Nineteenth- and early twentieth-century condemnations of mass violence proclaimed a moral obligation to speak out against barbarism elsewhere in the name of "laws of humanity," but these were often pleas by distant spectators to show pity for their victims. Abolitionists, who organized around victims' struggles, used the language of sympathy.[7] International humanitarian missions in the interwar period, often under the aegis of the League of Nations (founded in 1920) and spearheaded by committed activists, sought to inspire their audiences by appealing to their "human conscience," itself the moral achievement of an abstract comity of "civilized" nations and empires.[8]

The trials I discuss began to alter this picture. They recast victims' survival as a redemptive force, placing their suffering and their perspective center stage in place of humanitarian spectators and their dismay, and making the restoration of victims' dignity eventually vital to an international global image of the right and good.[9] Their proceedings articulated how and why victims' suffering mattered, and how most properly to memorialize the unburied. They explained Hannah Arendt's postwar contention that being stripped of the symbolic trappings of dignity—"being nothing but human"—facilitated rather than hindered statelessness, torture, mass murder, and want of refuge.[10]

---

was employed by Russia's foreign minister Sergei Sasanov in 1915 to describe the genocide of the Armenians). Once "genocide" became more widely used in the late 1960s and 1970s, I refer to "genocide" where applicable. On the origins of "crimes against humanity" as a response to the Turkish massacres of Armenians, see Gary Jonathan Bass, *Stay the Hand of Vengeance: The Politics of War Crimes Tribunals* (Princeton, NJ: Princeton University Press, 2000), 115, and Peter Holquist, "'Crimes against Humanity': Genealogy of a Concept, 1815–1945" (unpublished manuscript consulted in February 2016).

7. See, for example, Lynn Festa, *Sentimental Figures of Empire in Eighteenth-Century Britain and France* (Baltimore: Johns Hopkins University Press, 2006).

8. The idea that "humanity" should be defended by international order, including the protection of civilians in war, traces its roots to the sixteenth century. Later, humanitarian order and international law as they were codified in The Hague Conventions of 1899 and 1907 recognized "laws of humanity" in the context of imperialism and national sovereignty.

9. See Sara Kendall and Sarah Nouwen, "Representational Practices at the International Criminal Court: The Gap between Juridified and Abstract Victimhood," *Law and Contemporary Problems* 76, no. 3-4 (2014): 235–62.

10. Hannah Arendt, *The Origins of Totalitarianism* (New York: Harcourt, 1968), 298, 300.

The moral witness forged in the trials on which I focus drew on victims' testimonies but was a composite of survival only loosely attached to particular individuals and experiences. Witnesses are symbols of darkness and hope that have an ideological and memorial function, erase some realities and distort others; most problematically, especially after the 1970s, witnesses transfigured victims into quasi-sacred signs. Like all symbols, they condense specific survival stories to convey a broader message. Witnesses' positive traits cannot overcome deep-seated racism, antisemitism, or political interests: the Rousset trial redeemed witnesses deported for political opposition at the expense of Jewish ones; the Eichmann trial's redemption of Jewish victims hardly eradicated antisemitism; and recent cases before the International Criminal Court target disproportionally non-Western perpetrators, revealing the economic, political, and racial hierarchies embedded in the international justice system.

The definition of who is and is not a moral witness varies from one location to another and is always linked to cultural projections that may have a tenuous relationship to real victims. That definition also depends on whether there develops a moral consensus around victims whose suffering can be universalized and whose presence no longer inspires guilt, denial, and displacement—most victims, after all, will not have their day in court. All the trials I analyze shaped moral witnesses by incorporating former victims into broader but restricted definitions of humanity. In the interwar period victims were integrated into European "civilization" represented by a comity of nations; after World War Two, they became part of the universalized Western image of suffering humanity embodied by the patriotic anti-fascist survivors of Nazi camps; and later, after the Eichmann trial, Jewish survivors of the Holocaust became the quintessential witnesses to genocide, not because of their anti-fascist heroism, but because they survived an assault on their collective existence. In the postcolonial period, now that every victim matters and all of humanity is theoretically entitled to equal justice, the moral witness is, ironically, less likely to be a survivor than a humanitarian who works on his or her behalf.

A durable Western moral consensus formed around the Jewish Holocaust survivor, a consensus itself belated, extremely fragile, and contested by Holocaust denial. In the aftermath of the Eichmann trial, Jews, once berated for not having resisted their persecutors and suspected of complicity in their own deaths, were recast as innocent survivors of unspeakable violence. Because Western powers still rationalized imperial conquest as subduing savagery and repressing rebellion rather than violating humanity, the Holocaust survivor, rather than colonized victims of genocidal violence, came to represent Western Europeans' and North Americans' discovery of their own murderousness and to reflect their shocked self-recognition. By the 1960s there was a thin consensus against the violence colonized victims had suffered but not against the colonial regimes that perpetrated it. In contrast, the consensus that developed around the Nazis' attempted annihilation of European Jewry rendered Holocaust survivors relatively uncontested reminders of the destruction of which human beings were capable.[11]

In this book, my aim is not to make the Holocaust more or less central to the historical unfolding of contemporary Western witnessing. Such arguments inform recent discussions of the history both of international human rights and comparative genocide.[12] From within a longer genealogy of the symbolic witness, I ask instead by what figurative process the Holocaust became the self-evidently representative genocide and Holocaust survivors its icons, and why this dubious privilege persisted even as other moral witnesses have emerged.

In what follows I identify four iterations of the witness to genocide and devote a chapter to each: the righteous avenger in the interwar period, the concentration camp survivor in the immediate postwar period, the Holocaust survivor in the 1960s and 1970s, and now, in the postcolonial era, the global victim and the counterwitness. I analyze how, over the last hundred years, witness figures represented a distinction between genocidal killing and the mass violence associated with imperial conquest and conventional warfare.[13] I also explore how witnesses to genocide came to

---

11. International human rights proclamations like the Universal Declaration of Human Rights (1948) and the Genocide Convention (1948) recognized the historical significance of the Holocaust as a vast exterminatory program proper to authoritarian states, but also preserved state sovereignty in national and colonial undertakings, making it unlikely that genocide perpetrated by imperial powers would be prosecuted, at least in the short term. Moral witnesses emerged in colonial conflicts, such as Djamila Boupacha, who in 1962 publicized her torture at the hands of the French army during the Algerian War. Such witnesses were heroes to some and remained the enemies of others. Without a clear consensus about the wrongness of colonialism, the humanity of the victims might be acknowledged, but violence against them was often justified by logics of raison d'état and racism, effectively minimalizing the real impact of persecution and repression. See G. Daniel Cohen, "The Holocaust and the 'Human Rights Revolution': A Reassessment," in *The Human Rights Revolution: An International History*, ed. Akira Iriye, Petra Goedde, and William I. Hitchcock (Oxford: Oxford University Press, 2012), 53–72; A. Dirk Moses, "Raphael Lemkin, Culture, and the Concept of Genocide," in *The Oxford Handbook of Genocide Studies*, ed. Donald Bloxham and A. Dirk Moses (Oxford: Oxford University Press, 2010), 1–27; Rebecca Jinks, *Representing Genocide: The Holocaust as Paradigm?* (New York: Bloomsbury, 2016); Simone de Beauvoir and Djamila Boupacha, *Djamila Boupacha: The Story of the Torture of a Young Algerian Girl Which Shocked Liberal French Opinion*, trans. Peter Green (New York: Macmillan, 1962). See also Erik Lindstrum, "Facts about Atrocity: Reporting Colonial Violence in Postwar Britain," *History Workshop Journal* 84 (2017): 108–27.
12. Paul Gordon Lauren, *The Evolution of International Human Rights: Visions Seen* (Philadelphia: University of Pennsylvania Press, 2003), 204–7, emphasizes political realism of the Great Powers but also argues that the Holocaust gave rise to human rights. Cohen, "Holocaust," 53–72, contests the continuity between the Holocaust and the founding of international human rights.
13. The trauma diagnosis is another medical and cultural vehicle that shaped our understanding of the impact of genocide, which Didier Fassin and Richard Rechtman analyze in *The Empire of Trauma: An Inquiry into the Condition of Victimhood*, trans. Rachel Gomme (Princeton, NJ: Princeton University Press, 2009), 70–76.

symbolize a Western moral culture in which crimes against humanity and genocide are identifiable, actionable, and frequent occurrences. The chapters examine repeated but historically differentiated features and concepts that have forged a narrative about witnessing, and illuminate how the narrative changed after the 1990s, when witnessing became the obligation of all responsible citizens. The book focuses on "family resemblances" rather than on causal connections among various witness figures; it identifies significant patterns of cultural representation rather than demonstrates the particular impact of this or that trial.[14]

The Trials

I address the distinctive historical formation of a witness to genocide by analyzing interwar and postwar trials that recognized victims of mass atrocities in courts at a time when no tribunals would try the perpetrators, among them the Turkish, Soviet, and German governments.[15] None of the trials I examine aimed to provide justice for victims of mass violence other than the one of Eichmann in 1961–62, and all occurred in the absence of an international tribunal specifically tasked to try crimes against humanity or genocide. The first four trials I analyze were trials for homicide and libel that turned into judgments of violence against Armenians, Jews, and people imprisoned in the Soviet Union.

The courtroom, as has often been noted, is a particularly powerful arena for the making of new meanings, and trials are a rich source for tracing new narratives about mass atrocities and genocide: witnesses tell their stories, lawyers shape them, and formal rules constrain testimony and shape its meaning.[16] What victims could say in courtrooms and how they could say it constituted new narratives about human suffering and survival that were as important to the outcome of the trials as legal argument alone. Similarly, in the circumstances

---

14. Ludwig Wittgenstein used "family resemblances" to describe the multiple meanings signified by a word in his *Philosophical Investigations*, trans. G.E.M. Ancombe, P.M.S. Hacker, and Joachim Schulte (Oxford: Wiley-Blackwell, 2009), xcv.

15. An Ottoman court under British pressure was to try Turkish perpetrators of the Armenian genocide in Constantinople in 1919. For various reasons, and in spite of some courts-martial, the effort finally collapsed and ended with a swap of the prisoners for British ones taken hostage by Kemal Atatürk's nationalist forces in 1921. See Bass, *Stay the Hand*, 106–46. The Allies tried German war criminals successfully at Nuremberg in 1945–46, but the German government itself was reluctant to try perpetrators.

16. As Peter Brooks and Paul Gewirtz note, "storytelling in law is narrative within a culture of argument." See their introduction in *Law's Stories: Narrative and Rhetoric in Law*, ed. Brooks and Gewirtz (New Haven, CT: Yale University Press, 1996), 5.

common to all of these trials, truth claims made by individual witnesses—even when they could not be established as true or false—generated higher, transcendent, seemingly unimpeachable truths about the effects of violence in radically dehumanizing conditions.

In all of these trials, political forces tried hard to hijack the proceedings, turning them into spectacles in which witnesses' suffering took center stage. Much testimony was ancillary to the charges brought before the courts. All of these trials spotlighted mass atrocities, used victim testimony in highly unusual if defensible ways, put victims center stage to teach the public about their plights, and provided multilingual forums for their revelations. The Eichmann trial had more in common with these earlier trials than not. Though it put a Nazi perpetrator on trial, the Israeli prosecution of Eichmann, like the other trials I examine, used victim testimony in an unconventional fashion, made victims' voices central, and unfolded as a moral lesson about the Holocaust. Concerns about the Eichmann trial's legality at the time are well known; such concerns were also raised about the other trials.[17] This book does not aim to ascertain the inevitable limits of legal proceedings from victims' points of view—it is not a legal history. My interest is rather in the common rhetorical features of the five trials and the moral witnesses they shaped.[18]

Together these unusual legal proceedings forged a narrative about the terror wrought by murderous twentieth-century political regimes that their proceedings defined as qualitatively different from tyrannical states. Each trial told variations of the same story regardless of the crimes it adjudicated and the context in which courts addressed the victims. The trials refashioned the witness figure adopted by nineteenth- and early twentieth-century witnesses, who spoke with respect to and on behalf of the suffering and dead; the experiences victims recounted in the trials did not only affront the humanity of audiences but also

---

17. For a rigorous defense of the Eichmann trial's legal integrity, see Lawrence Douglas, *The Memory of Judgment: Making Law and History in the Trials of the Holocaust* (New Haven, CT: Yale University Press, 2001), 97–182. Leora Bilsky has gone further than Douglas, arguing that the court developed a legal rationale for the variety of victim testimonies. Bilsky, "The Eichmann Trial: Toward a Jurisprudence of Eyewitness Testimony of Atrocities," *Journal of International Criminal Justice* 12, no. 1 (2014): 27–57.

18. On how figuration in Primo Levi's work makes empirical realities more "real," see Hayden White, "Figural Realism in Witness Literature," *Parallax* 10, no. 1 (2004): 113–24. For a nice summary of the work of figures, see Sarah Hammershlag, *The Figural Jew: Politics and Identity in Postwar French Thought* (Chicago: University of Chicago Press, 2010), 7–16, which treats the figure of the Jew in postwar French thought (from Emmanuel Levinas to Jacques Derrida) as a critique of the particular/universal binary so predominant in French approaches to politics. Baucom, *Specters of the Atlantic*, 297–305, also offers a critique of Derrida's concept of witnessing in light of an account of abolitionist witnesses.

strained to their limits the traditional tropes used to describe atrocities. And all these trials took place when the term "genocide," a neologism formulated by the Polish Jewish lawyer Raphael Lemkin in 1942 to define the state-sponsored extermination of Jews by the Nazis, was not available or rarely invoked, and when the particular nature of Jewish death under Hitler was still a subject of vast ignorance.[19]

None of these five trials is a landmark of human rights law or history. Two overlap incidentally with interwar humanitarianism, two with postwar crimes against humanity, and one with genocide, but none fits into the history of international law on human rights or has a significant relationship to Nuremberg except as a reference point.[20] Indeed, Nuremberg is famous for the mountains of documents it wielded against the defendants and its minimal reliance on witness testimony.[21] Robert H. Jackson, associate justice of the US Supreme Court and chief prosecutor for the United States at Nuremberg, feared witnesses could be brought "by defense lawyers to waver in their statements."[22] In his diary, the British judge Sir Norman Birkett wrote that testimony of the camps at the Nuremberg tribunal was ample. Though moving in its "horror" and

---

19. On Lemkin and the formulation of "genocide" see Douglas Irvin-Erickson, *Raphaël Lemkin and the Concept of Genocide* (Philadelphia: University of Pennsylvania Press, 2017), which dates the coining of the term to the winter of 1942 (1).

20. In a book on the interwar development of international law, Mark Lewis does not mention either trial. Lewis, *The Birth of the New Justice: The Internationalization of Crime and Punishment, 1919–1950* (Oxford: Oxford University Press, 2014), 1–21. More generally, historians increasingly locate the modern commitment to "humanity" in the progressive modernization processes of nation-states and empires and conceive Nuremberg as part of longer-term efforts to combat "crimes against humanity" in the name of civilization—Russian diplomats introduced the term into the penal lexicon already in 1915 to address Ottoman crimes against the Armenians. For examples of this view, and most prominently on the Russian role, see Holquist, "'Crimes against Humanity'." See also Michelle Tusan, "'Crimes against Humanity': Human Rights, the British Empire, and the Origins of the Response to the Armenian Genocide," *American Historical Review* 119, no. 1 (2014): 47–77. Samuel Moyn displaces Nuremberg implicitly from its moral if not legal pulpit to argue that contemporary human rights emerged only in the 1970s, when the nation-state model of a "politics of citizenship at home" eroded in favor of a "politics of suffering abroad." Moyn, *The Last Utopia: Human Rights in History* (Cambridge, MA: Harvard University Press, 2010), 12.

21. There is an ample discussion of the absence of Jewish testimony at Nuremberg in particular. See Donald Bloxham, "Jewish Witnesses in War Crimes Trials of the Postwar Era," in *Holocaust Historiography in Context: Emergence, Challenges, Polemics, and Achievements*, ed. David Bankier and Dan Michman (Jerusalem: Yad Vashem, 2008), 539–56; Rebecca Whitman, "'A Lost Voice'? Jewish Witnesses in Nazi Trials in West Germany," in *Holocaust Historiography*, 555–65; Laura Jockusch, "Justice at Nuremberg? Jewish Responses to Nazi War-Crime Trials in Allied-Occupied Germany," *Jewish Social Studies* 19, no. 1 (2012): 107–47. For a balanced view that takes a less critical attitude of Nuremberg's treatment of Jewish death, see Michael R. Marrus, "The Holocaust at Nuremberg," *Yad Vashem Studies* 26 (1998): 5–41.

22. Cited in Douglas, *Memory of Judgment*, 18.

"inhumanity," he wrote, "from the point of view of this trial it is a complete waste of valuable time."[23]

Of course, trials of former Nazis after the war treated victims as witnesses in standard juridical terms (though there was also a great deal of summary justice, from purges of collaborators to high-profile military trials, such as the 1945 judgment of Pierre Laval in France). Witness testimony was particularly important when other forensic evidence was lacking, and it proved essential in some postwar trials, such as the British-led Hamburg trials of Ravensbrück guards, held from 1946 to 1948.[24] In such cases, testimony replaced or supported documentary evidence. The 1963–65 Auschwitz trial in Frankfurt best exemplifies proceedings in which the victims' testimony made a media splash but did not alter collective memory of war crimes in West Germany.[25] The shock to German memory would come more than ten years later in the form of a US television series.[26] The Frankfurt trial and those of former Nazi war criminals held in Düsseldorf and elsewhere in the 1970s were important for Germans' coming to terms with the past, but were standard legal proceedings in which lawyers used witness testimony to highlight the sadism of some guards rather than their culpability for industrialized murder, and often ended with startlingly lenient sentences.[27]

---

23. Cited in Telford Taylor, *The Anatomy of the Nuremberg Trials: A Personal Memoir* (New York: Knopf, 1992), 306.

24. For a discussion of trials other than the 1945–46 International Military Tribunal (IMT) that tried high-level Nazi perpetrators, see Michael J. Bazyler and Frank M. Turkheimer, *Forgotten Trials of the Holocaust* (New York: NYU Press, 2014). They include the Soviet Kharkov trial of 1943, the Ravensbrück trial, and the 1946 trial of Amon Göth in Poland (15–44, 129–57, 101–27). On how the Polish trials, in contrast to Nuremberg, emphasized cultural genocide, see Leora Bilsky and Rachel Klagsbrun, "The Return of Cultural Genocide?" *The European Journal of International Law* 29, no. 2 (2018): 373–96. The daughter of Geneviève de Gaulle Anthonioz wrote that her mother and Germaine Tillion, who had both been imprisoned at Ravensbrück, were deeply disappointed by the "nearly general indifference" to the Ravensbrück trials in France when they took place. De Gaulle Anthonioz and Tillion, *Dialogues: Présentés par Isabelle Anthonioz-Gaggini* (Paris: Plon, 2015), 15.

25. On the discrepancy between the media coverage and German public indifference or hostility, see Devin O. Pendas, "'I Didn't Know What Auschwitz Was': The Frankfurt Auschwitz Trial and the German Press: 1963–1965," *Yale Journal of Law and the Humanities* 12, no. 2 (2000): 397–446. Trial testimony was also recounted in a famous 1965 play: Peter Weiss, *The Investigation*, English version by Jon Swan and Ulu Grosbard (New York: Atheneum, 1966).

26. Bazyler and Turkheimer, *Forgotten Trials*, 227–45, summarizes all the relevant historical literature.

27. The charges against the defendants were brought under German domestic law, in particular an amended version of the German Penal Code of 1871. The use of domestic law and the judge's past under the Third Reich contributed to the relatively light sentences given to mass murderers. Both Devin O. Pendas and Rebecca Whitman in different ways conclude that in spite of their accomplishments, the Frankfurt trials limited recognition of the genocide to deeds committed by particularly sadistic men. Pendas, *The Frankfurt Auschwitz Trial, 1963–65: Genocide, History, and the Limits of the Law* (Cambridge: Cambridge University Press, 2006); Whitman, *Beyond Justice: The Auschwitz Trial*

In the alternative story I recount, the proceedings were inventive and didactic. They were embedded in particular contexts, and courts were sites where lawyers and judges questioned claims about mass atrocities. Smart lawyers staged eyewitness testimony to bring crimes to light even when there was no one, except in Jerusalem, on trial for perpetrating atrocities. The trials were not a failure of legal procedure; either they represented the absence of an established legal category with which courts could prosecute state-directed mass murder or, in the case of the Eichmann trial, sought to tell a story about Jewish death that the Nuremberg tribunal's emphasis on "crimes against humanity" tied to "aggressive war" could not.[28] Thus victims' advocates in these five trials strove in every way possible to put victims' suffering front and center even when that suffering was peripheral to the cases at hand.

The trials on which I focus are, moreover, insignificant for the development of legal norms and tangential to legal history because they left little mark on lawmaking.[29] They represent rather how the very absence of a legal concept of genocide created a moral imperative to make some crimes of mass violence legible in new ways or to create a narrative about genocide. Indeed, one iteration of the moral witness, the Jewish Holocaust survivor, captures a dimension of genocide sidelined in the legal codification of the term—the "tear in politics and culture" produced by what Lemkin termed cultural genocide.[30] The proceedings contributed

(Cambridge, MA: Harvard University Press, 2005). On the impact of the trial on a younger generation, see Daniel Levy and Natan Sznaider, *The Holocaust and Memory in a Global Age*, trans. Assenka Oksiloff (Philadelphia: Temple University Press, 2005) 98–99.

28. Douglas, *Memory of Judgment*, 48–53.

29. Devin O. Pendas argues that the Eichmann trial is not now "recalled mainly for its legal pedagogy": Pendas, "The Eichmann Trial in Law and Memory," in *Political Trials in Theory and History*, ed. Jens Meierhenrich and Devin O. Pendas (Cambridge: Cambridge University Press, 2016), 206. Other discussions render certain forgotten trials more central to legal history than they are usually considered or envision the Eichmann trial within a longer legal narrative. Lawrence Douglas suggests that an alternative "atrocity paradigm" that was more victim-centric than Nuremberg emerged in the neglected Nuremberg Military Tribunals (NMT) that followed the 1945–46 IMT. Douglas, "From IMT to NMT: The Emergence of a Jurisprudence of Atrocity," in *Reassessing the Nuremberg Military Tribunals: Transitional Justice, Trial Narratives, and Historiography*, ed. Kim C. Piemel and Alexa Stiller (New York: Berghahn Books, 2012), 276–95.

30. For the emphasis on cultural genocide as a "tear," see Hannah Pollin-Galay, *Ecologies of Witnessing: Language, Place, and Holocaust Testimony* (New Haven: Yale University Press, 2018), 3. International law does not, as Bilsky demonstrates, treat attacks against cultural heritage as genocide but as the destruction of property, even though there is a clear relationship between such attacks and physical violence toward particular groups. The Eichmann trial convicted Eichmann under the Nazi Punishment Law, or as "a crime against the Jewish people" modeled on the definition of genocide in the 1948 Genocide Convention. Bilsky notes that Lemkin's concept of "cultural genocide" was never adopted as part of the legal definition of genocide because it "undermined the clear distinction between totalitarian states and democratic states." See Bilsky, "The Return of Cultural Genocide?," 395.

to the broader historical and symbolic processes by which a moral vernacular for symbolizing crimes of mass violence became available.

These trials often went off script in spite of expert staging, the statutes they invoked did not always fit the crimes, lawyers wanted to teach moral and political lessons, and the publics were large, enthralled, and sometimes stunned by the testimony. The courts' failure to restrain witness testimony was a central feature of all these trials, and was the most common criticism leveled at the prosecution of Eichmann. The contrast between formal legal procedure and distraught witnesses turned the courts into forums in which the witnesses were given unusual latitude to speak or spoke in ways that amplified their testimony. Those testifying were conceived by publics and juries as messengers for the dead and persecuted. Most important, in the process of clarifying what happened and why, each trial, with the exception of Kravchenko's nonetheless significant libel suit, represents the victim's survival as a newly discovered source of honor, vitality, or wisdom.

Although they did not fully redeem victims in the eyes of everyone, to varying degrees the trials performed the symbolic work Terrence Des Pres demanded later in his 1976 book, *The Survivor: An Anatomy of Life in the Death Camps*: "We require a heroism commensurate with the sweep of ruin in our time: action equal to situations in which it becomes less self-indulgent and more useful to live. . . . The grandeur of death is lost in a world of mass murder, and except for special cases the martyr and his tragic counterpart are types of the hero unfit for the darkness ahead."[31] In addition to empowering the victim, the trials also developed a "mythology" of heroism outlined by Robert Jay Lifton in a discussion of witnesses to Hiroshima and the Holocaust: the witnesses, he said, have "a knowledge of death and therefore a knowledge of life, to bring back. It's a profound new knowledge. So in that sense the survivor has lived out the mythology of the hero, but not quite."[32]

The witness who emerged from these trials revised heroism in terms commensurate with the ruins created by particular events and experiences: the Armenian genocide, the Ukrainian pogroms, the Soviet Gulag, and the Holocaust of European Jewry. By seeking recognition for victims, the trials recast tragic heroism in the wake of mass murder, concentration camps, and genocide. To redeem victims from their humiliation, to integrate them into national

---

31. Terrence Des Pres, *The Survivor: An Anatomy of Life in the Death Camps* (Oxford: Oxford University Press, 1976), 6.

32. Cathy Caruth, "Interview with Robert Jay Lifton," in *Trauma: Explorations in Memory*, ed. Cathy Caruth (Baltimore: Johns Hopkins University Press, 1995), 135.

or human communities, however defined, lawyers struggled to fashion victims rhetorically as models of heroic humanity in contexts where human beings had been stripped of their humanness and resistance was driven by desperation when it emerged at all. The Eichmann trial restored dignity to every style of dying or enduring—suicide, exploitative or senseless labor, gas chambers, and bare survival—most of which, other than resistance, had until then inspired no broad understanding, let alone respect for those who returned alive. Many of its observers turned Jewish survivors' experiences of terror and death into a source of moral clarity that underpinned constructions of Holocaust survival by the 1970s and after.

All the trials in one way or another laid the groundwork for abstracting from the experience of real victims of mass violence to create a symbolic witness who possessed unprecedented experience of a human-made, unfathomable darkness. It is this dimension of the trials—the struggle to conceptualize suffering, degradation, and cultural annihilation distinct from the horror of conquest and war—that is their most innovative, and most revelatory of their limitations. A historically particular incarnation of Western human conscience, the witness serves as a constant reminder of all the evil in the world against which we are called to be vigilant. The analysis of these trials together suggests that orchestrated and yet disruptive public legal forums were critical if hardly the only sites for making meaning out of mass atrocities and genocide; they allotted unusual and extraordinary space to the didactic dimension of testimony, and, most important, they were forums for performatively creating new worlds of meaning. Though the moral witness may emerge in other arenas—I will argue in the last chapter that it also emerges in certain kinds of critical literature—the intersection of the juridical, moral, and historical registers of witnessing are on particularly powerful display in courtrooms. It is perhaps not surprising that moral witnesses appear there.

This book analyzes the trials' legacy by establishing patterns of representation in the United States and Western Europe that became increasingly legible and even self-evident over time, including the icon of the Holocaust survivor and the secular imperative to "bear witness." By placing the Holocaust witness in a longer trajectory of moral witnesses, I reject a teleological account that culminates in the icon of the Holocaust survivor, asking instead how witnesses became symbols of "human conscience." I use the trials as evidence that mass atrocities demanded a new vocabulary and constituted new ways of imagining moral sensibility, as well as collective violence and its victims. The moral witness shapes affronts to "human conscience" and tracks the changing Western cultural meaning attributed to victims' suffering, from the Armenian genocide to contemporary human rights violations. The witness figure is an unremarked part of a larger narrative one historian has called the "genocide script."[33]

Histories of Witnessing

There are many accounts of witnesses and witnessing, but few historical narratives of how the witness to genocide became a prominent icon during the twentieth century and witnessing a central activity in Western moral culture. Many works about the Great War address soldiers as witnesses to war because they experienced combat as a revelation about life and death in which they were tragically implicated.[34] This form of witness, however, invokes the morally transformed soldier and merges with but differs from the witness to genocide, who symbolizes the distinctive physical and cultural violence associated with ideologically motivated mass murder that often occurs under cover of war.[35] Historians of modern Europe have recently written about communities of Jewish survivors in the aftermath of the genocide, tracing their organizations and efforts to document their experiences in France, Poland, Germany, and elsewhere. They are mostly concerned with the evidentiary and memory-preserving role of actual witnesses and their restorative and moral function, treating only tangentially the figure of the witness.[36] Finally, there are also myriad recent treatments of human-

---

33. Jinks, *Representing Genocide*, 30.

34. The volume of literature on this general topic, which spans interwar art and culture as well as pacifist movements, is tangential to my project. Much of this literature focuses on how witnesses experience and express the impact of war and its meaning. For a moving account of witness testimony by Great War veterans whose reflections are particularly insightful, see Leonard V. Smith, *The Embattled Self: French Soldiers' Testimony of the Great War* (Ithaca, NY: Cornell University Press, 2007).

35. Irvin-Erickson helpfully notes that "'genocide'" did not signify "a particular type of violence." Lemkin was "trying to create a new juridical and philosophical category of 'different actions' that, 'taken separately,' constitute other crimes but, when taken together constitute a type of atrocity that threatened the existence of social collectivities and threatened a peaceful and cosmopolitan social order of the world." He also writes that Lemkin conceived groups in terms of shared thinking and imagined cohesiveness between people rather than in terms of "objective relations." Irvin-Erickson, *Raphaël Lemkin and the Concept of Genocide*, 7, 9.

36. See Laura Jockusch, *Collect and Record! Jewish Holocaust Documentation in Early Postwar Europe* (New York: Oxford University Press, 2012); Margaret Taft, *From Victim to Survivor: The Emergence and Development of the Holocaust Witness* (Portland, OR: Vallentine Mitchell, 2013). The witness to genocide was also a "survivor," a term drawn from biblical allusions to Jews saved from destruction that is not only a noun but also a cultural identity of Holocaust survivors. The term "survivor" is now increasingly used to define almost anyone who has triumphed over certain forms of adversity, such as sexual abuse. Alina Both and Markus Nesselrodt, "Survivor: Towards a Conceptual History," *Leo Baeck Institute Yearbook* 61 (2016): 57–82. The authors provide a good overview of the use of the term "survivor" as it emerged out of the Americanized "global culture of Holocaust

itarianism (caring for the sick and wounded) and human rights (struggling for justice on victims' behalf) that discuss contemporary witnessing as both a moral and political activity, but do not for the most part address the witness to genocide as a historical phenomenon it its own right.[37]

Arguments about how a moral witness emerged appear mostly in the standard narrative about the development of Holocaust consciousness after the 1960s, and with it, the recognition not only of actual Holocaust survivors but of an icon, the Holocaust survivor. That narrative tells a story about the increasing awareness of the genocide and the emergence of the Jewish Holocaust survivor as exemplary witness. After the Eichmann trial in Jerusalem, which emphasized the Jewish dimension of the genocide, public attention focused on the Holocaust. The trial came on the heels of the publication of many Jewish memoirs of the camps, including Primo Levi's *If This Is a Man*, which came out in 1947 in a small print run and was finally reprinted to greater acclaim in 1958.[38] The Jerusalem trial recounted the fate of the Jews and stirred increased interest in their suffering after a long period of postwar silence punctuated by some Jewish voices—even prize-winning memoirs, including not only Levi's works, but also Elie Wiesel's

---

memorialization" (58). Emma Kuby, *Political Survivors: The Resistance, the Cold War, and the Fight against Concentration Camps after 1945* (Ithaca, NY: Cornell University Press, 2019). Kuby's book, to which I will return in chapter 2, focuses on another concept of witnessing by way of an institutional history.

37. Didier Fassin provides a historical dimension that I discuss extensively in chapter 4, but his work is not, strictly speaking, a history of witnessing. Fassin, *Humanitarian Reason: A Moral History of the Present*, trans. Rachel Gomme (Berkeley: University of California Press, 2012), 200–222. In *Mengele's Skull: The Advent of a Forensic Aesthetics* (Frankfurt am Main: Sternberg, Portkus, 2012), Thomas Keenan and Eyal Weizmann too discuss a new form of witness, "forensic witnessing," but the book is mostly suggestive. The literature on humanitarianism is otherwise vast and includes works concerning abolitionism and nineteenth-century philanthropy. For studies of humanitarianism that provide a critical perspective on witnessing, see, among others, Eleanor Davey, *Idealism beyond Borders: The French Revolutionary Left and the Rise of Humanitarianism, 1954–1988* (Cambridge: Cambridge University Press, 2015), 3; Estelle d'Halluin, "Between Testimony and Expertise: How Immigration Policies Challenge the Humanitarian Ethic," in *Nongovernmental Politics*, ed. Michel Feher, Gaëlle Krikorian, and Yates McKee (New York: Zone Books, 2007), 419–31; Michal Givoni, *The Care of the Witness: A Contemporary History of Testimony in Crises* (Cambridge: Cambridge University Press, 2016); Robert Meister, *After Evil: A Politics of Human Rights* (New York: Columbia University Press, 2011); Miriam Ticktin, *Casualties of Care: Immigration and the Politics of Humanitarianism in France* (Berkeley: University of California Press, 2011); Keith David Watenpaugh, "The League of Nations' Rescue of Armenian Genocide Survivors and the Making of Modern Humanitarianism," *American Historical Review* 115, no. 5 (2010): 1315–19; Eyal Weizman, *The Least of All Possible Evils: Humanitarian Violence from Arendt to Gaza* (London: Verso, 2011).

38. Primo Levi, *If This Is a Man*, trans. Stuart Woolf, in *The Complete Works of Primo Levi*, ed. Ann Goldstein, 3 vols. (New York: Penguin Classics, 2015), 1:1–205. For details on the book's publication, see Robert Gordon, *The Holocaust in Italian Culture, 1944–2010* (Stanford, CA: Stanford University Press, 2012), 65–68.

much-praised memoir, *Night*.[39] *Night* was first printed in 1956 in Yiddish by an Argentinian publisher, but earned renown only in its much-abbreviated French version, published in 1958 with a preface by the Catholic writer François Mauriac.[40]

In the United States, the struggle for civil rights and the Vietnam War led to new soul-searching about the effects of racism and violence, which in turn provoked interest in the destruction of European Jewry. The Arab-Israeli Six-Day War of 1967 intensified engagement with Holocaust memory, especially within Jewish communities, by raising the specter of Israel's destruction. As in Europe, where antiestablishment students cried "We are all German Jews" in demonstrations against the French state, protesters in and outside the United States used symbols of Nazism to condemn the Vietnam War.[41] When, in 1967, Bertrand Russell convened a citizens' tribunal to denounce the Vietnam War, participants claimed over and over that US bombing represented an "indignation of the human conscience" comparable to Nazism.[42] Jean-Paul Sartre's contributions, including his short piece "On Genocide," presumed that the US bombing in Vietnam was comparable to Hitler's genocide of the Jews. In his inaugural statement to the tribunal, he used Oradour, a French town whose inhabitants the Nazis had cruelly massacred in 1944, and Auschwitz as points of reference.[43] Ralph Schoenman, secretary general of the citizens' tribunal and head of the Bertrand Russell Peace Foundation, insisted that we should "no more regard the Vietnamese resistance a crime than we would the rising of the Warsaw Ghetto."[44]

---

39. André Schwarz-Bart, *The Last of the Just*, trans. Stephen Becker (New York: Overlook, 2000), and Anna Langfus, *The Lost Shore*, trans. Peter Wiles (New York: Pantheon, 1964) won the Prix Goncourt in 1959 and 1962, respectively; Elie Wiesel, *Night*, trans. Marion Wiesel (New York: Hill & Wang, 2006).

40. For a discussion of the Yiddish work and a trenchant critique of Mauriac's treatment of Wiesel as a Christ figure, see Naomi Seidman, "Elie Wiesel and the Scandal of Jewish Rage," *Jewish Social Studies* 3, no. 1 (1996): 1–19.

41. Jeremy Varon, *Bringing the War Home: The Weather Underground, the Red Army Faction, and Revolutionary Violence in the Sixties and Seventies* (Berkeley: University of California Press, 2004), 98–100. For an outraged rebuttal to the comparison of the Holocaust and Vietnam, see Dorothy Rabinowitz, *New Lives: Survivors of the Holocaust Living in America* (New York: Knopf, 1976), 193–94.

42. Italian politician Lelio Basso, "Summary of the First Two Charges," in *Against the Crime of Silence: Proceedings of the International War Crimes Tribunals*, ed. John Duffett (New York: Clarion, 1968), 301. For other mock trials organized by intellectuals as protests against political regimes, see Arthur Jay Klinghoffer and Judith Apter Klinghoffer, *International Citizens' Tribunals: Mobilizing Public Opinion to Advance Human Rights* (New York: Palgrave, 2002). Mock trials were entirely staged and relied heavily on the star power of their conveners.

43. Jean-Paul Sartre, "On Genocide" and "Inaugural Statement to the Tribunal," in *Against the Crime of Silence*, 612–26, 41.

44. Ralph Schoenman's foreword in *Against the Crime of Silence*, 9.

Widespread awareness of the genocide of European Jewry began with the Eichmann trial and peaked with Wiesel's 1977 declaration that Jewish witnesses had "invented a new literature." One critic famously remarked that the Holocaust represented an earthquake of unprecedented magnitude for Western observers, for whom European culture was supposed to be a bulwark against the perpetration of such crimes. By virtue of the brutal and targeted violence the Nazis inflicted on Jews in the heart of Europe, the Holocaust became a Western reference point for inexplicable, unprecedented evil.[45] Wiesel became the public face of the Holocaust survivor in the US and was appointed chair of the Holocaust Memorial Council by President Jimmy Carter in 1980. By the time he won his Nobel Prize in 1986, the Cold War was waning and Western Europeans had begun to look critically at their complicity in Nazi antisemitism, spurred in part by a Hollywood miniseries about ostensibly average German and Jewish families that had been televised in the US and Germany in 1978 and 1979, respectively.[46] The iconic status of the Holocaust came into focus again in 1999, when the United States bombed the former Yugoslavia, an act of war legitimated by critics who had earlier published photos of Bosnian prisoners looking very similar to Margaret Bourke-White's famous images of Holocaust victims in Buchenwald. One journalist titled his 1993 compilation of Pulitzer Prize–winning news reports on ethnic cleansing during the breakup of Yugoslavia *A Witness to Genocide*.[47]

By 1998, when French historian Annette Wieviorka published her powerful condemnation of Holocaust-related media sensationalism, *The Era of the Witness*, witnessing was not only the task of actual witnesses but had also become part of Holocaust pedagogy from museums to memorials that made up the memory culture of the West since the 1970s, some of which involved the conversion of witness testimony into kitsch.[48] The biblical quotation "You are my witnesses" (Isaiah 43:10) adorns the walls of the United States Holocaust Memorial Museum in Washington, DC, and combines religious and secular

45. In *Remembering to Forget: Holocaust Memory in the Camera's Eye* (Philadelphia: University of Pennsylvania Press, 1999), Barbie Zelizer traces how Auschwitz became iconic and protests the inevitable analogies between the Holocaust and other crimes, not because of the Holocaust's so-called uniqueness, but because icons congeal time and mask the historical specificity of events.

46. For a more elaborate discussion of Holocaust consciousness, see Jinks, *Representing Genocide*, 30–36; and Levy and Sznaider, *Holocaust and Memory*, 117–18.

47. Gutman, *Witness to Genocide*, calls a Serbian camp (Omarska) for Bosnian Muslims a "death camp" (xii). He notes that *Newsday* publicized his story with the title "The Death Camps of Bosnia" (xiii), and expresses confidence that Omarska was a "death factory" (xiv).

48. Annette Wieviorka, *The Era of the Witness*, trans. Jared Stark (Ithaca, NY: Cornell University Press, 2005).

meanings: images and artifacts of twentieth-century suffering constitute a sacred presence to which visitors must testify. In 2000, at a meeting of the Stockholm International Forum on the Holocaust sponsored by member nation-states and international organizations, the Holocaust was, according to two sociologists, "free of any moral ambiguity, and its universal form, coming out of America, has helped Europeans redefine themselves."[49] There is no doubt that the Holocaust had become a touchstone of moral culture. As the German cultural affairs minister Michael Naumann proclaimed at the Stockholm forum, if the Holocaust was past, it left central questions in its wake: "What constitutes the dignity of humanity if not that of life? How can it be protected from future genocidal attempts? In the remembrance of the Holocaust we must find the right answer for politics and society."[50]

This narrative about Holocaust consciousness thus begins with an increasing awareness of the Jewish fate and ends with the saturation of US and Western European culture by Holocaust memory, from revelation in the Eichmann trial to a flood of memoirs, films, video testimonies, museums, memorials, and a wave of mostly English- and German-language scholarship that probed everything from Holocaust history to conceptions of trauma and witnessing. Literary theorists analyzed survivor memoirs and video testimonies as forms of bearing witness.[51]

---

49. Levy and Sznaider, *Holocaust and Memory*, 184. See also Pendas, "The Eichmann Trial," 227, who argues that continued interest in the Eichmann trial is "less about the history of the Nazi genocide of the Jews" than about the universal "human capacity for evil under dictatorship and the need to prevent genocide and other mass atrocities."

50. Cited in Levy and Sznaider, *Holocaust and Memory*, 198.

51. On theories of trauma and witnessing, see also a vast literature that increasingly addresses video testimonies and their curation: Shoshana Felman and Dori Laub, *Testimony: Crises of Witnessing in Literature, Psychoanalysis, and History* (New York: Routledge, 1992); Cathy Caruth, *Unclaimed Experience: Trauma, Narrative, and History* (Baltimore: Johns Hopkins University Press, 1996); Giorgio Agamben, *Remnants of Auschwitz: The Witness and the Archive*, trans. Daniel Heller-Roazen (New York: Zone Books, 1999); Michael Elm and Gottfried Kössler, eds., *Zeugenschaft des Holocaust: Zwischen Trauma, Tradierung und Ermittlung* (Frankfurt am Main: Campus Verlag, 2007); Dominick LaCapra, *Writing Trauma, Writing History* (Baltimore: Johns Hopkins University Press, 2001); Jean-François Lyotard, *The Differend: Phrases in Dispute*, trans. Georges Van Den Abbeele (Minneapolis: University of Minnesota Press, 1989), 56–57 for the famous reference to the Holocaust as an immeasurable earthquake; Michael Rothberg, *Traumatic Realism: The Demands of Holocaust Representation* (Minneapolis: University of Minnesota Press, 2000); Thomas Trezise, *Witnessing Witnessing: On the Reception of Holocaust Survivor Testimony* (New York: Fordham University Press, 2013). On "secondary witnessing," see Dora Apfel, *The Holocaust and the Art of Secondary Witnessing* (New Brunswick, NJ: Rutgers University Press, 2002), esp. 21 for a summary of artworks as secondary witnesses; Marianne Hirsch, *Family Frames: Photography, Narrative, Postmemory* (Cambridge, MA: Harvard University Press, 1997) on the concept of "postmemory"; and Eva Hoffman, *After Such Knowledge: Memory, History, and the Legacy of the Holocaust* (Cambridge, MA: Public Affairs, 2004) on children of survivors.

Historians studied survivor testimonies and analyzed their proper uses.[52] Others now explore the transnational "archive" of Holocaust images and keywords to understand how it has framed non-Western representations of genocide.[53] Most scholars take the Holocaust survivor as an object of explanation and telos, and construe witnessing as a self-evidently moral task inscribed in secular Western culture.

Some scholars have criticized how North American Jews transformed Jewish witnesses into sacred objects, criticizing the hallowed image of the survivor. They often condemn the veneration of the Jewish survivor as one more component of an overwrought attention to Holocaust memory that after the 1970s transformed the Holocaust into a "civil religion" with its own commemorative rituals, relics, saints, and pilgrimage sites—Auschwitz, Treblinka, Belzec, and other camps. In Western Europe, where the memory of World War Two focused initially on those men and women who fought in Resistance movements, the resurgent attention to Jewish death led some Europeans to argue that the memory of the Holocaust was blotting out the memory of other struggles, including battles by Resistance forces against the Nazis, thereby generating resentment and envy. The French writer Pascal Bruckner quipped in 1985 that "the whole world wants to be Jewish."[54] In the United States, where the Holocaust survivor was dubbed a "secular saint," the criticism of Holocaust memory was no less fierce, though on other grounds: North American Jews, critics insisted, overestimated the force of antisemitism; younger Jews fantasized about being victims as a surrogate

---

52. The literature is abundant, but Saul Friedländer's works have been crucial in forging a narrative that incorporates victims. See his *Nazi Germany and the Jews: The Years of Persecution, 1933–1939* (New York: Harper Perennial, 1997) and *Nazi Germany and the Jews: The Years of Extermination, 1939–1945* (New York: Harper Perennial, 2007).

53. Jinks, *Representing Genocide*, 32.

54. Pascal Bruckner, *La tentation de l'innocence* (Paris: Grasset, 1985), 131–32. These themes were particularly salient in France. See Tzvetan Todorov, *Les abus de la mémoire* (Paris: Arléa, 1995), 33. The 1987 Paris trial of Klaus Barbie (an SS officer in Lyon who deported Jewish children and tortured, among others, the Resistance leader Jean Moulin) pitted Jewish victims against partisans who wanted crimes against the Resistance to count in the indictment of crimes against humanity. The partisans won the right to be considered victims in this juridical category, even though they were harmed as combatants. I have discussed this ambivalence in the recent French context in Carolyn J. Dean, *Aversion and Erasure: The Fate of the Victim after the Holocaust* (Ithaca, NY: Cornell University Press, 2010), 30–100. In Italy, as the controversy around Roberto Vivarelli's memoir makes clear, right-wing thinkers have equated the crimes of the anti-fascist Resistance fighters and anti-Communist fascists. Vivarelli, *La fine di una stagione: Memoria 1943–1945* (Bologna: Il Mulino, 2000). In Germany, the topic of the Holocaust became less sacrosanct, especially after Martin Walser's 1993 Frankfurt Book Prize speech about how, in Germany, the Holocaust had become a "moral cudgel." Walser, *Erfahrungen beim Verfassen einer Sonntagsrede* (Frankfurt am Main: Suhrkamp, 1998) and Frank Schirrmacher, ed., *Der Walser-Bubis Debatte: Eine Dokumentation* (Frankfurt am Main: Suhrkamp, 1999), 7–17.

identity; the religion of the Holocaust substituted for a lack of adherence to organized Jewish religion; and commemorative rituals evacuated memorialization
of substance and substituted cheap sentiment for a real engagement with Jewish
death.[55] When the Holocaust survivor and writer Ruth Kluger tells us facetiously
that she does not "hail from Auschwitz, I come from Vienna," she criticizes the
transformation of her life into an icon of suffering that cannot convey the com-
plexities of who she is.[56]

Analyses of the Holocaust as a Jewish and non-Jewish civil religion are persuasive, and they account for the particular power the Holocaust survivor image once
exerted in the United States, as well as for a strain of ambivalence toward Jewish
memory in the United States and especially in Western Europe. The trenchant
criticism of survivor witnesses as secular saints, objects both of identification
and envy, retrieves the survivor's experience from appropriation and projection.
The scholar David Roskies reconstructs Jewish responses to catastrophe that
did not, as he sees it, bend to myth or endow "survivors with almost mystical
powers."[57] But this interpretation nonetheless risks reducing the survivor icon
merely to a distorted image, and isolating the figure of the Jewish Holocaust witness from other twentieth-century accounts of bearing witness to mass violence
that fashioned survivors as particular embodiments of human suffering.[58] As the
Holocaust witness begins to fade and the urgency of such arguments to dimin-
ish, moreover, other moral witnesses have emerged.

The symbol of the Holocaust witness not only reflected a distorted experience
of death and destruction that must be corrected. It was also part of a broader effort
to formulate norms governing twentieth-century moral culture in the shadow of
state-sponsored deportation and murder. That symbol condensed the meaning of
the near physical and cultural extermination of a people, and conveyed the Nazi
camp system as a caesura, one already implicit in Rousset's formulation of the
concentration camp survivor. By envisioning the witness icon in a broader field

---

55. The term "secular saints" appears in David G. Roskies, *Against the Apocalypse: Responses to
Catastrophe in Modern Jewish Culture* (Syracuse, NY: Syracuse University Press, 1999), 7. For these
arguments, see Peter Novick, *The Holocaust in American Life* (New York: Houghton Mifflin, 2000),
201, and Gary Weissman, *Fantasies of Witnessing: Postwar Efforts to Experience the Holocaust* (Ithaca,
NY: Cornell University Press, 2004). This analysis of memorialization has by now become a cliché,
though there exist many subtle arguments about Holocaust commemoration. Zeitlin, "Vicarious
Witness," offers a particularly nuanced discussion of identification with victims of the Holocaust.

56. Ruth Kluger, *Still Alive: A Holocaust Girlhood Remembered* (New York: Feminist Press,
2003), 112.

57. Roskies, *Against the Apocalypse*, 7.

58. Both and Nesselrodt, "Survivor," 57–82, argue that the term "survivor," self-applied over time
by various networks of survivors, was preferred over "victim" for its more positive connotations.

of representation instead of only as a true or false perception of survivors, we can determine how and why it came to represent the moral affront of genocide. We can also place less heralded efforts to conceive genocide alongside prominent figures who play a role in this story: Lemkin and Arendt commented on the interwar trials, and Arendt looked to Rousset for a blueprint of the concentration camp experience.[59]

The courtroom scenarios in which audiences strained to comprehend victims' testimony constituted the speakers as moral witnesses, each a variation on a narrative about a particular kind of mass killing that ascribed moral meaning to victims' experiences of pogroms, concentration camps, and extermination. Brought into presence by the act of testimony and the symbolic solidarity it constitutes, the witness possesses similar features across different trials that makes victims' experiences of mass violence culturally legible before they were called genocide. Though both male and female victims testified, observers cast the witness primarily as a portrayal of weary and sober masculinity, with broader consequences for reimagining heroism and defiance. The witness also represents the universal violence inflicted on humans by way of the particular violence imposed on certain groups. A genealogy of the witness asks how it does so and with what effects, querying how and why some groups—anti-Nazi camp laborers, Jewish Holocaust survivors—became Western stand-ins for all of human suffering.

The Global Witness and the Counterwitness

By the time the Cold War ended, global proxy wars fought by the United States and the Soviet Union were winding down, postcolonial regimes were in power, and international legal, moral, and political responsibility for suffering others began to challenge the preeminence of state sovereignty. Genocide and other forms of global mass violence became increasingly identifiable, actionable, and visible in images of atrocity so pervasive that journalists invented a phrase to describe their numbing effects: "compassion fatigue."[60] The *Diagnostic and Statistical Manual* of the American Psychiatric Profession, the DSM-3, added post-traumatic stress disorder (PTSD) in 1980 to account for the stress that accompanied exposure to an external, usually catastrophic event. PTSD, diagnosed under other names

---

59. Arendt, of course, analyzed the specificity of totalitarian states and was interested in concentration camps as an expression of totalitarian government. Arendt, *Origins of Totalitarianism*.

60. Susan Moeller, *Compassion Fatigue: How the Media Sell Disease, Famine, War, and Death* (New York: Routledge, 1999).

since the Great War and in reference to Holocaust survivors, provided a short-hand reference for the symptoms experienced by victims of all sorts of extreme violence, including war, genocide, and assault.[61] The International Criminal Court (ICC), founded in 1998 but not operational until 2002 except for ad hoc trials to prosecute crimes in the former Yugoslavia (1993) and Rwanda (1994), assumes that survivors' testimony is key to remedying victims' trauma and restoring their dignity. The ICC also instituted protections, however inadequate, to acknowledge the vulnerability of those witnesses who continued to live in the same locations as their former persecutors.[62] As Didier Fassin and Richard Rechtman have argued, during the 1980s and 1990s medical and broader cultural narratives abstracted the diagnosis of trauma from the bodies of those who bore its impact. They also described the symptoms of those who may have come into contact with traumatized persons as secondary trauma—that of children of survivors, of observers at scenes of catastrophe, and even of guilty perpetrators.[63]

Thirty years after the Eichmann trial, a new international language and infrastructure, including courts, humanitarian organizations, and media devoted to recognizing, remedying, and alleviating victims' suffering has generated another symbol of mass atrocities and genocide. By virtue of the urgency of their needs, their ubiquity, and the now politically salient demand that victims be healed, this human rights and humanitarian infrastructure and its committed activists recast Holocaust survivors as one group among other blameless victims represented by the global victim of contemporary catastrophes like wars, genocides, and famines. The global victim's symbolic power now authorizes the work of institutions and persons who address victims' grievances, document their wounds, prosecute their tormentors, and mobilize concern about their plight. It is no coincidence that such activists are often referred to as supplementary "witnesses."[64]

The global victim and the witnesses who supplement the victim's testimonial role appear as two sides of the same coin, the latter invoking the political and

---

61. Matthew Friedman, "PTSD History and Overview," US Department of Veterans Affairs, accessed December 11, 2016, http://www.ptsd.va.gov/professional/PTSD-overview/ptsd-overview.asp.

62. Fassin and Rechtman, *Empire of Trauma*, esp. 77–97; Eric Stover, *The Witnesses: War Crimes and the Promise of Justice in The Hague* (Philadelphia: University of Pennsylvania Press, 2005), 29, 78–109.

63. Fassin and Rechtman, *Empire of Trauma*, 72–96; Fassin, *Humanitarian Reason*, 200–222.

64. In *Humanitarian Reason*, 207, Didier Fassin called attention to "the second age of humanitarianism" that "corresponds to the emergence of the witness—not the witness who has experienced the tragedy, but the one who has brought aid to its victims."

moral status of the former to pursue an agenda on the victim's behalf. The network of institutions and those who labor for them—the ICC, NGOs, exhibitions, museums, and myriad other humanitarian and human rights organizations and publications—now exist as symbols of the urgency, cultural preeminence, and necessity of witnessing and as literal forums for bearing witness, the activity that best describes the promise they hold out to victims. Many scholars have claimed that this symbolic victim merely stands in for actual victims, whose voices are muted by activists who wish to help them.[65] I take up this claim to argue that the global victim is related to but represents a historically new incarnation of the Holocaust witness. I also speculate that the persistence of the Holocaust as an icon of evil in the West owes something to the continued symbolic power of the Jewish survivor in spite of the recognition of colonial genocides and their victims—the legacy of the Jewish survivor is diminished, but nonetheless identifiable.

Activists are now second- and third-party witnesses, professionals or otherwise concerned spectators who fulfill the widespread political, social, and ethical commitment to victims' care and empowerment. Journalists, photographers, and humanitarians in danger zones are witnesses, and away from danger zones, exhibits bear witness to photographs, transforming spectators into witnesses of human rights violations from a distance.[66] The French humanitarian medical organization Doctors Without Borders (Médecins Sans Frontières) defined its moral and political activism as a form of witnessing, contrasting its work with organizations like the Red Cross, which profess neutrality. After the 1967–70 Biafran War, the group broke with its conventionally neutral stance and condemned the Nigerian government for manipulating food aid.[67]

Apolitical humanitarian witnessing like Red Cross operations still exists, but activist witnesses have proliferated, and they have become a subject in their own

---

65. Kendall and Nouwen, "Representational Practices," make this argument about the International Criminal Court. Other critics of humanitarianism make a parallel argument. Most accounts of such witnesses take their role for granted and offer strategies for improving their effectiveness (see chapter 4). Only Didier Fassin, in *Humanitarian Reason*, because he is interested in trauma, draws any sort of line from the Holocaust to this "global victim."

66. Several examples that suggest the breadth of this phenomenon are cited in note 1. See chapter 4 for myriad references to photographers and spectators of photographs as "witnesses."

67. Givoni, *Care of the Witness*, 181–203, offers a new interpretation of Doctors Without Borders' ethical discourse. The witness has also expanded to include forensic witnesses who gather facts on behalf of groups like Human Rights Watch. On the rise of "forensic witnessing"—international experts who assess forensic evidence in the aftermath of a crime against humanity—see Weizman, *Least of All Possible Evils*, and Keenan and Weizman, *Mengele's Skull*. On humanitarian doctors confronting these dilemmas, see d'Halluin, "Between Testimony and Expertise."

right. Their agonizing work and proximity to atrocities prompt questions about how they manage the stress and what ethical dilemmas they face in their capacity as "surrogate voices."[68] "Bearing witness to atrocity" refers increasingly to the moral, legal, psychological, and physical labor of second- and third-party witnesses, as well as to the testimony of traumatized victims; it describes the hard work of physicians and journalists in the field and the act of spectators looking at atrocity photographs. Witnesses now document, alleviate, and mobilize on behalf of victims' suffering. All of critic James Dawes's protagonists working in the fields of human rights and humanitarianism transfer locations to avoid "burnout" once their assignments are over; but as soon as they recover they are sent to work in yet another setting—after Bosnia there was Rwanda, after Rwanda there was Darfur.[69]

The argument that the traumatized victim is central to contemporary Western culture is hardly new, and critics across the political spectrum have long bemoaned the victim's centrality in debates by referring (in various iterations) to a "victim competition" in which victim groups ostensibly compete for a piece of the pie rather than submit their claims to reasoned historical and policy analysis. Others argue that images of traumatized victims in humanitarian fundraising, among other images mobilized for political purposes, encourage sentimentalism and turn real victims into powerless objects of philanthropic condescension.[70] Rather than reiterating or engaging these arguments directly, in the last chapter I address some of the literature, including debates about the ICC, humanitarian organizations, and atrocity photography, that map the emergence of the global victim and the activist witness in tandem—one a symbolic figure and the other laboring on behalf of all the victims the global victim represents. In the process I outline a new

---

68. James Dawes, *That the World May Know: Bearing Witness to Atrocity* (Cambridge, MA: Harvard University Press, 2007), 4, 80.

69. Dawes, *That the World May Know*, 80.

70. This literature is extensive. I will discuss this in more depth in chapter 4. I have addressed the problem of "victim competition" and the debates about it in Dean, *Aversion and Erasure*. On human rights and humanitarianism specifically as forms of consumer culture, see, among others, Mary Mostafanezhad, *Volunteer Tourism: Humanitarianism in Neoliberal Times* (Farnham, UK: Ashgate, 2014); Lecia Rosenthal, *Mourning Modernism: Literature, Catastrophe, and the Politics of Consolation* (New York: Fordham University Press, 2011); Keith Tester, *Humanitarianism and Modern Culture* (University Park: Pennsylvania State University Press, 2010). Wendy Brown and Lauren Berlant argue that identity politics involves an unintentional surrender of self-definition to others. See Berlant, "The Subject of True Pain, Privacy, and Politics," and Brown, "Suffering the Paradoxes of Rights," in *Left Legalism / Left Critique*, ed. Wendy Brown and Janet Halley (Durham, NC: Duke University Press, 2002), 105–33 and 420–34, respectively; Brown, *States of Injury: Power and Freedom in Late Modernity* (Princeton, NJ: Princeton University Press, 1999).

figure that appears, however dimly, in this literature. I call it the counterwitness, in order to capture its implicit criticism of institutionalized compassion.

In the work of critics of contemporary institutionalized attitudes toward, representations of, and policies regarding victims of state violence, the counterwitness symbolizes the recent failures of activist witnesses and institutions to live up to their promises to victims. It figures the witnesses in court who leave more wounded than before they appeared or who are never able to speak, the recipients of humanitarian aid who become pawns in larger political games or to whom experts do not listen, and victims whose injuries become the subject of voyeuristic gazes far from the location of the violence done to them. The counterwitness is fashioned in the image of a fragile but stoic victim who accuses the world of betrayal. It remains limited to a particular strain of argument and is not a generalized phenomenon, but it accords with more general criticisms of contemporary political and institutional failure to stop crimes against humanity and genocides from occurring. The counterwitness may emerge more fully formed as a figure on behalf of which newer struggles for racial equality and social justice as well as against genocide are waged. This latest moral witness is one more symbolic restoration of dignity that represents how victims experience their suffering. But as I will argue, it represents—at least in important criticism—the perceived structural weaknesses of global justice. It also reflects the deep stigma associated with powerlessness.

A genealogy of the witness to genocide from the interwar period to the present reveals patterns of cultural representation that might otherwise be obscured. The family resemblances it traces, even if each instance is contingent, suggest that responses to mass atrocities over time delineated parameters of moral responsibility and accountability that shaped conditions within which victims' suffering could be acknowledged and mourned. The forging of the witness is deeply political: it makes cultural concerns about victims' suffering central to narratives of justice and right but also articulates the cultural and ethical limits of those concerns. The witness embodies particular genocidal violence against which we are compelled to be militant and makes other forms of violence, including that which we might qualify as genocidal, less legible as such. The witness cannot, however, control entirely the power of victims' self-representations when they are able to speak for themselves. The icon of the witness to genocide is one key to the development of contemporary Western moral culture, for better and for worse. The witness symbolizes not only a moral cause but also violence that we perceive now to be so ubiquitous that "witnesses to genocide" are pervasive gauges of moral responsibility and images of human conscience.

1

THE RIGHTEOUS AVENGERS /
The Tehlirian and Schwarzbard Trials, 1921 and 1927

When we read that the Assyrian or Babylonian Government "carried into captivity" such and such a broken people or tribe, we hardly seize the meaning of the statement. Even when we see the process portrayed with grim realism on the conqueror's bas-reliefs, it does not penetrate our imagination to the quick. But now we know. It has happened in our world, and the Assyrian's crime was not so fiendish as the Turk's. "Organized and effective massacre"— that is what such a deportation means, and that must always have been its implication.

—Arnold Toynbee, *Armenian Atrocities: The Murder of a Nation* (1916)

In the midmorning of March 15, 1921, Soghomon Tehlirian shot Talaat Pasha in an affluent neighborhood in Berlin. Talaat, one of the men responsible for planning the 1915 Armenian genocide, had been one of the highest-ranking officials at the Ottoman court. Talaat fled to Berlin after the defeat of the Ottoman Empire to avoid trial by the Allies, but was targeted for assassination by the Armenian Revolutionary Federation, an important Armenian political party. The plotters in the party assigned the job to Tehlirian, whose family had perished in the genocide. The would-be assassin rented a room across the street from the former minister and got to know his routine. Tehlirian shot Talaat through the back of the head and ran, but he was cornered by bystanders who hailed the police as he protested, in halting German, that the incident was merely a dispute between foreigners. The Armenian shooter was arrested and brought to trial a few weeks later on charges of premeditated murder.[1] After a hasty preliminary investigation, the June trial lasted two days.

---

1. *Der Prozess Talaat Pascha (Stenographischer Bericht)* (Berlin: Deutsche Verlagsgesschaft für Politik und Geschichte, 1921). I cite pages in the text from the English version except where I have

FIGURE 1.1 / Soghomon Tehlirian, June 1922.
Ara Oskanyan's Family Archive.

Five years later in Paris, Samuel (Scholem) Schwarzbard, a Bessarabian Jewish watchmaker, committed a similar crime of vengeance. He had come to France in 1910 to escape political repression in Russia, fought in the Great War, won the Croix de Guerre in 1916, and acquired French nationality. He returned to Odessa in 1917 to fight with anarchist forces assisting the Bolsheviks to take over the city. Several years later, back in Paris, Schwarzbard learned that Symon Petliura, former head of the short-lived Ukrainian National Republic, was living there in exile. Petliura had been the commander of the Ukrainian Directory's army and had allegedly organized the 1917 pogroms that took some fifty to sixty thousand Jewish lives, and wounded or orphaned many more.[2] He settled in Paris in 1924 as the head of the Ukrainian government in exile and published a Ukrainian-language newspaper. On May 25, 1926, Schwarzbard shot him five times in the rue Racine outside of a bistro and a few more times after he was dead. When the police showed up, Schwarzbard proclaimed that he had killed a "great butcher (*massacreur*), a great assassin."[3] He was arrested and put on trial for eight days from October 18 to October 26 in 1927 after a pretrial investigation that lasted seventeen months.[4]

These are likely the first major trials in Western Europe featuring victims of interethnic violence and state-sponsored mass atrocities seeking justice. They

---

modified the translation: *Armenian Political Trials Proceedings 1: The Case of Soghomon Tehlirian*, trans. Vartkes Yeghiayan (Los Angeles: A.R.F. Varantian Gomideh, 1985). For various accounts of Tehlirian, see also Edward Alexander, *A Crime of Vengeance: An Armenian Struggle for Justice* (New York: Free Press, 1991); Eric Bogosian, *Operation Nemesis: The Assassination Plot That Avenged the Armenian Genocide* (New York: Little, Brown, 2015); Stefan Ihrig, *Justifying Genocide: Germany and the Armenians from Bismarck to Hitler* (Cambridge, MA: Harvard University Press, 2016); Jacques Derogy, *Resistance and Revenge: The Armenian Assassination of Turkish Leaders Responsible for the 1915 Massacres and Deportation*, trans. A.M. Berrett (London: Transaction, 1990); Raymond Kevorkian, *The Armenian Genocide: A Complete History* (London: I.B. Tauris, 2011); Ronald Grigor Suny, *"They Can Live in the Desert but Nowhere Else": A History of the Armenian Genocide* (Princeton, NJ: Princeton University Press, 2015).

2. From 1918 to 1920 Ukraine was under a provisional government called the Directory of the Ukrainian National Republic.

3. Testimony of Scholem Schwarzbard, October 18, 1927, Institute for Jewish Research, Center for Jewish History, New York (hereafter YIVO), formerly Elias Tcherikower Archives, now RG85, folder 486, fol. 39494–95; David Engel, ed., *The Assassination of Symon Petliura and the Trial of Scholem Schwarzbard 1926–1927: A Selection of Documents* (Göttingen: Vandenhoeck & Ruprecht, 2016), 351. I have consulted the microfilm of the transcripts of the trial that took place at the Cour d'Assises de la Seine, beginning on October 18, 1927, which is held at YIVO. Short segments of the French transcript, as well as additional documents, in all of their original languages, are reproduced in Engel, *Assassination of Symon Petliura*.

4. David Engel discusses the context of this trial in depth from a Jewish and a Ukrainian perspective. His focus is less on the actual trial than on how political players outside the courtroom influenced or were influenced by it. Introduction, in Engel, *Assassination of Symon Petliura*, 7–102.

FIGURE 1.2 / Samuel (Scholem) Schwarzbard, Paris.
Archives of the YIVO Institute for Jewish Research, New York.

brought these crimes into public view.[5] In Berlin, the defense defended Tehlirian by proclaiming the importance of humanitarian justice. In Paris, Schwarzbard's defense lawyer, Henry Torrès, invoked French republican nationalism and the rights of man on behalf of his client, as if the case were as momentous as the Dreyfus affair. Both trials took place at a particular moment in interwar politics: international imperialism, national self-determination, and claims about minority rights framed debates in the League of Nations about Armenian statehood and the denationalization of Jews in the East. Jewish organizations pressured the league to protect Jews in the newly created nations of Eastern Europe. Germany lobbied to join the League of Nations and wished to ward off charges of complicity with the Armenian genocide (which was not yet called by that name) as domestic politics became increasingly polarized, while the French Left sought to rally around a cause in a rightward shifting political landscape.

Both Tehlirian and Schwarzbard were acquitted of murder after juries heard blood-curdling accounts of the Armenian massacres and the military invasions of Ukrainian villages. The verdicts decreed that the shooters had momentarily lost control of their free will, in both cases because the defense showcased the atrocities that had pushed each man to lose his composure rather than the murders they had committed. Polish Jewish lawyer Raphael Lemkin, who coined the term "genocide" in 1942, mentioned both trials in the same breath, referring to the "absence," as he put it, of "any law for the unification of moral standards in relation to the destruction of national, racial, and religious groups."[6] But since the trials' official purpose was not to seek justice for victims of pogroms or

5. For an account of the assassination of a Bolshevik functionary by a White Russian émigré, see Alfred Erich Senn, *Assassination in Switzerland: The Murder of Vatslav Vorovsky* (Madison: University of Wisconsin Press, 1981) and *L'affaire Conradi: Plaidoirie de M. Theódore Aubert* (Geneva: Droz, 1924). There were many other interwar political trials, but none of which I am aware that addressed state-sponsored mass murder targeting ethnic minorities, with the exception of the court-martial of the Armenian assassin Misak Torlakian by a British tribunal in Harbiye, Turkey, for the murder of a Tatar leader responsible for killing Armenians. See note 51.

6. Raphael Lemkin, *Totally Unofficial: The Autobiography of Raphael Lemkin*, ed. Donna-Lee Frieze (New Haven, CT: Yale University Press, 2013), 21. See also the discussion in James Loeffler, "Becoming Cleopatra: The Forgotten Zionism of Raphael Lemkin," *Journal of Genocide Research* 19, no. 3 (2017): 347–48; and Douglas Irvin-Erickson, *Raphaël Lemkin and the Concept of Genocide* (Philadelphia: University of Pennsylvania Press, 2017). On Lemkin and the Armenian genocide, see Annette Becker, "Raphael Lemkin, l'extermination des Arméniens, et l'invention du mot 'génocide,'" in *Le génocide des arméniens: Cent ans de recherche, 1915–2015*, ed. Becker, Hamit Bozarsian, Vincent Duclert, and Raymond Kévorkian (Paris: Armand Colin, 2015), 192–202; Olivier Beauvallet, "Lemkin et le génocide arménien sous l'angle juridique," in *Le génocide des arméniens*, which notes, apropos of Lemkin's commentary on Tehlirian and Schwarzbard, that Lemkin viewed these trials as episodes in which "the massacred victims had been essentially an informal judgment before human conscience" (207).

genocide, they do not overlap easily with the categories of international criminal law or even with the history of human rights; advocacy and political mobilization were important—and Schwarzbard's trial spurred Jewish organizations to defend him—but from an official perspective they were secondary to adjudicating a crime, and from the defendants' perspective, secondary to vengeance.

The two trials are part of the broader phenomenon, during and after the Great War, of using testimonial practices to denounce atrocities committed against suffering others. Veterans of the Great War generated an enormous literature about the brutality of industrialized warfare alongside interwar art and literary production, from Dada to the works of Louis-Ferdinand Céline, which ironized war heroism. Jews and Armenians produced volumes of photographs and narratives documenting the violence to which they had been subjected for a wide variety of audiences and issued broad calls for attention to these crimes.[7] Non-Armenians such as the historian Arnold Toynbee and the German missionary Johannes Lepsius also wrote important works about the Armenian genocide that documented and denounced the crimes.[8]

The Tehlirian and Schwarzbard trials depended on victim testimony, whose use was controversial, partly because audiences equated atrocity literature with state propaganda and partly because the educated public believed victims' perspectives were overly subjective. Toynbee and Lepsius thus had more credibility than eyewitnesses who were victims, spurring victims to back up their claims as meticulously as possible.[9] Toynbee, worried about the use of anonymous victim testimony, which he knew might compromise his effort, contrasted Armenians' industriousness, commercial talent, and civility with the "savagery" of their Muslim tormentors.[10] The trials, however, provided a forum for publicizing

---

7. Alexandra Garbarini, "Document Volumes and the Status of Victim Testimony in the Era of the First World War and Its Aftermath," *Études arméniennes contemporaines* 5 (2015): 113–36. On the literature of denunciation and the emergence of "humanitarian rights" in the interwar period, see Bruno Cabanes, *The Great War and the Origins of Humanitarianism* (Cambridge: Cambridge University Press, 2014).

8. James Bryce and Arnold J. Toynbee, *Armenian Atrocities: The Murder of a Nation* (London: Hodder & Stoughton, 1916); Johannes Lepsius, *Bericht über die Lage des armenischen Volkes in der Türkei* (Potsdam: Templeverlag, 1916). Toynbee was a member of the British Foreign Service and on the British Armenia Committee's propaganda subcommittee. See Gary Johnson Bass, *Stay the Hand of Vengeance: The Politics of War Crimes Tribunals* (Princeton, NJ: Princeton University Press, 2000), 113.

9. Garbarini, "Document Volumes," 114–16, demonstrates that the use of victims' voices was controversial.

10. Toynbee, *Armenian Atrocities*, 17–20. In "Document Volumes," Garbarini discusses Toynbee's worry about the anonymity of his sources, which he had ensured to protect their identities, noting that in his preface to Toynbee's work, Lord James Bryce took care not to identify Armenians as "'moral witnesses'" (123).

atrocities in the defendants' words, in court, and to the press. Each trial provided a forum for the dissemination and discussion of atrocities.[11]

Lawyers' invocation of temporary insanity defenses to argue for acquittals made victim testimony extremely significant. By putting the Armenian genocide and the Jewish pogroms on trial, the lawyers hoped to prove that their clients had acted without premeditation, gripped by forces beyond their control. The more harrowing the testimony about defendants' suffering, the more likely they were to gain jurors' sympathies. The invocation of temporary insanity was nonetheless a stretch, given how much time had lapsed since both defendants were said to have witnessed the violence and other evidence of premeditation. In order to rationalize the homicides as expressions of temporary insanity, the trials subtly differentiated forms of organized violence not only from combat but also from generic invocations of barbarism and its oft-invoked abstract synonyms—horrors, vile crimes, outrages, and unimaginable indignities.

The trials defined the terms of defendants' innocence or guilt in the absence of a legal consensus about how to prosecute the massacres they had avenged, and clarified the conditions necessary for redeeming even assassins from shame. The defendants' own communities mostly celebrated the verdicts, but the public acquittals were very controversial because the jury refused to condemn men who had taken the law into their own hands. The juries may have grudgingly admired or simply understood the men's desire for vengeance. But in retrospect, the creative, pedantic, uncannily similar defense strategies turned the defendants into moral witnesses. The trials harnessed the defendants' harrowing stories to a legal argument about temporary insanity, producing a rationale for acquittal that was embedded entirely in an assessment of the defendants' suffering. Tehlirian and Schwarzbard became moral witnesses because they testified to crimes against their people, and the trial proceedings turned them into righteous avengers whose witness mattered.

In so doing, the trials redeemed Tehlirian's and Schwarzbard's injuries, justifying the defendants' acts by the violence done to them and their families, cleansing them of guilt for their crimes and placing the violence to which they had been subjected center stage. In order to ensure the defendants' acquittals, the trials transformed extralegal violence and vigilante justice rhetorically into a higher form of moral expression they characterized as dignified, manly, and humanitarian, motivated by the defendants' experience of extreme indignity.

---

11. Comité des Délégations Juives, *Les pogromes en Ukraine sous les gouvernements ukrainiens (1917–1920)* (Paris: n.p., 1927). On the use of this document book, a compilation of evidence about the pogroms, see Garbarini, "Document Volumes," 127–32.

The lawyers' rhetoric turned vengeance into a quest for humanitarian justice. By voting to acquit, juries declared that the assassins' own suffering and its debilitating effects were an exculpatory factor in their crimes. The trials could recast the assassins as righteous avengers because their rhetoric—the witnesses' stories and how the lawyers shaped those stories—created a narrative about the crimes that was exculpatory and redemptive at once.

Lax Courts and the Press

In *Eichmann in Jerusalem* Hannah Arendt refers to both trials to assess the Israeli handling of Eichmann's capture and prosecution. She distinguishes between these trials and Eichmann's because the Berlin and Paris proceedings were not "spectacles with pre-arranged results."[12] The "*j'accuse*," she argues, "so indispensable from the point of view of the victim, sounds, of course, much more convincing in the mouth of a man who has been forced to take the law into his own hands than in the voice of a government-appointed agent who risks nothing."[13] In Arendt's view, Israel took no such risks when it kidnapped Eichmann. And though she contrasted the boldness of risk-taking avengers with Israel's ostensibly no-risk strategy, she mostly lamented the absence of an international tribunal that might have tried Eichmann instead of forcing the Israelis to take their own measures. During Schwarzbard's trial, others had made Arendt's argument about how the existence of an international tribunal might have prevented the murder of Petliura; Tehlirian's trial, too, highlighted the inadequacy of any legal remedy for collective murder.[14]

Neither Tehlirian's nor Schwarzbard's trial has received much scholarly attention in its own right. David Engel argues that Schwarzbard's trial unified the Jewish diaspora around the question of minority rights at the cost of Jewish-Ukrainian relations, as each side demonized and caricatured the other and the pogroms took precedence over the murder of Petliura.[15] Historians of the Armenian genocide

---

12. Hannah Arendt, *Eichmann in Jerusalem: A Report on the Banality of Evil* (1963; repr., New York: Penguin, 1994), 266.

13. Arendt, *Eichmann in Jerusalem*, 266. She also notes that "in the Schwartzbard trial especially, methods very similar to those in the Eichmann trial were used" (265). The transliteration of "Schwarzbard" makes for different spellings of his name.

14. Testimony of Professor Paul Langevin (Collège de France), October 19, 1927, YIVO RG85, folder 488, fols. 39872–73.

15. Engel, *Assassination of Symon Petliura*, 7–102. Engel argues that the trial reflected a new chapter in the transformative mobilization of Jews in the diaspora and Jewish public opinion, and contrasts Schwarzbard with Captain Dreyfus, who led a private life once he was finally released.

mention Tehlirian's trial as an important moment in publicizing crimes against Armenians for better or worse; the trial, Stefan Ihrig argues, played a central role in writing a new chapter in German "genocide debates" as German nationalists' justification of the murders replaced their earlier denials.[16] Others treat Tehlirian's acquittal as a triumph of the Armenian Revolutionary Federation, whose members assassinated Turks they blamed for the genocide.[17]

While there is little scholarship on these specific trials, legal historians who study this period focus on the importance of lawyers and juries and, in such cases, the nature of acquittals, which were increasingly common. Both the German and French legal systems used juries only for the most serious crimes, in part because of complaints about laymen's susceptibility to manipulation by lawyers and witnesses, which allegedly led to frequent acquittals.[18] Historians also attribute the increased laxity of courts in murder cases to the importance of new psychological theories of compromised free will, jurors' sympathy for defendants, and their deference to medical experts, who often focused on the psychological impact of social deprivation.[19] Lawyers in the United States sometimes invoked an "honor defense" to shield men accused of murdering their wives' "seducers."[20] The honor

---

Schwarzbard, in contrast, became an international Jewish celebrity (53–71). Others have also addressed the trial, but more peripherally: Alexandra Garbarini refers to Torrès's strategy during the Schwarzbard trial as exemplary of narrative and testimonial strategies that have been insufficiently explored. Garbarini, "Power in Truth Telling: Jewish Testimonial Strategies before the Shoah," in *Kinship, Community, and Self: Essays in Honor of David Warren Sabean*, ed. Jason Coy, Benjamin Marschka, Jared Poley, and Claudia Verhoeven (New York: Berghahn, 2014), 175. The trial is also covered in the context of a biography of Schwarzbard in Kelly Scott Johnson, "Biography of a Jewish Assassin: Sholem Schwarzbard" (PhD diss., Harvard University, 2012). It is mentioned in Henry Abramson, *A Prayer for the Government: Ukrainians and Jews in Revolutionary Times, 1917–1920* (Cambridge, MA: Harvard University Press, 1999), 136–37, 168–72. Howard M. Sachar, *Dreamland: Europeans and Jews in the Aftermath of the Great War* (New York: Knopf, 2002), 3–19, is based on secondary sources and is often inaccurate.

16. Ihrig, *Justifying Genocide*, 235.

17. Bogosian, *Operation Nemesis*, 200.

18. Napoleon brought the jury system to Germany. For a discussion of judges' attitudes toward juries in Germany, see John H. Langbein, "Mixed Court and Jury Court: Could the Continental Alternative Fill the American Need?" *Law and Social Inquiry* 6, no. 1 (1981): 195–219; Benjamin Carter Hecht, *Death in the Tiergarten: Murder and Criminal Justice in the Kaiser's Berlin* (Cambridge, MA: Harvard University Press, 2004), 167. On André Gide's commentary on jury leniency, see Edward Berenson, *The Trial of Madame Caillaux* (Berkeley: University of California Press, 1992), 33–34.

19. See Berenson, *Madame Caillaux*, 30–42; Hecht, *Death in the Tiergarten*, 8–9, 179–219. For an overview of the constitutional crisis under the Weimar Republic, see Peter Caldwell, *Popular Sovereignty and the Crisis of German Constitutional Law: The Theory and Practice of Weimar Constitutionalism* (Durham, NC: Duke University Press, 1997). On the impact of lawyers and public opinion on "staging" that crisis, see Henning Grunwald, *Courtroom to Revolutionary Stage: Performance and Ideology in Weimar Political Trials* (Oxford: Oxford University Press, 2012).

20. Hendrik Hartog, "Lawyering, Husbands' Rights, and the 'Unwritten Law' in Nineteenth-Century America," *Journal of American History* 84, no. 1 (1997): 67–96, argues that this "unwritten"

defense was articulated in France and Germany as the loss of self-control caused by extreme and momentary passion—most commonly a husband murdering his adulterous wife, but also a wife murdering her husband's defamer, or a woman retaliating against a stalker who abused and tried to blackmail her.[21]

Most contemporary commentary understood that in the end Tehlirian's and Schwarzbard's trials were, for better or worse, revelations about suffering humanity as much as they were efforts to determine the assassins' guilt. As the media became an increasingly important component in shaping public opinion, lawyers and even judges played to the press and transformed trials into political flashpoints: the political Left rallied predictably around verdicts favorable to progressive defendants, and the Right embraced acquittals of their own representatives. Both trials reiterated interwar rhetoric in which lawyers invoked the defendants' willingness to sacrifice themselves for a cause, whether for social justice or national honor.[22] The trials followed formal legal procedure to establish the assassins' responsibility for their crimes, and both relied heavily on translators for some of the witnesses and, in Tehlirian's case, for the defendant himself. Each called forensic and medical experts to the stand and asked eyewitnesses to testify about the shootings.

The tension between the sympathy for victims of mass atrocities and a commitment to law and order was reflected in the press coverage, which made the Armenian genocide and the pogroms causes célèbres even as mainstream papers winced at the verdicts. In Germany, left-wing journalists such as Maximilian Harding in the weekly *Die Zukunft* reviled Talaat and used his murder as an opportunity to discuss Armenian suffering, German guilt, and the evils of war.[23] *Die Zukunft* devoted two full issues to Tehlirian's story and referred to extensive documentation of the massacres, acknowledging that no verdict could adequately judge Tehlirian's real motives, which eluded the laws on criminal responsibility. For the same reason, Harding did not condemn the acquittal.[24]

---

law, which was a statute in only three states, was enforced at a moment when men's legal power over women was diminishing. Lawyers defended their murderous clients with honor defenses by appealing to tacit assumptions about male authority, pitting moral conservatives against progressive reformers.

21. Hartog, "Lawyering," 67–69, explains that in the United States, the murder had to be committed in (or at least construed as committed in) the "heat of passion," not after a cooling-off period. Madame Caillaux murdered her husband's defamer. See Berenson, *Madame Caillaux*; the stalker incident is recounted in Hecht, *Death in the Tiergarten*, 203–13.

22. On this rhetoric of sacrifice, see Grunwald, *Courtroom to Revolutionary Stage*, 194–97.

23. See "Tehlirian" and "Zwischen Ost und West: Armenien in Moabit," *Die Zukunft*, June 4 and June 11, 1921, 273–94 and 295–322, respectively. Moabit refers to the location of the high court in Berlin.

24. "Zwischen Ost und West," 297.

The Socialist *Vörwarts* applauded the acquittal and proclaimed it "the first trial of the real war guilty."[25] Most other papers were ambivalent. Whether centrist or conservative, they interwove stories of Talaat's murder with accounts of the Armenian genocide either consciously to evoke sympathy for the Armenian plight or simply by virtue of reporting on the trial. The headline in the liberal *Vossische Zeitung*, "The Murder of Talaat Pasha," was subtitled "The Sorrows of the Armenian People," and yet the story also described Tehlirian as having the "head of an intellectual" and "shifty Oriental eyes."[26] The conservative-nationalist *Deutsche Allgemeine Zeitung* sought to rationalize the massacres of Armenians and deplored the interpretation of article 51 of the penal code that had been used to acquit the Armenian shooter by virtue of temporary mental incapacitation.[27] Almost all but the most virulently nationalist conceded, as did the *Berliner Volkszeitung*, that the trial and acquittal were ultimately about the murder of the Armenians, and almost all reported sympathetically on Tehlirian's personal sufferings.[28] Even the *New York Times* pointed out that the jury was between a rock and a hard place. If they acquitted Tehlirian, they would rightly condemn the massacres, but they would also sanction extralegal murder: "This dilemma cannot be escaped: all assassins should be punished; this assassin should not be punished. And there you are!"[29]

These responses mirrored the press reaction to Petliura's murder in France, where the Communist paper *L'Humanité* celebrated Schwarzbard's acquittal, but most newspapers conceived it as the outcome of a focus on the pogroms and mourned the verdict as a stain on the French judicial system. A Republican newspaper in Normandy, *L'Ouest-Éclair*, asked whether French courts would always allow cold-blooded killing in the "name of humanity and the rights of man." While expressing sympathy for Jewish victims of pogroms, the editorial asked if revolutionaries who sought vengeance would simply be able to plead their political cause by marching "a parade of slaughtered corpses into the court."[30] In Paris, *Le Temps* claimed that the acquittal was understandable given the pogroms and lawyer Torrès's ability to evoke their horrors, and a hostile Polish-French

---

25. Cited in Derogy, *Resistance and Revenge*, xxiv.
26. "Die Ermordung Talaat Pashas: Leiden des armenischen Volkes," *Vossische Zeitung*, June 2, 1921.
27. "Der Freispruch des Mörders," *Deutsche Allgemeine Zeitung*, June 4, 1921.
28. "Der Freispruch im Talaat-Prozess: Die Tragödie eines Volkes," *Berliner Volkszeitung*, June 4, 1921.
29. "They Simply Had to Let Him Go," *New York Times*, June 6, 1921. The *New York Times* reported on German complicity in the Armenian massacres. For a fuller account of the press aimed at understanding German attitudes toward the genocide, see Ihrig, *Justifying Genocide*, 226–33, 263–69.
30. "L'affaire Schwartzbard," *L'Ouest-Éclair* (Caen), October 27, 1927.

paper friendly to Petliura stated outright that the jury "in no way judged the accused, but the pogroms."[31] Even *Le Petit Parisien* grudgingly acknowledged that the horror of the pogroms overdetermined the outcome of the trial.[32] In the United States, *Time* magazine interpreted Schwarzbard's acquittal the same way: "the outcome of the trial, which gripped all Europe, was regarded by the Jews as establishing proof of the horrors committed against their co-religionists in the Ukraine under the dictatorship of Simon Petlura. Radical opinion rejoiced; but conservatives saw justice flouted and the decorum of the French courts immeasurably impaired."[33]

The witness testimonies did not overwhelm the trials—only a few eyewitnesses to the massacres testified in each one. Schwarzbard's attorney Henry Torrès renounced his right to call eighty more witnesses in addition to those who had already testified. In his closing statement he played up the atrocities by seeming to downplay them: he stated that because the jury was already familiar with the pogroms' horrors, he would spare them the "hundreds and hundreds" of photographs in his possession, including one in which they would recognize the "unfortunate young woman bent over a wounded child" who had testified previously.[34] In his memoirs he claimed that the trial turned in Schwarzbard's favor at a crucial moment when the jurors could not hide their emotions; it was not necessary to prolong the testimony, which he feared might prove "tiresome."[35] In Tehlirian's case it took the prosecution half of the trial to protest the relevance of some shocking witness testimony; by the time the prosecution argued that it was not within the court's jurisdiction to determine Talaat's guilt or innocence, only that of Tehlirian, the damage had been done. The defense called no further eyewitnesses.[36]

31. "L'assassinat de l'ataman Petlioura," *Le Temps*, October 29, 1927; "Le procès Schwartzbard," *Le bulletin périodique de la presse polonaise* 180, October 21–November 24, 1927, 4.

32. "Schwartzbard est acquitté aux applaudissements de l'auditoire" and "Pour et contre," *Le Petit Parisien*, October 27 and October 29, 1927, respectively. For more discussion of the Schwarzbard trial press, see Schor, *L'opinion française et les étrangers en France, 1919–1939* (Paris: Publication de la Sorbonne, 1985), 488–89.

33. "Petlura Trial," *Time*, November 7, 1927. I should point out what is perhaps obvious: Schwarzbard was on trial, not Petliura. Similarly, the German transcript of Tehlirian's trial is called "The Trial of Talaat." These inversions suggest how much the alleged crimes of those assassinated overtook the focus on the accused's deeds.

34. Henry Torrès, "Plaidoirie," in "L'assassinat de l'ataman Petlioura," *Revue des grands procès contemporains* 5–6 (May–June 1929): 336. This is Torrès's closing argument in the trial. The witness to which he referred was Haya Greenberg.

35. Henry Torrès, *Souvenir, souvenir, que me veux-tu?* (Paris: Del Duca, 1964), 131–32. He also claims that Albert Einstein provided a preface to an edition of his closing argument. He reproduces the laudatory preface, which celebrated Schwarzbard's acquittal (133).

36. *Case of Soghomon Tehlirian*, 92.

In each case the defense and even the prosecution thus emphasized the atrocities suffered by Armenians and Jews. Tehlirian's and Schwarzbard's own purported suffering in particular occupied center stage, and each gave his own testimony. Even more important, the defense focused on the nobility and resilience of the shooters, who managed not only to survive, but also to avenge the suffering of their respective "nations." This rhetorical strategy afforded a public tribunal for victims of collective suffering that focused extensively on the injured victims and their avengers.

These trials cannot be extricated from the pressing political issues and legal and social debates of the period, just as they depend on those contexts for their outcomes. In the historical literature they are unsurprisingly treated like other trials for homicide during the period, reflecting broader cultural battles about immigration, international politics, and domestic politics, and in the case of Germany, even the domestic politics of mass murder.[37] But their narratives also turned assassins into righteous avengers, augmenting not only the evidentiary power of victims' voices but also amplifying their moral role in condemning the violence to which they had been subjected—hence Lemkin's insight that the two trials had a lot in common. Indeed, the rhetorical dimension of these trials has been neglected almost entirely, perhaps because from a legal and political perspective, they appear predictable and have thus not inspired further probing.

While the interwar trials do not fit within the trajectory of human rights law, some critics have claimed that they paved an unheralded path to the Nuremberg tribunal. Edward Alexander writes that Tehlirian's trial fell short of international justice, but inspired a commitment to an international forum in the mind of

---

37. David Engel, "Being Lawful in a Lawless World: The Trial of Scholem Schwarzbard and the Defense of East European Jews," *Simon Dubnow Institute Yearbook* 5 (2006): 83–97. Engel defines what the trial meant to a French audience by reference to the many other political trials of the period, a judicial system for the most serious crimes that leaned toward leniency, and interwar politics that were not only increasingly anti-immigrant but also polarized, pitting Communists against the monarchist Action Française (53–71). On trials of foreigners for murder in France, see Schor, *L'opinion française*, 477–90. Schor, on whose account Engel, *Assassination of Symon Petliura*, 484, relies, lists fourteen trials and acquittals from 1920 to 1930, including Schwarzbard's. Schor argues that these trials represent heightened anxiety over immigration and political murders, antipathy toward foreigners, and lax courts, and conceives Schwarzbard's case as particularly revelatory of diverse strains of public opinion. But Schwarzbard's and Tehlirian's trials focus on a combination of interethnic and state-sponsored violence. They were more than political murders, and revealed in exemplary fashion the political tensions at the time and received international attention. Henry Torrès's autobiography suggests that he saw his most famous case, the trial of Germaine Breton—one of the four that Engel mentions here in the same breath—and Schwarzbard's very differently, even though they both involved political murders and had a similar outcome. See Torrès, *Souvenir, souvenir*, 98–132. On the German context, see Ihrig, *Justifying Genocide*.

Robert M.W. Kempner, a German Jewish lawyer who later became a US prosecutor at Nuremberg.[38] The former US ambassador to the United Nations Samantha Power notes that Tehlirian's trial motivated the young Lemkin to try to understand mass murder in new terms. She conceives of the verdict as an anticipation of Nuremberg, though British and US lawyers pushed Lemkin and his arguments aside in that trial.[39] Lemkin, who believed Tehlirian "had acted as the self-appointed legal officer for the conscience of mankind," worried about the implications of extralegal vengeance. But he was so moved by "the sufferings of hundreds of Jews ... displayed like an open wound before the world" that his qualms diminished in reference to Schwarzbard, whose crime, he exclaimed, was "beautiful," and could "only be executed by people with sublime feelings, pure souls and huge hearts, who take upon themselves the pain of their brothers, often of all of humanity, even of entire generations."[40]

Though the trials inspired Lemkin, from a legal point of view they do not anticipate Nuremberg in any formal sense—they did not develop a legal category to convict the perpetrators of mass murder—though anticipation of the successful Nuremberg proceedings is one way to conceive their moral significance. Their importance lies elsewhere: by the end of each trial, the defendant was a righteous man of honor, a humanitarian, and most surprisingly, a locus of human conscience, not only because the trials confirmed or challenged tacit assumptions about male authority, xenophobia, individual criminal responsibility, and political accountability, but also because the creative interpretation of existing statute and the brilliant manipulation of familiar rhetoric reconstituted their crimes as morally unimpeachable. The rest of this chapter traces the trials' rather startling transformation of vigilantes into righteous avengers, of assassins into witnesses of terrible crimes and heroes of humanity, though contemporaries only used "witness" in its juridical meaning when they used it at all.[41] In this period, human

---

38. Alexander, *Crime of Vengeance*, 196.

39. Samantha Power, *"A Problem from Hell": America and the Age of Genocide* (New York: Basic Books, 2002), 17–20.

40. Lemkin, *Totally Unofficial*, 20, 21, quoted in Loeffler, "Becoming Cleopatra," 348. The trial was an expression of Lemkin's view of Schwarzbard—the rendering of vigilante justice as a righteous act by a "pure" soul who suffers on behalf of his "brothers." When the young David Frankfurter shot a Swiss Nazi in 1936 as revenge for Jewish suffering, the December 8, 1936, issue of the Communist newspaper *L'Humanité* likened his gesture to Schwarzbard's. Jewish newspapers later hoped that Schwarzbard's defense lawyer would represent Frankfurter. See *L'univers israélite*, February 12, 1937, and *Paix et droit: Organe de l'Alliance israélite universelle*, December 1936.

41. French and German both use "witness" in moral and juridical senses. Tehlirian is now sometimes referred to as a "witness" in the moral sense. Ihrig treats him both ways in *Justifying Genocide*, 234–69, as does Sévane Garibian, who stresses the moral dimension of his testimony, in "Ordonné par le cadavre de ma mère: Talaat Pacha ou l'assassinat vengeur d'un condamné à mort," in *La mort*

conscience, such as Lemkin's reference to Tehlirian as the "conscience of mankind," represented the dismay of distant and civilized spectators observing the barbarism of others, not moral and psychological pressure to remedy victims' injuries. This representation would begin to change over the course of the next twenty-five years.

The Trial of Soghomon Tehlirian

Tehlirian's hasty trial lasted from June 2 to June 3, 1921. It became an exercise in teaching the German people about the horrors of the Armenian genocide. During the preliminary investigative phase Tehlirian admitted he had killed Talaat, but insisted that he had acted on his own even though he was an operative in the Armenian Revolutionary Federation (ARF), which had orchestrated the assassination. He was later more pliant once he realized that the headlines were treating the assassination as a political murder. Worried about being condemned to death, he played the role of an anguished and isolated actor whose (very real) epileptic fits were brought on by memories of his family's murder. The prosecution never brought out his involvement in any organized plot to pursue Talaat, who was the first of several Turkish nationalists to be assassinated in a series of murders the ARF dubbed "Operation Nemesis."[42]

Correspondence between the German foreign office and one of Tehlirian's eminent defense lawyers, Adolf von Gordon, indicates that the Weimar government acted to limit, and in one case prohibited, the testimony of a diplomat at the trial in order not to expose the extent of German complicity in and knowledge of the Armenian genocide.[43] The foreign office may have hoped for a conviction in order not to alienate its former Turkish allies, but it was also concerned

---

du bourreau: Réflexions interdisciplinaires sur le cadavre des criminels de masse, ed. Sévane Garibian (Paris: Pétra, 2016), 207–31.

42. For an overview, see Bogosian, Operation Nemesis.

43. The defense nonetheless got hold of several documents signed by Talaat and had them translated into German for the court. Recent literature makes the German role clear, based in part on the publication of documents that were translated into English in 2016. For example, the German consul in Aleppo from 1910 to 1918, Walter Rössler, told the German Foreign Office that if called to testify he would have to indict Talaat. He was not allowed to testify. Wolfgang Gust, ed., The Armenian Genocide: Evidence from the German Foreign Office Archives, 1915–1916 (New York: Berghahn Books, 2014), 91, 768–69. Most secondary sources treat Tehlirian as an Armenian hero and understand the trial through that prism. This is the case with Bogosian, Operation Nemesis, and Alexander, Crime of Vengeance. On German culpability in the genocide, see Osik Moses, "The Assassination of Talaat Pascha in Berlin: A Case Study of Judicial Practices in the Weimar Republic" (PhD diss., California State University—Northridge, 2012).

that the German army not be implicated in crimes against the Armenians. These government measures did not prevent the trial from becoming a cause célèbre, but shortened Tehlirian's time in the public eye and turned testimony away from the German army's misdeeds to the defendant's distress over what he said he witnessed—the murder of his mother and brothers and the kidnapping and rape of one of his sisters. Medical experts could not agree on whether Tehlirian was responsible for his act, but agreed with one exception that his epilepsy compromised his free will even though the condition had not sapped it entirely.[44] What never came out in the trial—and what the prosecution notably failed to establish—was that Tehlirian did not witness the genocide, but was in Tiflis (now Tbilisi) when the Turks murdered his family because he had volunteered to fight with the Russian army.[45] When he returned home, he found a brother alive and the town abandoned. Though by virtue of his losses and his grief he was a victim of the genocide, at the trial he insisted that he had witnessed the murders.

The trial's presiding judge was Erich Lemberg, the prosecutor was the district attorney Gollnick, and the defense attorneys were Adolf von Gordon, Theodor Niemeyer, and Johannes Werthauer. Niemeyer was a distinguished professor of international law at Kiel University, and the other defense attorneys were well known, guaranteeing the trial lots of attention. The judge's opening interrogation revealed his sympathy for the defendant, whom he probed gently about his traumatic experiences. Tehlirian recounted his story calmly and deliberately, beginning with the Ottoman order to leave his village in 1915, the robbery of their convoy by troops who stole their valuables—they had only been allowed to bring what they could carry—and then bursts of gunfire, at the sound of which a soldier dragged his sister away and his mother screamed, "May I go blind!" Tehlirian said he could no longer bear to think about their suffering: "I do not want to be reminded of that day. It is better for me to die than describe the events of that black day" (7). The judge urged him to try and recount what happened as best he could, and Tehlirian described how his brother's head was split open with an ax, his mother was shot, and he woke up surrounded by corpses. His entire family had almost all disappeared without a trace. In response to the judge's query about why he had initially admitted to having killed Talaat, he replied, "When did I say that?" When pressed, he insisted that he had had no plan to kill him and that "I do not consider myself guilty because my conscience was clear." "I have killed a man, but I am not a murderer," he claimed, acknowledging that

44. *Case of Soghomon Tehlirian*, 98–104. Page citations from this source are hereafter given parenthetically in the text.

45. Bogosian, *Operation Nemesis*, 194–201.

about two weeks before the murder, he kept "seeing over and over the scenes of the massacres. I saw my mother's corpse. The corpse just stood up before me and told me 'You know Talaat is here and yet you do not seem to be concerned. You are no longer my son'" (15). It was then that he decided to kill Talaat, but on further interrogation he claimed that he had made no such decision, did not know that Talaat was in Berlin, and he appeared dazed and confused.

The district attorney Gollnick played it safe, referring to the massacres as "killings known to us all" and avoiding questions about Talaat's relationship with the German army (114). He echoed the testimony of General Otto Liman von Sanders, head of the German military mission in the Ottoman Empire, who declared that the German army was shocked and surprised by the massacres, though it was "naturally understandable that the victors in such a war would be accused of massacring the vanquished" (83). The general, who had been the object of British criticism for having abetted the murders, worked to counter charges of German complicity by insisting that all the "officers up to the rank of general in the Eastern provinces were Turks," that most of the perpetrators were not of a "select class" of soldiers ("criminals or the perennially unemployed") and that the German government protested Turkish actions (83–84). Gollnick used von Sanders's testimony to portray the massacres as in keeping with the "savagery and bloodshed" that had "always been a tradition in Asia Minor," to deflect from Talaat's responsibility by portraying the murderers as rogue troops—"gendarmes, actually vagabonds"—and as an overheated but understandable response to fears of Armenian betrayal (114).[46] Although von Sanders's testimony defended the Germans, it also created sympathy for Tehlirian, who emerged as a victim of Ottoman "savagery."

The prominent Jewish and left-wing Social Democratic Party (SPD) defense attorney later attacked by the Nazis, Johannes Werthauer, also negated the real ties between Talaat and Germany. He argued disingenuously that Talaat, who was widely believed to be living in Berlin as a guest of the government, could not have been given refuge from the Allies by highly placed German officials because he lived under a false name (141). An Armenian bishop who had survived the genocide also distanced the Germans from the Turks even as he indicted Talaat. He described his atrocious experience and hailed the Germans in Ottoman lands who had saved him from certain death: "I would like to express my deep gratitude and heartfelt thanks, here, to those German engineers who granted me aid and comfort in my time of need" (90).

---

46. Ihrig, *Justifying Genocide*, 254, 256–57, claims that Gollnick was likely asleep on the job, "incompetent," and "unmotivated."

Testimonies came from a wide range of eminent doctors, academics, military men, Germans who had witnessed Talaat's murder or who had known Tehlirian, Armenians who had known him, and witnesses to the Armenian genocide. The testimony of the Protestant missionary Johannes Lepsius, a highly respected former state official, was essential to the defense, and outside the courtroom, he held rallies for the Armenian cause.[47] Lepsius was a German nationalist who had sought to further German colonial interests in Anatolia, and he provided powerful testimony about the genocide, which he had investigated on his own. He had also published books about the massacres. He implicated Talaat directly and repudiated references to the responsibility of rogue Ottoman troops, while also insisting that the Germans would never have condoned the massacres (76–82).

Even before these experts spoke on the stand, a few Armenian witnesses had testified to their own experience of Turkish brutality with harrowing reports that served to make Tehlirian's deed more comprehensible. Christine Terzibashian from Garin, Anatolia, and married to an Armenian living in Berlin, recounted how the deportations were carried out (72–73). She described how wealthy Armenians were given advance notice that they were to leave their homes, while the poor were told to gather with little time to spare. Four groups of five hundred families from her village were evacuated. As they filed out, they began to walk over corpses from other villages. At some point men were separated from the group, tied together, and thrown into the river, while those who remained watched. The presiding judge asked, "How do you know that?" to which Terzibashian responded, "I saw it with my own eyes" (73). She went on to describe how Turkish gendarmes murdered the remaining men with axes, threw them in the river, and killed by bayonet the women "selected" by gendarmes whose demands they refused. They "crushed the pelvic bones of pregnant women, took out their fetuses, and threw them away" (74). To great commotion in the courtroom, the witness declared, "I swear to you this is true" (74), and later, when the judge asked, as if to emphasize the horror of her story, "Is all this really true? You are not imagining it?" she swore that it was true, and even worse than she "could relate." The judge then asked who was "thought to be the person responsible for this terror," and she insisted that it was Talaat Pasha, because the Turkish guards forced some of their victims to kneel and cry "Long live the pasha" to thank him for sparing their lives. Only three members of her family survived. At this point, the defense attorney von Gordon underlined the

47. On Lepsius, see Ihrig, *Justifying Genocide*, esp. 47–53.

veracity of her testimony by arguing that she had described the massacres in such detail that no more Armenian eyewitnesses need be called other than the bishop Krikoris Balakian, who would recount the deportations and indict Talaat directly (75).

Once evidence of the atrocities had been established and confirmed by credible authorities, Tehlirian's lawyers sought to exculpate their client. Werthauer, careful not to cast aspersions on a former German ally, acknowledged that Talaat may have been a "decent fellow," but called him a member of a "militarist cabinet":

> A militarist is a person opposed to justice. The militarist is not an individual who is a member of the military by calling. It is possible to be an officer or a soldier, wear a uniform, use weapons and, at the same time, not be a militarist. The officer or soldier himself can uphold the principles of right and justice and perform his duties as a member of the military at the same time. On the other hand, there are countless militarists who have never put on a uniform. They sit at a desk, write articles, and fiercely defend the flag of brute force. (145)

The lawyer then strove to alter the image of Tehlirian from a murderer into a noble figure by making a dramatic distinction between humanitarian patriots and coldhearted "militarists." The militarists "annihilated the Armenians": they were not the Turkish people, they were not even soldiers—here again he made a crucial distinction between legitimate and illegitimate warriors. The militarists were "well-trained animals that will never be able to have human feelings," and formed a distinctive new cast capable of deporting "a whole nation"; they resembled the Bolsheviks, those with "influence across the Rhine," and even some Germans who had provided military training to Turkish soldiers (146). In contrast, Werthauer proclaimed, Tehlirian was like the Swiss patriot William Tell: "Of all the juries in the world, which one would have condemned Tell if he had shot his arrow at [the tyrant Albrecht] Gessler? Is there a more humanitarian act than that which has been described in this courtroom?" (148). By associating him with Tell, the defense associated Tehlirian's act with honor and humanitarianism, displaced the German army's responsibility for murderous deeds onto Turks cast as "militarists" rather than soldiers, and realigned German loyalties from the Ottoman Empire to the murdered Armenian nation. Werthauer reminded the jury that the genocide was aimed against Armenians because they were Christians (148), though defense attorney Niemeyer also argued that Armenians had "Eastern" rites similar to those of "Islamic washing and daily prayers" (152). Like the Turks, they are a "people of the East who have a different approach than we do to the legality or illegality of an action," but they also have "a wholesome family life" (155).

The cynical mission of the German government—to prosecute Tehlirian quickly while using the opportunity to redeem German conduct—inadvertently transformed Tehlirian into a symbol of human conscience tragically compelled to gun down a murderer for want of justice. Defense attorney Werthauer urged the jury to declare the defendant not guilty, because when Tehlirian descended to the street, revolver in hand, he acted in the name of human conscience. He was "the representative of humanity vs. inhumanity, of justice vs. injustice. He steps forward as the representative of the oppressed against the collective representative of the oppressors; for the one million killed against the one who, along with others, is to blame for those crimes. He stands as the representative of his parents, his sisters, his brothers, his brother-in-law, and finally, as the representative of his sister's two-and-a-half year old child" (149). Werthauer had already stated dramatically, "The whole world is watching us. . . . Therefore, even the function of the defense counsel has to give way before the responsibility to humanity" (134–35). Niemeyer, too, pleaded, "We of the Third District Court and this jury are obliged to maintain a broad view of this case and to render a well thought-out decision which will be recognized for its justice and humanitarian quality" (155). Pressing the case, he declared that "we can be opposed to it [Talaat's murder], but this is not like an ordinary trial. It takes us beyond the confines of this courtroom and obliges us to widen our horizons. Try to understand other nationalities, other peoples, other circumstances, and be fair to them" (155). And more dramatically, he added, "If you condemn him to death, we know what will happen. He will declare steadfastly and with a clear conscience and noble conviction: 'If this is what you want, I am ready to die.' He will put his martyred head on the scaffold, his mother will appear to him and aid him, and he will have an enviable death. If he were to be set free, that would not revive his parents, his sisters, and his brothers. It would not make him well again; he will never be normal like other people" (155). Asked by the judge to respond to these pleas that he be set free, Tehlirian responded: "I did not understand what the defense attorneys said. But I am convinced that whatever they have said suffices. I have nothing to add" (162).

In keeping with centuries' worth of appeals to the laws of humanity, these references to German honor were extensions of the civilizing mission, and it would be easy to interpret them only as efforts to whitewash the German army. Niemeyer, after all, had appealed directly to the jury's patriotism, arguing that if they condemned Tehlirian, they would confirm the West's worst fears about Germany: "We Germans have been held responsible with the Turks for the crimes committed against the Armenians." A finding of not guilty, he went on, "would put an end to the misconception the world has of us" (162). Yet the defense also insisted that saving Germany's honor depended on the recognition of Tehlirian's righteousness. Tehlirian had been "forced," to quote Arendt, "to take the law into his own hands," and it is the absence of any other forum for justice that was ultimately put on trial.[48] The verdict did not really pronounce on whether the assassin had done what he did since that question was settled, but on his right to have done it. The defense requested the jury to declare Tehlirian unfit under paragraph 51 of the German Penal Code, which held that punishable conduct was not present if the defendant had a temporarily compromised will.

The German government's opportunism may have contributed to the verdict, but so too did the way in which Armenian suffering was on trial, embodied by its avenger. Since any focus on Tehlirian's suffering did little to help the prosecution because it risked generating sympathy for the defendant, prosecution lawyers sought instead to contrast the vigilante Tehlirian with the good soldier Talaat. "Members of the jury," said the district attorney Gollnick,

> The psychological roots of this crime go back to the bloody and savage events that took place in Asia Minor, and it is as if we have to hear the thunder of the World War again. Furthermore, the personality of the victim gives the crime its particular significance. From a nameless and unknown mass of people rose a hand that struck down a man. This man [Talaat], himself a son of the people, steered his country through a world struggle, and walked the heights of history as a true ally of the German people.[49]

While conceding that Tehlirian's act of vengeance was "not ignoble" (115), and that the war formed the background for the assassination, the prosecution also implied that Talaat "steered his country" with honor and that Tehlirian, also from a humble background, chose a less honorable path.

Turning the comparison between Tehlirian and Talaat to their advantage—both were engaged in the war, both played their parts—the defense refused to blame Talaat entirely for the "sea of blood" spilled by one million "children, women, the elderly, healthy and brave males" and ascribed war atrocities to "demons" and "mass impulses" that "move[d] people around as if they were pawns" (132). Werthauer's association between the forces gripping soldiers

---

48. Arendt, *Eichmann in Jerusalem*, 265.
49. Translation modified. *Der Prozess Talaat*, 83–84. Standard translation in *Case of Soghomon Tehlirian*, 111.

in combat and those that moved Tehlirian treated his crime implicitly as a symptom of war gone awry. Moreover, he argued, if we cannot fully blame Talaat for the "extermination of the Armenian people"—he had not done the actual killing—then surely the jury could not blame Tehlirian for the "one more drop of blood" he added to this bloodshed. (132). If there were any doubt left about the defendant's compromised will, Werthauer compared the assassination to a husband's fury if he discovered his wife with another man. Who, he asked, would "even imagine condemning such a man?" (160).

The trial cast Tehlirian as an unconventional soldier whose lapse was explained as a sign of the reign of "demons" and as a response to a "militarist" enemy, distinguishing between the soldier's demons and the militarists, who were not soldiers at all. His analogy between the assassination and honor killing reframed Talaat's murder as Tehlirian's response to the loss of control over the "property" that a man believes is rightfully his, and transformed Tehlirian's murder of Talaat into a struggle to restore his sovereignty and his human dignity. Even the prosecution distinguished between revenge and premeditated murder, conceding that perhaps revenge would be understandable under the circumstances, but insisted—since the case turned on his state of mind—that Tehlirian had murdered intentionally (115). The defense instead represented his act of vengeance as an act of conscience, as a "humanitarian" gesture worthy of William Tell, and as a symptom of wounded honor by a man who could not have possibly been in his right mind (148).

But how did the court reconcile a compulsively committed, unintentional act with an honorable one? Tehlirian became a combatant, and yet not quite. Though he was like a soldier, his mind was gripped by darkness, by an uncontrollable revolt against the memory of his and his family's submission to the militarists' whims. He had to wreak vengeance at all costs to survive psychologically the deaths of those with whom his life was once entwined and to uphold the wrongness of their murder. The assassin was an unconventional warrior against an unconventional enemy who abandoned soldierly conduct in his mission to annihilate his adversaries. Tehlirian was a survivor whose heroism consisted in his quest, however belatedly, for vengeance, now transfigured into a righteous act of humanitarian justice. This fight, in which the perpetrators neglected the rules of war and the victim struggled to dissipate the demons that tormented him, is not patriotic combat defined by bravely fighting the enemy—impossible under the circumstances—but rather a mode of struggle driven by the compulsions of human conscience, by the necessity that right and justice must triumph no matter what, no matter how belatedly. That is why the defense called him a representative not only of the Armenian people but of humanity.

In this reformulation of the patriotic soldier, the trial constituted a new kind of hero battling a seemingly novel type of crime—"militarists" signed writs decreeing the annihilation of a people. But Tehlirian's honor was restored on terms that were ambiguous in a case that used a temporary insanity defense for what many believed was a cold-blooded crime. German conservative nationalists and genocide denialists bemoaned the verdict because it rewarded a man who had murdered a wartime German ally.[50] For those who celebrated Tehlirian's release in Germany and elsewhere, the trial restored his honor by fashioning him as a humanitarian warrior shocked by what he had witnessed and unable to act any other way. Tehlirian (in the story he told on trial) never contemplated revenge, and his wounds were deep. If the defense lawyers' strategy hardly convinced everyone, it accomplished its goal. An Armenian assassin on trial for murder turned the proceedings into a verdict on Armenian suffering and walked out of the courtroom a free man.[51]

The Trial of Scholem Schwarzbard

The Schwarzbard case drew many comparisons to that of Tehlirian, none more powerful than Schwarzbard's defense attorney's Henry Torrès's claim that Talaat's order to massacre Armenians was analogous to Petliura's alleged instigation of pogroms against the Jews. Torrès insisted that, like Tehlirian, acquitted by a "bourgeois jury in Berlin," Schwarzbard must also be declared not guilty.[52]

---

50. Ihrig, *Justifying Genocide*, 266–67.

51. The Armenian assassin Misak Torlakian was part of the same group, Operation Nemesis, that had sent Tehlirian to murder Talaat. Torlakian killed Behoud Khan Javanshir, former minister of the interior of Azerbaijan until 1918, on July 18, 1921, barely two months after Tehlirian was acquitted. Khan Javanshir had assisted the Ottomans in murdering twenty thousand Armenians in Baku, which later fell to the Bolsheviks. Torlakian, claiming that his family was killed, was handed over by French occupation soldiers to the British and found guilty by a British military tribunal in Harbiye in 1921, but he was not sentenced (for reasons of mental incompetence) and was expelled to Greece. Torlakian had borrowed the script from Tehlirian's trial and called witnesses from the scene of the crime. But absent a European setting for the crime and closed the military tribunal, the proceedings had little general impact abroad. American Jewish Historical Society, New York, *Raphael Lemkin Collection*, box 9, P-154: Misak Torlakian's trial transcript, 1921. Thanks to Charlotte Kiechel for this reference. See also Derogy, *Resistance and Revenge*, xxv, 115–17.

52. Torrès, *Le procès des pogromes: Plaidoirie suivie des témoignages* (Paris: Les Éditions de France, 1928), 340. The Berlin jury was actually a mix of social classes: pharmacists, masons, roofers, merchants, painters, jewelers, and locksmiths. Torrès later published excerpts of letters and famous witness testimony from Schwarzbard's trial in Torrès, "Plaidoirie." There were several references to the Armenian genocide in the Schwarzbard trial and in the correspondence around it. On the witness stand on October 25, 1927, Leo Motzkin proclaimed, "Another nation has suffered as much: the

Torrès proclaimed that like Schwarzbard, Tehlirian had cried, "I am pleased to have done what I did! I avenged my people; I've killed an assassin!"[53] That Tehlirian made no such declaration is beside the point. Audiences understood both trials to be about the inhumane treatment of a minority population with no recourse to the usual tribunals of justice.

Schwarzbard's trial was an important chapter in Jewish-Ukrainian relations because it highlighted in a public forum the routinized violence to which Ukrainian Jews had long been subjected. Moreover, though Torrès wisely stressed the political diversity of his witnesses in order to avoid being tarnished by a pro-Soviet or pro-"Jewish" bias—he was Jewish—the trial nonetheless played out as a struggle between pro- and anti-Soviet French factions. Torrès was a left-wing lawyer who had tried some famous political cases and was later a consultant to the lawyer for Herschel Grynszpan, the Polish Jew whose 1938 murder of a Nazi in Paris sparked Kristallnacht.[54] Like Tehlirian's trial, Schwarzbard's too provided a forum for political warfare of various kinds and condemned mass violence. It did so by celebrating French "civilization" and denouncing Slavic "barbarism" in the rhetoric of the civilizing mission, just as the Berlin defense team had celebrated German honor and denounced Turkish brutality. The trial transformed an extralegal act into a gesture of righteous humanity that offered the French court an opportunity, as the Comité des délégations juives declared, to stigmatize "the murderers, inciters to murder, and authors of rape and acts of hardly imaginable acts of bestiality." Like Tehlirian, Schwarzbard embodied human conscience, and his trial would "serve not only as a way to compensate the hundreds of thousands of victims but also as a prophylaxis in the future."[55]

In Schwarzbard's case, too, the trial eventually revolved less around Schwarzbard's deed than around the atrocities committed in pogroms and whether Petliura had really organized and sanctioned them. The state brought the case against Schwarzbard on behalf of Petliura's widow and brother. Judge

---

Armenian nation! We were the first to cry out for the Armenian cause." YIVO, RG85, folder 492, fol. 40519. Engel cites the Zionist Yehoshua H. Yeivin, who spoke disdainfully about how Jews gathered statistics while the Armenians avenged their dead. Engel, *Assasination of Symon Petliura*, 79.

53. Torrès, "Plaidoirie," 340.

54. On Grynszpan and Torrès, see Jonathan Kirsch, *The Short, Strange Life of Herschel Grynszpan: A Boy Avenger, a Nazi Diplomat, and a Murder in Paris* (New York: Liverlight, 2013), 183–84. For a personal account of Torrès and his influence by one his most prominent students, see Robert Badinter, *L'exécution* (Paris: Fayard, 1998).

55. Both citations above are quoted from a memo attributed to the *Comité des délégations juives* in Engel, *Assassination of Symon Petliura*, 84. Defense attorney Torrès, in a letter to Justice Louis Marshall, then head of the American Jewish Committee, insisted that the trial should be a trial of the pogroms (277–79).

Georges Flory presided over the trial, and the Corsican César Campinchi represented the prosecution. The lawyers were seasoned, and the defendant was unbowed. When the judge interrogated Schwarzbard at the beginning of the trial, the defendant remained defiant and headstrong, in marked contrast to Tehlirian. When asked by the judge if he had really acted alone, since the prosecution insisted that he was part of a Soviet conspiracy, Schwarzbard insisted he had, and explained his motive by focusing on the horror of the Ukrainian pogroms.[56] He claimed that a non-Jewish Russian acquaintance in Paris had told him about having overheard officers from the White Russian army ("or the Army of Petliura, because it's the same thing") talking about their exploits in a hospital waiting room. One claimed that he had raped thirty-seven Jewish women, and the other boasted that he had killed fifteen Jews in a single day. The acquaintance told Schwarzbard that he was so shaken by the terrible stories that he left without finishing his medical treatment. Schwarzbard told the judge, "You can imagine the state that I, too, was in. I was present at some pogroms, I saw atrocities committed and I forced myself to forget them. But this Russian who came to tell me these things awakened in me all the memories, and that had a huge impact on me."[57]

The judge, as was customary in order to establish the facts of the case, proceeded to describe how Schwarzbard located the Ukrainian exile, and how the hetman had been killed. Through the entire narrative, Schwarzbard merely responded "yes" or "yes, exactly," and only spoke to contest a detail here and there. In a later session, the judge confirmed that Schwarzbard was in his right mind and fully understood him. He then asked: "You said you wanted to avenge your coreligionists who were victims of pogroms in the Ukraine, pogroms organized, according to you, by Petliura." When Schwarzbard once again replied yes, the judge asked him why he believed that Petliura was responsible for the pogroms. Schwarzbard responded with a long narrative about the violence, claiming that he had seen several pogroms. He offered a short history lesson—Petliura took Ukraine by force against the Bolsheviks and the first thing his men did was to massacre Jews. "It has been three centuries since massacres in these valleys of

---

56. The historian Henry Abramson has noted that it is impossible to know if Schwarzbard, as the prosecution contended, was really a Soviet agent, or whether Petliura had ever given a direct order to his troops to conduct pogroms. Abramson, *Prayer for the Government*, 136–37, 171–72. Engel arrives at the same conclusion in *Assassination of Symon Petliura*, 20n48, 96.

57. YIVO, RG85, folder 486, fols. 39482–83, October 18, 1927; Engel, *Assassination of Symon Petliura*, 348–49. In Engel's account, small portions of the more than twelve hundred–page French transcript appear as documents 62–65 (pp. 345–406). Whenever my citations overlap with his, I cite the page number in his text.

blood and tears began." Calling Petliura's men "true brutes," he stated that they surprised people in their homes as they slept "because they knew that the Jewish population had no defense." They "raped women in front of their husbands, daughters in front of their fathers and their brothers. They burned and pillaged, they planned pogroms; pogroms are assassinations, pillage, and rape. Voilà the pogrom." When he saw a third pogrom he alleged was directed by Petliura, he claimed that Petliura's soldiers had a slogan on their armbands and hats: "Kill the Jews and save Ukraine."[58]

Other witness testimony bore out Schwarzbard's claims, not only about the atrocities committed in pogroms, but also about Petliura's responsibility. Among them, Elias Tcherikower, a pioneering Jewish historian from Kiev, had gathered documents and photographs of Ukrainian pogroms and brought them to Paris for the purpose of the Schwarzbard trial. This collection of documents, assembled by the Comité des délégations juives, consisted of detailed accounts of pogroms from all over Ukraine.[59] Tcherikower, through an interpreter, spoke as an eyewitness and in precise detail, even when subjected to the grandstanding of prosecutor Campinchi (though Torrès and sometimes Schwarzbard punctuated the prosecutor's remarks with their own exhortations). Tcherikower alluded to the "Bolshevik terror" he had fled—since the Bolsheviks suppressed Jewish autonomy—countering prosecution witnesses' insinuations that Jews had all allied with the Bolsheviks. When the prosecutor asked him if Petliura was "at least partially" responsible for the pogroms, he responded that "no one in Ukraine" doubted his responsibility, and recounted the Jewish community's multiple pleas with Petliura to stop the pogroms to no avail: "The assurances Petliura gave about his opposition to pogroms can be compared to calling the doctor after the sick person dies, or to calling the firemen after the fire has already been snuffed out."[60]

Another eyewitness, "Mademoiselle Grimberg" (Haya Greenberg), a medical student, testified about the 1919 Proskurov pogrom. She said that she left her office one evening only to hear "savage cries" as Ukrainian soldiers approached the Jewish parts of the city. The next afternoon, she went to care for the wounded and found there had been a massacre. The survivors had lost entire families, including young children, all murdered by soldiers wielding bayonets. A young

58. YIVO, RG85, folder 487, fols. 39513, 39514, 39516, October 18, 1927; Engel, *Assassination of Symon Petliura*, 357–58.

59. He brought these archives to New York and they are now a part of YIVO, the institute devoted to the study of Yiddish culture that was originally founded in 1925 in Vilna (now Vilnius). On Tcherikower and the Schwarzbard trial, see Cecile Esther Kunitz, *YIVO and the Making of Modern Jewish Culture* (Cambridge: Cambridge University Press, 2014), 26, 87–88.

60. YIVO, RG85, folder 492, fols. 40461, 40462, 40468.

woman of nineteen who witnessed her mother's murder saw the Ukrainians throw themselves on her and cry, "This is for our father Petliura!"[61]

Her own grandparents' home had been turned into a hospital. There she cared for more wounded children, their mothers, and later, a woman with a bullet lodged in her throat who died in Greenberg's arms; many of them died, had limbs amputated, or were struck dumb by terror.[62] She went on to claim that some of Petliura's soldiers stopped by the makeshift hospital to express their shame at the senseless murders while others sang and played music in the streets. She testified that the Jewish council of the town, of which her father was a member, went eventually to plead with Petliura to leave them in peace, but he did nothing to stop the pogroms or punish his men. She did not know of an order by Petliura and did not see him herself, but insisted that he was responsible for the atrocities.[63]

The prosecution called witnesses to prove that claims about Petliura's responsibility were exaggerated or false. These were men who had served in the military with Petliura and civilians who testified to his great affection for the Jewish people. But they proved not to have the same credibility as Schwarzbard and other witnesses for the defense. The prosecution set the stage by arguing that in Ukraine and Russia, pogroms were simply a fact of life and Jews were among their many victims.[64] They underlined the chaos of the period, during which the Germans fought with Ukrainians against the Bolsheviks, the Bolsheviks fought to control Ukraine, and the Ukrainians were split into many groups, some of whom fought with Petliura for independence.

In this environment, in which troops of various loyalties battled ferociously, the prosecution witnesses claimed that the Bolsheviks engaged in pogroms, as did rogue elements of an otherwise honorable Ukrainian military. A Ukrainian ex-military man, a certain Procopovitch, proclaimed that he had personally struggled both to prevent the "Jewish colonization" of Ukraine and to stop the Bolsheviks from creating a "Jewish Republic."[65] Others, also denying Petliura's responsibility, justified the pogroms because, they claimed, the Bolsheviks had killed members of their own families, in yet one more reiteration of the

61. YIVO, RG85, folder 491, fols. 40342, 40343, October 24, 1927; Engel, *Assassination of Symon Petliura*, 396.

62. YIVO, RG85, folder 491, fol. 40342, October 24, 1927; Engel, *Assassination of Symon Petliura*, 396.

63. YIVO, RG85, folder 491, fols. 40348, 40351, 40352, October 24, 1927; Engel, *Assassination of Symon Petliura*, 396–400.

64. YIVO, RG85, folder 487, fol. 39713, October 19, 1927; Engel, *Assassination of Symon Petliura*, 385.

65. YIVO, RG85, folder 488, fol. 39893, October 19, 1927.

antisemitic cliché that all Bolsheviks were Jews.[66] In the same breath as he swore
that Petliura had opened his arms to Ukrainian Jews, a French engineer who had
lived in Ukraine for some thirty years referred to "Jewish agents" whose dishonest
business practices angered local gentiles.[67] In one of the most dramatic moments
of the trial, Colonel Alexandre Boutakow denied Petliura's responsibility for any
massacres but stated that he regarded the pogroms against Communist Jews to
be the work of "divinely inspired revenge."[68]

Torrès made hay of these statements, mocking the reference to "divinely
inspired revenge" and skillfully weaving a narrative about the pogroms into his
cross-examinations. He insisted that Petliura had not sanctioned one of his officers until a year and a half after the worst pogrom, undermining testimony that
the sanction demonstrated Petliura's compassion for Jews. When asked if his witness Haya Greenberg had not simply relied on public rumors about who was
responsible for the pogroms, Torrès argued that the violence was systemic and
organized and, in a dig against the so-called rogue troop argument (also made in
Tehlirian's case), reminded the court about Greenberg's claim that Petliura's soldiers cried, "This is for our dear father Petliura" (as the Turkish gendarmes had
cried that their deeds were in honor of the pasha).[69] His point was that even if
Petliura did not participate in deadly pogroms, the murderers invoked his name
and presumed his approbation. As Schwarzbard had also testified, if Petliura
were commander of the Ukrainian Directory's army, was he not responsible?[70]

Torrès also deftly compared the civilized values of the French command to
the barbarity of Ukrainian troops, turning the rogue troop claim into a characterization of Ukrainian brutality rather than an assertion about a few groups
of hooligans. In France, he argued, military promotions were based on merit,
while in the Ukrainian Directory, army titles were given away as spoils of war. He
implied that since the officers testifying likely did what they were told in order to

---

66. YIVO, RG85, folder 489, fol. 39942, October 21, 1927.

67. YIVO, RG85, folder 490, fol. 40216, October 22, 1927.

68. YIVO, RG85, folder 488, fol. 39785, October 19, 1927. The Russian names in the trial are all
gallicized.

69. YIVO, RG85, folder 491, fol. 40355, October 24, 1927.

70. In a letter published by the defense, the Russian Jewish writer Joseph Kessel, also a French
citizen, argued against the prosecution's suggestion that Petliura was not fully in control of events
by reference to Pontius Pilate (pointedly echoing and elaborating on an allusion Schwarzbard had
made to Pilate and lending it his authority): "Everyone knows of a case in which a Roman magistrate
washed his hands of the blood of a crucified man. History and human conscience have in no way
pardoned him. A chief does not have the right to make the same gesture as Pontius Pilate. The Bolshevik commissars are responsible for those executed by the Cheka. None of them can say: 'I did not
want this to happen.' The same goes for Petliura." Kessel cited in Torrès, *Le procès des pogromes*, 158;
Schwarzbard's comment is in YIVO RG85, folder 486, fol. 39524, October 18, 1927.

reap rewards, it was hard to imagine that Petliura was ignorant of what his men were doing.[71] Torrès later claimed that Boutakow's remark about a pogrom motivated by "divinely inspired revenge" likely moved the jurors definitively toward Schwarzbard's side.[72] In the course of the trial, the defense lawyer almost never called attention to the casual antisemitism of the prosecution explicitly. The jury may or may not have had a few second thoughts about references to "Jewish atavism" in the prosecution attorney's closing statement or his insistence that the Russian Revolution was mostly a "Jewish oeuvre," but they clearly judged the prosecution's argument to be weak or disingenuous.[73]

Torrès put to rest any questions about Schwarzbard's character by reference to his time as a French solider, invoking Schwarzbard's service in the Great War and his French nationality as guarantors of his integrity. Jews ("this race"), he declared, "subdued by an ancestral habituation to domination, eventually adapted to the organization of terror against them. But when one becomes a French citizen, as Schwartzbard has done, when one rubs elbows with freedom-loving Parisians, when, with the hands of a French soldier one holds a rifle in the hot trenches, a new soul, ardent and quaking, awakens, one willing to strike out for justice."[74]

The experience of trench warfare is thus rhetorically linked not to senseless killing but to an honorable murder (a "strike" in the name of justice). Having absorbed French honor on the battlefield, Schwarzbard repudiated Jewish passivity and demanded justice. The Comtesse de Noailles echoed the same theme in her letter for the defense, in which she did not even pretend that Schwarzbard was afflicted by temporary insanity: "we are in France, the country of Corneille. Of course, there is a commandment, 'thou shalt not kill.' But does the life of nations and of men really permit accepting passivity in the face of unpunished savagery? The humble watchmaker who fought for France, home of justice and liberty, would not resign himself to that view, which his work made easy: he waited."[75]

This version of Schwarzbard's suffering and valor, like Tehlirian's own at trial, was not quite faithful to the real story. Schwarzbard was surely deeply affected by the pogroms he witnessed, but his parents had not died in one, though Torrès told the American Jewish Committee president Louis Marshall that they had, and the implication of all the testimony was that Schwarzbard had lost them to

---

71. YIVO, RG85, folder 489, fol. 40042, October 21, 1927; YIVO, RG85, folder 488, fol. 39798, October 19, 1927.

72. Torrès, *Souvenir, souvenir*, 131–32.

73. Prosecuting attorney Albert Willm, "Plaidoirie," in "L'assassinat de l'Ataman Petlioura," 293, 300.

74. Torrès, "Plaidoirie," 337.

75. Torrès, *Le procès des pogromes*, 195.

the violence.[76] Most French or immigrant Jews saw him as an avenger, though some French Jews worried that the trial would intensify antisemitism and called the murder of Petliura an act of "humanitarian justice" rather than revenge.[77] Schwarzbard wrote to his wife from prison that she should tell his "brothers and sisters in wretched Ukraine" to go to his father's grave and etch on his tombstone "Rest in peace, great Jewish soul! Your son has avenged the innocent blood of your brother Israel, the saint, and of your Jewish people, all of them."[78] Though Schwarzbard was a vigilante, and though he proudly proclaimed what he had done, the assassination was treated as a crime of passion, the legal category usually used to acquit enraged husbands or wives who murdered their adulterous spouses.[79] His madness, as the narrative went, was temporary, and like Tehlirian's, driven by his insatiable passion for justice.

Unlike Tehlirian, however, Schwarzbard was not docile, perhaps because his assassination of Petliura was not a planned hit meant to remain anonymous, but a less carefully carried out killing by a man who sought the limelight. Both men were nonetheless acquitted by reference to a temporary loss of will in verdicts that were akin to US jury nullifications.[80] The juries delivered these results even though Tehlirian had shot Talaat from the back and fled, and Schwarzbard killed Petliura as the Ukrainian held up his cane in self-defense.

In his memoirs, Torrès rationalized Schwarzbard's acquittal. His crime, he claimed, was honorable and necessary since "European public opinion remained indifferent" to the pogroms. He contrasted the Schwarzbard case to another one he had argued with similar, spectacular results in 1923: he had defended the anarchist Germaine Breton, who avenged the murder of Jean Jaurès by assassinating Maurius Plateau, secretary of the far-right Ligue d'Action Française. Breton was also acquitted on the grounds of having committed a *crime passionnel*. In his closing argument, Torrès refused to condone

76. Engel, *Assassination of Symon Petliura*, 279. On the biographical details, see Samuel Schwarzbard, *Mémoires d'un anarchiste juif*, présentées et préfacées par Michel Herman (Paris: Éditions Syllepse, 2010), 29. The text notes that his mother died when he was a child. This is a French translation of multiple Yiddish works by Schwarzbard (with no clear dates of origin of any particular document). Yiddish sources are used by Engel to assert that Schwarzbard's father died of an illness in 1917 and his mother died when he was a child (*Assassination of Symon Petliura*, 279n117). Johnson's "Biography of a Jewish Assassin" makes the same claims (63, 31).

77. Johnson, "Biography of a Jewish Assassin," 166. Schwarzbard's crime was also the inspiration for a short story by Yiddish writer Dovid Bergelson, "Among Refugees" (1928), in *The Shadows of Berlin: The Berlin Stories of Dovid Bergelson*, trans. Joachim Neugroschel (San Francisco: City Lights Books, 2005), 21–44.

78. Schwarzbard, *Mémoires d'un anarchiste juif*, 270.

79. Berenson, *Trial of Madame Caillaux*, 28–36.

80. Thanks to Sam Moyn for this observation.

her violence and attributed it to her psychological instability—her father had died when she was fourteen, and her mother abandoned her, rendering her acutely sensitive to matters of social justice. He proclaimed that, like the infamous Madame Caillaux, who had murdered a man who impugned her husband's reputation, some women kill but must be let free: "It is not a matter of knowing if they strike because their honor, sensibility, or vanity was tainted; they strike because they believe that they have the right to seek retribution in the name of an idea for which they have sacrificed their lives." He went on to say that in the "long jurisprudence concerning *crimes passionnels*, there is no other crime that so dignifies an acquittal."[81]

Torrès claimed that Breton was in the grip of a delusion when she murdered Plateau, thus rendering her political violence a matter of psychological instability. His argument was strategic because he could not condemn the Action Française's celebration of violence and then laud an assassination. In Schwarzbard's case, the pogroms were sufficiently distant and so brutal that an act to avenge them might evoke far more sympathy. Still, he proclaimed, employing tacit assumptions about gender, Schwarzbard was a "good and simple man lacking the vanity of vigilantes like Breton and her ilk." He was "attached to his family, his race, and his religion, [and] would have lost his self-esteem if he had had not punished the perpetrator." If Schwarzbard had been condemned, he mused, "France would no longer be France."[82] Schwarzbard's crime was a redemptive act carried out in the name of the rights of man and thus in the name of the principles of freedom, equality, and brotherhood embodied by French republicanism. Like Tehlirian, he was a soldier but not quite. His act could not be legally recognized as a courageous self-sacrifice and was thus portrayed as a crime of passion, an uncontrollable response to memories dredged up of his family's and his people's suffering. By arguing that Schwarzbard's compulsive quest for "self-esteem" was the act of a combatant fighting in the name of "humanity," Torrès recast vigilantism as a quest for justice, transfiguring the murder of Petliura into a righteous act. In the trial narrative, Schwarzbard became a righteous avenger.

These two interwar trials did not develop new legal categories of crimes or secure rights for victims. The acquittals suggest that the courts were befuddled

81. Torrès, *Souvenir, souvenir*, 98.
82. Torrès, *Souvenir, souvenir*, 128, 129, 132. In his account of the "unwritten law" in the United States that defended husbands who killed their wives, Hartog references clichés about female vanity as they were used to acquit male defendants, "Lawyering," 80. In France and Germany, but not in the United States, women could be acquitted of having committed honor crimes.

about how to hold the perpetrators of pogroms and mass murders accountable except by showing mercy to their victims. The trials extended to the courtroom and popular press the "literature of denunciation" that drew public attention to mass atrocities and intensified after the Great War.[83] The defense's invocation of "humanity," "humanitarianism," "liberty, justice, courage, and the dignity of man" legitimated the defendants' acts in the name of universal principles of justice and right.[84] Unlike other political murders in the interwar period, which the Right rationalized in the name of patriotic duty and the Left in the name of social justice, the circumstances of these two trials generated particular moral pressure on the court to judge in favor of wounded witnesses whose acts lawyers claimed transcended debates of Right against Left. Lawyers rendered the defendants selflessly patriotic by referencing universal "humanity" and "civilization."

Of course, political factions used the verdicts to make arguments or lobby for or against the recognition of Armenian and Jewish suffering. Jews and Armenians mostly celebrated the risks the avengers took in order to bring attention to their plights, and Turkish nationalists, Ukrainian nationalists, far-right Germans, far-right Frenchmen, and anti-Communists all derided the verdicts. The trials' rhetoric invoked patriotic humanism before Germany descended into chaos and France grew ever more polarized a decade later. That is why so many centrist papers abhorred the verdicts all the while underlining their inevitability; they were committed to a vision of the "rights of man" or "the laws of humanity" in the name of patriotic honor and "civilization," if such lofty ideals could legitimate the acts of the defendants.

The trials also point elsewhere. Tehlirian's and Schwarzbard's lost and restored honor provided a legal resolution in court to shocking crimes for which no one could be held accountable. In spite of their differences, the courts in each case developed strikingly similar modes of addressing justice for victims of mass violence and genocide in the absence of established legal categories defining the offense caused by the crimes. The trial turned Tehlirian into a soldier, alluding to the Great War and praising the humanitarian justice with which he dispatched his enemy. Torrès made Schwarzbard sympathetic by invoking the war's redemptive power, arguing that he committed his act in defense of the rights of man. Both appeals worked, and mercy was made more viable, not only because spectators took pity on the defendants, as Torrès demanded they should do for his other client, Breton. The trials also redeemed the accused by transforming the vigilantes into righteous avengers who fought for humanitarian ideals against barbaric

---

83. Cabanes, *Great War*, 303–4.
84. Torrès, "Plaidoirie," 343.

enemies. One trial informed a generous nation that it should have more sternly judged its brutal allies; the other celebrated French army service for inspiring a passive man to fight his ignoble enemies. In so doing, they turned "Eastern" victims into witnesses of unspeakable suffering within a European nationalist and imperialist framework.

Lawyers made the suffering witness on the stand the protagonist of the story rather than its object; the testimony of the sufferer was as important as the "civilized" spectator's perspective. Appeals to humanity's suffering diminished the particularity of Armenians' or Jews' struggles, but also commemorated the victims and mourned their deaths. These appeals were themselves startling: victims were center stage, and assassins were recast as righteous avengers and humanitarian warriors. The trials portrayed these men as heroes, but not quite. For the source of Tehlirian's and Schwarzbard's conscience, and hence their humanitarian war on barbarism, was not the heroes' determination, but an injury, one originating in an unrelenting subjection to powerful memories of violence that overtook their lives; even if they had already endured the worst, their psychic wounds caused such extreme disorientation that under certain circumstances they might not be in their right mind when they pulled the trigger. The trial narratives pitted these injured men rhetorically against their enemies: Tehlirian and Schwarzbard, disoriented by suffering, confronted the men they killed; the Turkish "militarists" and the Ukrainians had low-level troops who did their dirty work. The Armenian and the Jewish avengers had pure, humanitarian motives; the "militarists" committed calculated, organized crimes of annihilation or, like the Ukrainians, perpetrated systematic mass atrocities motivated by animus and cruelty.

As Lemkin wryly noted about Schwarzbard's trial, unable to "punish a man who had avenged the death of hundreds of thousands of his innocent brethren, including his parents," but also unable to "sanction the taking of the law in one's own hands[,] . . . ingenious legal minds found a compromise similar to that in the trial of Tehlirian: 'The perpetrator is insane and must therefore go free.'"[85] Lawyers using versions of temporary insanity defenses cast the defendants as noble avengers in a David and Goliath struggle between "militarists" and their impossibly vulnerable victims. Fusing the psychically wounded victim's compulsion with the willful self-sacrifice and nobility of the humanitarian avenger, the

---

85. Lemkin, *Totally Unofficial*, 21. Loeffler, "Becoming Cleopatra," 348, contrasts Lemkin's contemporaneous articles about the trial with his later reflections, suggesting that Lemkin later underplayed his enthusiasm for vigilante justice.

lawyers had it both ways: Tehlirian and Schwarzbard had committed murder and yet they were shining exemplars of civilization.

This recognition transfigured premeditated murder long after a crime took place into a form of soldierly honor no longer defined as glory on the battlefield. The avenger was the survivor of an unspeakable war waged deliberately against helpless people who could not fight back, and risked his life—the penalty for murder was death—to restore the dignity of his people and in so doing restore human dignity *tout court*. The conventional soldier goes to war to prove his mettle and too late realizes either his complicity in its horrors or despairs of a better opportunity to demonstrate his patriotism and honor. He narrates his experience as tragic revelation or thrilling self-discovery.[86] The righteous avenger instead suffers persecution as an insuperable wound he can no longer bear, and goes to "war" to stanch the bleeding. He is a survivor not of war between nations but of national attacks on stateless groups, and embodies the psychological effects of wounds left by the experience of mass victimization for which there was no remedy other than his own action. Both the conventional and the unconventional soldier bear witness, and both derive moral authority from their experience of organized violence, but they testify to different experiences, including some for which the avenger had no recognizable names other than "horrors."

In the process of proving the cases, the trial proceedings attributed new meanings to old crimes and fashioned new kinds of heroes, portraying assassins as victims and as enemies of barbarism. As much of the press coverage suggested, however, in the eyes of many, the defendants remained ambivalent figures, sympathetic perhaps, but marred by their vigilantism. No matter how popular the image of the righteous avenger was among Jews and Armenians, vigilante justice was very hard to condone. Moreover, the particularity of the victim's suffering—its precise geography, history, and causes—was diminished by the language of barbarism and humanism. The trials integrated the particular suffering of Jews and Armenians into a broad vision of "civilized" humanity. But they did so because the avenger was not only a juridical but also a moral witness who symbolized the suffering of wounded humanity. This outcome was consistent with Lemkin's portrayal of Schwarzbard as a "beautiful soul," but its appeal to civilized humanity could not entirely mute concerns about the acquittals of murderers.

The trials' rhetoric thus made mass murder recognizable as an affront to human dignity by integrating the victims of such violence into the universe of

---

86. Smith, *Embattled Self*, 196–97.

civilized humanity. In so doing, the trials conceptualized state-sponsored murder against Jews and Armenians as a legible crime so heinous it justified acquittal. They defined humanitarian justice in terms of pity for sufferers elsewhere
and dismay on their behalf. But they also recognized victims' narratives about
their suffering and held their persecutors morally accountable. This is what is
most extraordinary about these trials: they imagined a new kind of crime and
formed a novel, victim-centered concept of a witness who demands not pity or
empathy, but justice.[87]

87. For this reason, I disagree with Anna Schur, who believes that the particular violence against
Jews was erased by the rhetoric of the Schwarzbard trial. There is no question that the specificity of
that violence is erased—humanist rhetoric is always more concerned with integration than with the
effects of marginality. And yet the violence against Jews in the Schwarzbard trial is also recognized in
radically new terms. Schur, "Shades of Justice: The Trial of Sholom Schwartzbard and Dovid Bergelson's 'Among Refugees,'" *Law and Literature* 19, no. 1 (2007): 15–43.

2

THE CAMP SURVIVOR /
The Libel Cases of Victor Kravchenko and David Rousset, 1949 and 1950–51

> The concentration camps are an amazing and complex mechanism of expiation.
>
> —David Rousset, *L'univers concentrationnaire* (1946)

The postwar French Communist Party remained fervently loyal to the Soviet Union and commanded a strong following during the Cold War, even as revelations about the Gulag became best sellers.[1] In this politically tense atmosphere, anti-Communists levied two libel suits in order to publicize the existence of Soviet concentration camps. The Ukrainian émigré Victor A. Kravchenko brought a suit against the French Communist literary magazine *Les Lettres françaises* in 1949, and the French Resistance member and writer David Rousset brought another a year later against the same journal. Kravchenko was a Soviet defector who had written a book on Stalin's crimes and sued the magazine for publishing lies about him and his book. Rousset, who was on the non-Communist Left, used his postwar stature to issue a formal appeal in *Le Figaro littéraire* to all "political deportees," inviting them to participate in an international commission of former inmates to explore the existence of prison camps in the Soviet Union.[2]

---

1. According to Tony Judt, Arthur Koestler's *Darkness at Noon* rivaled Kravchenko's book *I Chose Freedom* (1946) on the French best-seller list between 1945 and 1955. Judt, *Past Imperfect: French Intellectuals, 1944–1956* (Berkeley: University of California Press, 1992), 115n38. See Koestler, *Darkness at Noon*, trans. Daphne Hardy (1941; repr., New York: Modern Library, 1946); and Kravchenko, *I Chose Freedom: The Personal and Political Life of a Soviet Official* (New York: C. Scribner's Sons, 1946). Other memoirs of inmates of Soviet camps were available, among them Julius Margolin's *La condition inhumaine*, published in 1949 by Calmann-Levy and attributed to "Jules Margoline." The full version is Julius Margolin, *Voyage au pays des Ze-Ka*, trans. by Nina Berberova and Mina Journot, revised and complied by Luba Jurgenson (Saint-Just-la-Pendue, Loire: Le bruit du temps, 2010).

2. For a reprint of the text of the appeal, "Au secours des déportés dans les camps soviétiques aux anciens déportés nazis," in Émile Copfermann, *David Rousset: Une vie dans le siècle; Fragments d'autobiographie* (Paris: Plon, 1991), 197–209.

As Tony Judt pointed out, Kravchenko's 1949 defamation suit attracted interest partly because it took place as the Soviet Union was consolidating power brutally in Eastern Europe and purges were under way in Czechoslovakia, which, one dismayed French intellectual loyal to the party reported, was "almost" a "Western" nation.[3] Rousset's personal and political stature, gained from his award-winning 1946 book about his Nazi camp experience, *L'univers concentrationnaire*, guaranteed him a large audience.[4]

Both Kravchenko and Rousset used public trials to argue that Soviet camps were a locus of evil. They called on witnesses who had survived the Gulag to place the intransigence of French Communists in a harsh light, and their suits received widespread attention. These trials, ostensibly about libel, were opportunities to expose what Rousset called "crimes against humanity," invoking the Nuremberg tribunal and Nazi crimes in a forum with a full court press.[5] The Kravchenko trial put a parade of witnesses on the stand whose testimony often strayed from the charges against the editors of *Les Lettres françaises*, setting the stage for Rousset's approach in his own trial against the magazine. Rousset, too, called former Gulag detainees to testify and asserted confidently that his lawsuit would be "infinitely more important" than Kravchenko's; it would be "the trial of the Russian concentration camps."[6]

Once again, plaintiffs and defendants intentionally hijacked the courtroom in order to publicize or refute crimes the tribunal could not adjudicate, and former camp inmates dominated the courtroom drama even if they were not the only players. Witnesses for Kravchenko's and Rousset's side were there to provide evidence, but their role was political and moral; they confirmed and condemned the existence of concentration camps in the Soviet Union.[7] All trials are a form of theater, and all trials mobilize moral, political, and social assumptions

---

3. Judt, *Past Imperfect*, 112–13.

4. David Rousset, *L'univers concentrationnaire* (Paris: Les Éditions de Minuit, 1946). The English translation is David Rousset, *The Other Kingdom*, trans. Ramon Guthrie (New York: Reynal Hitchcock, 1947).

5. *Le procès concentrationnaire pour la vérité sur les camps: Extraits des débats, déclarations de David Rousset, plaidoirie de Théo Bernard, plaidoirie de Gérard Rosenthal* (Paris: Éditions du Pavois, 1951), 29.

6. Cited in Emma Kuby, *Political Survivors: The Resistance, the Cold War, and the Fight against Concentration Camps after 1945* (Ithaca, NY: Cornell University Press, 2019), 66.

7. Judt, *Past Imperfect*, 111–16 on the trial's significance. Rousset's trial was also the first postwar trial to publicize Stalin's crimes. John Dewey headed a "Joint Commission of Inquiry" in Mexico City in April 1937 organized by public intellectuals to defend Leon Trotsky against charges of terrorist conspiracy alleged in the August 1936 purge trial in Moscow. But this was a citizens' tribunal focused on exposing the show trials as a sham, not a court trial, and not aimed at the Soviet camp system. See Arthur Jay Klinghoffer and Judith Apter Klinghoffer, *International Citizens' Tribunals: Mobilizing Public Opinion to Advance Human Rights* (New York: Palgrave, 2002), 97–101.

to the advantage of one side or the other. No legal testimony is neatly extricable from the character of its narrator or the style of delivery. Yet these were not ordinary legal testimonies but moral reckonings that pitted the emotional intensity of witnesses' horror stories against dispassionate judges who sought to contain the proceedings within familiar legal boundaries. The defense's hostility to witnesses during cross-examination also amplified the harrowing testimonies. If Kravchenko's trial provided a public forum for the victims and their allies, the Rousset libel suit went much further: the plaintiff and his lawyers used the forum to interpret witness testimony as a unique vehicle of insight into human depravity that had been forged through suffering in the Nazi and Soviet camps.[8]

This chapter begins with the backdrop of Kravchenko's trial, without which it is difficult to understand the Rousset proceedings. For reasons we will see, Kravchenko's suit lacked a transcendent moral argument beyond its message that the Gulag existed and Stalin's Soviet Union was not what it promised to be. But the trial put victims center stage and used their testimony to great effect. Like the interwar defendants whose trials we analyzed in the previous chapter, Rousset won legally and morally because camp survivors were not only credible—most of them had credentials as former combatants in various anti-Nazi Resistance movements—but also proved themselves to be above all partisanship. They were allegedly concerned not with victory for one side or the other but with exposing and denouncing concentration camp systems wherever they occurred. Rousset's trial against the magazine was a performance of his masterwork *L'univers concentrationnaire* and cast the camp survivor as a new type of combatant against inhumanity he dubbed the "witness." He thus used the noun "witness" both to capitalize on the authority of Resistance heroes returning from Nazi camps who were "witnesses" (*témoins*) and to revise the meaning of the term.

The Kravchenko Trial

Victor Kravchenko was an engineer specializing in metals who had been appointed by the Soviet government to a Russian state committee, the Soviet Purchasing Commission, in Washington, DC. He defected to the United States

---

8. Another, earlier trial for murder in 1924 of the anti-Bolshevik assassin Maurice Conradi featured testimony against Bolsheviks and a dramatic closing argument by the defense lawyer Théodore Aubert. Conradi had murdered a Soviet government representative, Vatslav Vorovsky, and was acquitted. This trial belongs to the interwar period rhetoric, and was a referendum on the October Revolution rather than on prison camps. See *L'affaire Conradi, plaidoirie par M. Théodore Aubert* (Geneva: S.A. des Éditions Sonor, 1924), and Alfred Erich Senn, *Assassination in Switzerland: The Murder of Vatslav Vorovsky* (Madison: University of Wisconsin Press, 1981). See chap. 1, n4.

in 1944 and was aided by several anti-Soviet writers in the United States who facilitated the translation and publication of articles and his best-selling book, *I Chose Freedom.*[9] Winner of the prestigious Prix Sainte-Beuve in 1947, the book recounted starvation in the Ukrainian famine, party purges, and the arrest and torture of men and women who languished in forced labor camps.

On November 13, 1947, the pro-Soviet *Les Lettres françaises* published an article by Sim Thomas, who claimed to be a former US agent. He declared that Kravchenko was a US spy and a drunk, and accused him of making up or plagiarizing most of his book. In retaliation, Kravchenko named Claude Morgan, the editor of *Les Lettres françaises*, and two contributors, Sim Thomas and André Wurmser, in a libel suit against the magazine. The case went to court in Paris on January 24, 1949, with Communist defense lawyers Joë Nordmann, Michel Bruguier, and Léo Matarasso. André Blumel, a Socialist and former member of Léon Blum's Popular Front cabinet, also participated in the defense.[10]

The defense presumed the trial was a US propaganda operation: when Nordmann saw the international press outside the courtroom, he assumed the worst, and feared he had not adequately prepared.[11] It called former French Resistance fighters like Jean Cassou (director of France's modern art museum) and the novelist Vercors (the pen name of Jean Bruller) to attest to the credibility of *Les Lettres françaises*, hoping to discredit the other side's procession of mostly unknown former Gulag detainees.[12] Also appearing for the defense was Kravchenko's ex-wife and other Russians who represented the Soviet government—among them military men and party operatives, none of whom

9. Gary Kern, *The Kravchenko Case: One Man's War on Stalin* (New York: Enigma Books, 2007), 89–90; Frances Stonor Saunders, *The Cultural Cold War: The CIA and the World of Arts and Letters* (New York: New York Press, 1999), 68–70, discusses CIA help for anti-Communists in Western Europe, though does not mention Kravchenko. The trial was a Cold War proxy battle in its own right. The impact of the Cold War on the unfolding of the trial has been the focus of most scholarship.

10. *Le procès Kravchenko: Compte rendu sténographique*, 2 vols. (Paris: Éditions Albin Michel, 1949). See also Nina Berberova, *L'affaire Kravchenko*, trans. Irène Markowicz and André Markowicz (Arles: Actes Sud, 1990); Liora Israël, "Un procès du Goulag au temps du Goulag? L'affaire Kravchenko (1949)," *Critique Internationale* 3, no. 36 (2007): 85–100; Judt, *Past Imperfect*, 111–16; Kern, *Kravchenko Case*; Guillaume Malaurie, *L'affaire Kravchenko* (Paris: Éditions Laffont, 1982); Irwin Wall, *French Communism in the Era of Stalin: The Quest for Unity and Integration, 1945–1962* (Westport, CT: Greenwood, 1983), 93–96; Michel Winock, *Le siècle des intellectuels* (Paris: Seuil, 1997), 572–84.

11. Joë Nordmann with Anne Brunel, *Aux vents de l'histoire: Mémoires* (Arles: Actes Sud, 1996), 171. As Kuby shows, Nordmann was not wrong about Kravchenko's American support (*Political Survivors*, 52–3).

12. In *Postwar: A History of Europe since 1945* (New York: Penguin, 2005), 214, Tony Judt calls Kravchenko's witnesses "rather obscure."

could have appeared in a Paris court without the support of the Soviet regime.[13] The defense called several French intellectuals to the stand, nominally if not always on the Communist Left, who burnished their patriotic and combat credentials. They testified that they had seen none of the brutalities Kravchenko described in his book on their visits to the Soviet Union. Defendants Morgan and Wurmser invoked their own experience in the Resistance to contrast their heroism with Kravchenko's ostensibly traitorous flight from his country at war.

In addition to demonstrating its own credibility, the defense spent much of the trial trying to show that Kravchenko had not written his book alone. The defense lawyers, however, had trouble proving that Thomas's claims about Kravchenko were true. For one, Thomas could not be called to testify against Kravchenko because the American agent, as the defense team was well aware, did not exist. He was in fact André Ullmann, a French leftist journalist who used the pseudonym to write unflattering articles about the Soviet defector.[14] Without Mr. Thomas to call to the stand, the defense claimed that Kravchenko could not have written *I Chose Freedom* because it appealed to the lower instincts of a US public with whom he was not yet familiar. The lawyers also argued that the book was versed in the classics of Russian literature, whose elevated sensibilities were beyond Kravchenko's grasp.[15]

Kravchenko's side instead put the Stalinist regime on trial, arguing that the Soviet Union had an enormous prison system in which those who committed no crimes were sent to labor and die. With the help of his legal team, led by the lawyer and former Resistance fighter Georges Izard, a Catholic centrist, Kravchenko's side called witnesses who were ostensibly former Gulag detainees; many had survived the war in Russia or the Soviet camps and came to Paris from displaced persons (DP) camps in Germany. An aide of Kravchenko's had sent appeals to Ukrainian- and Russian-language camp newspapers, and helped bring several witnesses back to Paris.[16] Though Kravchenko was a democratic socialist whose politics were closer to Schwarzbard's than to those of the United States government, he stood with the side he believed to be the lesser of two evils.

---

13. See the discussion in Israël, "Un procès," 90–91. Nordmann asked the Soviet embassy to pull together a list of witnesses that could help his side, and was helped by the French Communist Party to research the list of those witnesses called by the prosecution (95).

14. Israël, "Un procès," 89n16. Based on correspondence between Nordmann and Morgan, Israël states that "there was obviously no doubt among the communist defense team that the so-called correspondent of the *Lettres françaises* did not exist." See also Nordmann with Brunel, *Aux vents de l'histoire,* 172.

15. *Le procès Kravchenko,* 1:144–55.

16. Malaurie, *L'affaire Kravchenko,* 42–45.

Kravchenko's witnesses testified in the second part of the trial about their imprisonment in the Soviet Gulag. Faced with their testimony, the defense resorted to sarcasm and character assassination. The defense lawyers were outraged by the charge that prisons comparable to Nazi camps might exist in the Soviet Union, and reminded their audience of the wartime alliance between France and the Soviet Union, arguing that an anti-Nazi ally could not now be equated to Hitler's Germany. Wurmser implied that witnesses modeled alleged Soviet camps on Nazi prisons. As he had declared at the opening of the trial: "We should not read books today in which [collaborator Maurice] Bardèche doubts the existence of Buchenwald, or at least the atrocities of which it had been the theater, in the same way that we should not learn from Kravchenko that if these atrocities did not take place in Buchenwald, they took place in Siberia! It is almost as if we were told that our deported comrades died in crematoria in Kuban!"[17]

Ignoring the violence described in much of the witness testimony, the defense insinuated that most of the witnesses ended up in DP camps because they had worked for the Germans willingly rather than as forced labor.[18] A particular witness, Kysilio (the trial transcript provides only last names), spoke in detail about his time in a Siberian camp, where it was forty degrees below zero centigrade. He testified that in those temperatures, sweat from hard labor froze inmates' clothes to their bodies. Wurmser, after having asked if he had correctly understood the witness, asked Kysilio again and again to repeat what he had said, as if it could not possibly be true. In response to the same witness's description of being evacuated to a displaced persons' camp in Vienna, the defense lawyers tried to trip him up as he recounted his story.[19] Defense lawyer Nordmann finally wrote off the whole testimony by stating that the witness "was trying to make us believe that Buchenwald was in Siberia."[20]

The defense treated witnesses with disdain. Nina Berberova, a Russian expatriate in Paris who reported on the trial, excoriated its tactics. She described how defense lawyers pummeled the Martchenkos, a married couple, who were "imperturbable, almost indifferent, without being intimidated in the least by

---

17. *Le procès Kravchenko*, 1:33.

18. Non-Jewish Eastern Europeans and Russians were pressed into labor service for Germany, which had been dependent on forced labor since the early years of the war. The majority of Polish Jewish survivors lived out the war in the Soviet Union, where Jews were also conscripted for labor or military work. Some ended up in Soviet camps. Jews who survived in the Soviet Union made up the largest group of survivors after the war. See Mark Edele, Sheila Fitzpatrick, and Atina Grossmann, eds., *Shelter from the Holocaust: Rethinking Jewish Survival in the Soviet Union* (Detroit: Wayne State University Press, 2017).

19. *Le procès Kravchenko*, 1:315–16.

20. *Le procès Kravchenko*, 1:319.

the public. . . . The Martchenkos responded to each question in a serious and dignified manner that impressed all those who listened to them."[21] The defense attacked particularly forcefully when witnesses backed Kravchenko's descriptions of the 1932–33 famine in Ukraine, including accounts of how cadavers lined the streets and starving peasants resorted to cannibalism.

When it came to the witness Margarete Buber-Neumann, a victim of both the Soviet KGB and the Gestapo, the defense lawyer miscalculated. Nordmann sought to discredit the now famous testimony of Buber-Neumann, a German ex-Communist.[22] Her book, *Deported to Siberia*, appeared in French translation the year of the trial.[23] Buber-Neumann had a particularly unusual experience because of her persecution and imprisonment by both the Nazi and Soviet regimes. She had joined her husband, Heinz Neumann, in Moscow in 1935. He was a former German Communist (KPD) leader sidelined for not toeing the party line. He was arrested in Switzerland for not having a regular passport, and when the Germans subsequently demanded his extradition, the Soviets stepped in to provide him refuge. He believed he had been welcomed back in the fold. Instead, he was arrested in 1937 and executed, though his wife did not learn of his death until 1961. Buber-Neumann was arrested in 1938 and spent several years in Karaganda, a camp in Kazakhstan, after which the Soviet secret police turned her over to the Gestapo. She survived Ravensbrück, the women's camp near Berlin where it is estimated that between thirty thousand and ninety thousand women died.[24]

She was the object of much adulation for her grace under pressure. *Le Monde* correspondent Camille Anbert wrote that she spoke with "vengeful precision."[25] Witnesses to the trial as well as members of the press were moved by her testimony, which, Nina Berberova exclaimed, "was worth ten years of anti-Communist propaganda."[26] Based on many sources, Tony Judt called her "the remarkable Margareta Buber-Neumann."[27] In 1982 Guillaume Malaurie, also writing about

21. Berberova, *L'affaire Kravchenko*, 49.

22. *Le procès Kravchenko*, 2:589–93.

23. Margarete Buber-Neumann, *Under Two Dictators: Prisoner of Hitler and Stalin*, trans. Edward Fitzgerald (1949; repr., London: Pimlico, 2008). Her first husband was Martin Buber's son.

24. Buber-Neumann, *Under Two Dictators*, ix–xv; Sarah Helm, *Ravensbrück: Life and Death in Hitler's Concentration Camp for Women* (New York: Anchor Books, 2016), xviii. Exact numbers cannot be determined because the Nazis destroyed most documents. Helm provides an account of Buber-Neumann's time in *Ravensbrück*, 73–77, 88–89.

25. Camille Anbert, "Une saisissante déposition au procès Kravchenko: Livrée par l'URSS au Reich Mme. Buber-Neumann, communiste allemande, passa de la Sibérie à Ravensbrück," *Le Monde*, February 25, 1949.

26. Berberova, *L'affaire Kravchenko*, 148.

27. Judt, *Past Imperfect*, 114.

the trial, described Buber-Neumann as "imperturbable." Unlike other witnesses, she knew "how to speak movingly by virtue of the clarity of her memories." He added that her "cold anger" made her "insensitive to the lowest sort of attacks."[28]

The presiding judge at the Paris trial did not appear to understand the importance of the witness's experience and asked her to keep it short after her first statement.[29] Unfazed, she gave clear and detailed testimony through a translator. She said that in Moscow she feared that the Soviet secret police would denounce both her and her husband. When the judge asked why, she described a party sponsored by a publishing house for which they worked as translators. The party, she said, resembled those later thrown by the Nazis, full of camaraderie. When a woman joined them at their table, they immediately suspected that she was an informer (*dénonciatrice*), and indeed, Heinz Neumann was called in a few days later and grilled about some things he was purported to have said that evening. He was eventually accused of being a "German fascist," asked to declare his errors, and arrested. Nordmann sustained a running commentary as Buber-Neumann testified, saying "maybe" the accusations leveled at her were "true," and other off-the-cuff remarks.[30]

In spite of his repeated and aggressive interruptions, she continued, telling the defense lawyer calmly that she was held in a prison camp two times the size of Denmark, from which escape was impossible. The defense advocate Blumel claimed that she could not have been in a camp because there were no walls, to which she replied that there were guards everywhere along the perimeter.[31] He insisted, and the judge pressed her to describe more precisely the conditions of her imprisonment, allowing her to go into a great deal of detail about the size of her living quarters, the millions of fleas and bedbugs who shared them, the regimentation of her days, and the "punishment block" (*bloc de représailles*) from which women often disappeared.[32]

As she told the story of her transfer by the Soviets to the Gestapo, the defense attorneys' disdain failed to upset her or undermine her testimony. Nordmann implied that she was a Nazi, and Blumel kept insisting that she had not really been in a camp. Yet with striking unanimity, except for the Communist paper *L'Humanité*, the press deferred to her testimony. Nordmann later expressed profound misgivings

28. Malaurie, *L'affaire Kravchenko*, 148–50.

29. *Le procès Kravchenko*, 2:261. The judge, Durkheim, happened to be the sociologist Émile Durkheim's nephew.

30. *Le procès Kravchenko*, 2:263–64.

31. *Le procès Kravchenko*, 2:268. This particular part of the testimony about a camp bigger than Denmark has been repeated in multiple accounts.

32. *Le procès Kravchenko*, 2:268–69. I use the term "punishment" rather than "retaliation" to translate *représailles* because "punishment block" is the standard English term for these unfortunately common features of concentration camps.

about the way he had treated Buber-Neumann, who now appeared "luminous" in his memory: "Faced with the unimpeachable Margarete Buber-Neumann, faced with her calm and her suffering, I comported myself like a blind and sectarian partisan. Her self-control on the stand and her admirable composure should have, however, made an impression on me, shaken my judgment. I didn't believe her."[33]

The defense had not countered Buber-Neumann's testimony effectively. The judge pronounced that Kravchenko had indeed been defamed but stated that the trial was insufficient to prove or disprove claims about the Soviet Union. In spite of Kravchenko's efforts, the trial could not adjudicate whether there were concentration camps there, since neither side had any definitive proof either way, and such a judgment was not the aim of the proceedings. The judge determined instead that most of the testimony about *I Chose Freedom*, including the manuscript copy submitted by the prosecution, was sufficient to prove that Kravchenko was the author, even if he had had help transforming his story into a more marketable tale. The judge also found it reasonable that Kravchenko would hire help to render his work in passable English and to make it accessible to a US audience. He clearly did not believe that Kravchenko was a drunk. Morgan and Wurmser were fined, and on appeal the penalty was reduced to a symbolic franc.

The verdict makes it easy to understand the trial merely as a lesson in the consequences of ideological blindness, especially in France: the Communist Party remained loyal to the Soviet Union until the invasion of Prague in 1968 and, despite internal discord, never openly condemned Soviet aggression. Historians rightly conceive the trial as an episode in the history of French communism or the Cold War in France: both sides played to the choir.[34] Tony Judt interpreted the Kravchenko trial as a Communist moral victory because the defense produced star witnesses, and the testimony of "obscure" former prisoners on the other side failed to move true believers.[35] Defense lawyer Nordmann believed that Kravchenko's suit was merely an attack on the Communist press and presumed the trial would be an unprecedented "ideological duel."[36] He remained loyal to the party long after the trial was over.

---

33. Nordmann with Brunel, *Aux vents de l'histoire*, 184–86. "She reached the end of her testimony. This small woman, dressed all in black, had just recounted that at the end of three years of imprisonment, at the end of 1939, her initial condemnation to five years of a camp had been commuted and she was expelled from Soviet territory. . . . Finally, she recounted her second deportation, by the Nazis, to Ravensbrück. She recounted all of that. Simply. Without bombast. And I didn't believe her. It's impossible to understand" (184–85).

34. Kern, *Kravchenko Case*; Wall, *French Communism*, 93–96; Winock, *Le siècle des intellectuels*, 572–84.

35. Judt, *Past Imperfect*, 113.

36. Nordmann with Brunel, *Aux vents de l'histoire*, 171.

Kravchenko won his battle, but he had not by any means won the war. Still, the trial provided a forum within which to articulate the injustice of collective suffering against ideological blindness, and to describe crimes that could not be adjudicated by any tribunal. It addressed unofficial mass detention in the Soviet Union, now in a legitimate court far from the scene of the crimes and the perpetrators, who remained out of reach. The plaintiff's studied use of witnesses turned them into vehicles of a message about the Soviet regime, and played into anti-Communist hands, making the trial a particularly fascinating Cold War drama. The role played by witness testimony was predictable given the plaintiff's intentions. But witness testimony was also turned into a spectacle by the defense, which lost the judge's sympathy and antagonized the audience with its aggressive interrogation of Buber-Neumann.

Since neither Kravchenko nor the defense side could substantiate the existence of the Gulag, the proceedings were above all a rhetorical battle between Communist Party loyalists (as well as fellow travelers) and anti-Communist victims of Soviet prisons. Even though the trial testimony was insufficient to persuade anyone to change their mind, the trial demonstrates under what circumstances and in what terms victim testimony could or could not transcend an "ideological duel" that no one was likely to win. It offered no narrative to establish victims' credibility other than the stories they told, which is likely why Buber-Neumann became a celebrity witness: she had a compelling story, and her sober comportment amplified the suffering she recounted. The defense's interrogation enhanced the effect of her testimony because of the contrast between their tone and her refusal to bend. But in spite of the defense's inadvertent aid to the opposition, she symbolized no truth—about suffering humanity, about dismayed human conscience—other than her own.

Kravchenko's lawyer used Buber-Neumann's past suffering in the framework of an aim to prove—which he could not do absent more documentation—that the Soviet Union imprisoned its citizens arbitrarily. Moreover, since the Communist editors insisted on a difference between Nazism and Stalinism, and no one, not even Buber-Neumann, could prove beyond a reasonable doubt that the two regimes were similar, the trial was simply the "duel" between two sides Nordmann anticipated it would be. In the absence of an innovative prosecutorial strategy to create at least one unimpeachable witness, the trial could not stage a story about the triumph of human conscience over the forces of darkness.

This was a Cold War battle in which witnesses' harrowing accounts of suffering moved only one side to tears. It demonstrates not only that trials' narratives depend on ingenious lawyers, and, at least in these cases, their clients' profound convictions, but also that only particular kinds of didactic trials, in the absence of a statute condemning crimes of genocide, possessed the elements necessary to forge a persuasive narrative about the distinctiveness of some forms of mass violence. The courtroom could become a forum for adjudicating crimes outside of its legal purview not simply when survivors' stories became the centerpiece of the trial. Smart lawyers and their star witnesses have to transform victims' testimony into a powerful truth impervious to shame or disdain.

Kravchenko's libel suit is the only one among the trials that I discuss in which this element was not present, but the trial is illuminating for that reason alone. In Kravchenko's case, the judge sought to keep to the facts of the libel regardless of witnesses' stories, and the defense lawyers' sarcasm violated only norms of civility. The witnesses were there to provide forensic testimony, but in the absence of other forms of documentation, their stories were insufficient to prove that inhumane hard labor camps existed in the Soviet Union, and no alternative narrative allowed them to claim higher ground. The indisputable brutality of Nazi camps put the onus on witnesses, in the face of denial, to prove that Soviet prisons were comparable, a dubious task. Buber-Neumann was herself exemplary, but again, as Nordmann's memory of how he viewed her at the time of the trial suggests, no overarching narrative rendered her symbolic of a universal truth transcending the courtroom's battle between French Communists and their detractors.

Nonetheless, the Kravchenko trial testimony had an impact on French public opinion, enough so that *Les Lettres françaises* unsuccessfully sought to circumvent another procession of witnesses when Rousset sued them for defamation a few months later. The magazine's defense team wanted to avoid the power of witness testimony on the audience and in the media.[37] Rousset ensured that his own libel suit avoided Kravchenko's efforts to use witnesses to prove the truth about camps in the Soviet Union and at the same time succeeded in elevating their stature and importance.

The Rousset Libel Case

On November 12, 1949, in *Le Figaro littéraire*, David Rousset issued a now famous appeal to former inmates of Nazi concentration camps urging them to join him in undertaking an investigation to establish whether or not there were similar kinds of camps in the Soviet Union.[38] Rousset had been imprisoned in Buchenwald, Neuengamme, and a few other German satellite camps for his

---

37. Pierre Daix, *J'ai cru au matin* (Paris: Opéra Mundi, 1976), 257; Winock, *Le siècle des intellectuels*, 579–80.

38. Copfermann, *David Rousset*, 197–209.

anti-Nazi activities. In addition to his novelistic account of concentration camp life, *Les jours de notre mort*, he had written the award-winning 1946 *L'univers concentrationnaire*, in which he described his dehumanizing experience so powerfully that the title of the book became a shorthand reference for life in the camps.[39] Now he called on men and women of all political persuasions to assist him in this investigation into Soviet camps.

That the appeal was published in *Le Figaro littéraire*, a right-wing paper, raised as many eyebrows as its content. In response, the writer and journalist Pierre Daix, who had been interned in Mauthausen, penned a vitriolic article in *Les Lettres françaises* accusing Rousset not only of distorting the Soviet penal code to make it appear that prisoners were sent to "reeducation" camps without trial—by administrative fiat—but also of basing false accounts of the Soviet Gulag on his knowledge of Nazi camps. Rousset sued the magazine for libel, and the trial opened on November 25, 1950.[40] Rousset's lawyers were anti-Soviets on the Left: Théo Bernard, formerly imprisoned in Drancy, and Gérard Rosenthal. Rousset had known both for years as friends and political brothers-in-arms and had participated with them and Jean-Paul Sartre in a short-lived alternative leftist revolutionary party, the Rassemblement Démocratique Révolutionnaire (RDR), which in 1948 charted a path between capitalism and communism.[41]

The trial ended in less than two months, on January 12, 1951, with a victory for Rousset. The judge found his adversaries Claude Morgan (still editor of *Les Lettres françaises*) and Daix guilty of libel and ordered them to pay a fine of 20,000 and 15,000 francs, respectively. Though the penalties were largely symbolic, since Rousset had asked for more, the judge did order them to pay an additional 100,000 francs to advertise the verdict in *Les Lettres françaises* and ten other periodicals Rousset would have the right to select (251–52).

Historians usually interpret the Rousset trial as a replay of the Kravchenko trial, involving the same defendant, the same lawyers, and another performance by Buber-Neumann. They claim, however, that it was more successful at stimulating serious debate about the Soviet Union.[42] The defense was much weaker this

---

39. David Rousset, *Les jours de notre mort* (Paris: Hachette, 1993); David Rousset, *L'univers concentrationnaire* (Paris: Les Éditions de Minuit, 1946); David Rousset, *The Other Kingdom*, trans. Ramon Guthrie (New York: Reynal Hitchcock, 1947).

40. *Le procès concentrationnaire*, 105 (hereafter page numbers cited in the text).

41. On the RDR, see Copfermann, *David Rousset*, 105–8.

42. Judt, *Past Imperfect*, 111–16. Judt claims that while the trial did not change the views of French Communist Party members, it encouraged real debate about Soviet camps. Kuby argues that the focus on the trial's short-term anti-Stalinist PR neglects Rousset's and the trial's longer-term mobilization of his appeal to concentration camp survivors. Kuby, *Political Survivors*, 80.

time around, partly because Rousset was a more formidable opponent, and also because the public had since become more skeptical of denials about Stalinist repression. The mainstream press was sympathetic to Rousset in a way it had not been to Kravchenko, reporting on the "fanaticism" of the defense and attacking its lack of "pity" for suffering men and women.[43] By 1950, more French Resistance figures and intellectuals, disturbed by purges in Eastern Europe, had moved to Rousset's side than Kravchenko's lawyers could rely on only a year before. The Catholic progressive and former camp inmate Louis-Martin Chauffier, who had testified against Kravchenko, now declared his loyalty to Rousset.[44] Others, like Albert Camus, who had called Kravchenko a "profiteer" of capitalism, acknowledged that the Gulag existed.[45] Rousset still had critics like Maurice Merleau-Ponty and Sartre, who also did not deny the existence of Soviet camps but argued that Rousset's appeal to former deportees to testify against the Soviet Union took a side in Cold War politics and absolved the "capitalist world" of its own crimes.[46] Rousset also alienated former comrades like Robert Antelme, who resented his focus on the Soviet Union to the exclusion of French imperialism in Algeria and Madagascar.[47]

Rousset retorted that his libel suit, unlike Kravchenko's, was not about the political views of each side toward communism, but was motivated by purely humanitarian concerns. *Le Monde* reported that Rousset, at lunch with the "Anglo-American press," had proclaimed that the challenge posed by the camps was a "human" rather than a "political" problem, one that should be addressed by the "organized will of the victims."[48] He used this argument about his apolitical aims strategically, because he was in fact helped by the British government, the American Federation of Labor, and the International Confederation of Trade

---

43. André Fontaine, "Le procès David Rousset Lettres Françaises est avant tout celui de fanatisme," *Le Monde*, November 12, 1950. Rémy Roure, "Après le procès," *Le Monde*, January 9, 1951. Roure was a former partisan who had been interned at Buchenwald and whose wife died in Ravensbrück. He testified at the trial on Rousset's side, so his articles in *Le Monde* should be treated as editorials.

44. Copfermann, *David Rousset*, 117–18.

45. Albert Camus quoted in Judt, *Past Imperfect*, 113. Camus asserted the existence of concentration camps in the Soviet Union in 1948 (115).

46. Maurice Merleau-Ponty and Jean-Paul Sartre, "Les jours de notre vie," *Les temps modernes* 51 (1950): 1154–56, 1163, 1167–68.

47. "J'accepte sous conditions," Antelme's response to Rousset's appeal was published in *Le Figaro littéraire*, November 19, 1949, and is republished in David Rousset, "Rapport sur les camps de concentration soviétiques," in *David Rousset: La fraternité de nos ruines; Écrits sur la violence concentrationnaire 1956–1970*, ed. Grégory Cingal (Paris: Fayard, 2016), 375–79.

48. André Fontaine, "Il ne s'agit pas de politique mais d'un problème humain, déclare M. David Rousset," *Le Monde*, November 24, 1950.

Unions, whose activities in Europe were funded by the CIA.[49] Like Kravchenko, Rousset was firmly on the political Left, but chose the side that would best help him accomplish his aims.

This time around, the defense, represented again by Joë Nordmann and also Pierre Vienney, resorted to many procedural delays. Nordmann argued that the judge was biased, that the press should not be admitted, and that the verdict in Kravchenko's trial proved it was not within the jurisdiction of a French court to judge the policies of a sovereign state, the Soviet Union.[50] In a desperate maneuver designed to rob the plaintiff of the need to call witnesses, the defense even declined to prove Daix's accusations against Rousset. Rousset's lawyers countered by claiming that the defense was acting in bad faith and that the plaintiff had cause to summon witnesses. Siding with the plaintiff, the judge ruled that witnesses were essential for assessing the libel charges and their impact on Rousset's reputation (47–49). He was exasperated by the defense's procedural arguments and later by the its pro-Soviet rhetoric. When the defendant Daix reminded the audience of his activities in the Resistance, associating the courtroom implicitly with German military and Vichy tribunals at which he had once appeared while the battle of Stalingrad was ongoing, the judge replied that "we are not at the battle of Stalingrad!" and reproached Daix for mocking the court (34).

Once the defense's procedural motions had been defeated and the witnesses took the stand, the entire trial centered on whether Rousset had distorted information about Soviet camps and the Soviet legal code, which had been translated for his side by the historian Léon Poliakov, and not whether the Gulag really existed.[51] The defense once again used all the weapons in its arsenal, claiming that Rousset sought to incite a war against the Soviet Union. This argument was in keeping with the Communist press's representation of West Germany as an aggressive power poised to strike the peaceful Soviet regime.[52]

---

49. According to Kuby, the US government provided Rousset's team with documents on Soviet forced labor and helped finance research assistance after 1951, and the AFL helped him during the *Lettres françaises* trial. Kuby, *Political Survivors*, 123.

50. Daix concedes in his own recollections that the defense used procedure to obstruct the media, and calls its legal strategy "inquisitorial." Daix, *J'ai cru au matin*, 257–58. In his memoirs Nordmann concedes that the defense was desperate and resorted to purely procedural measures in order to defuse the media coverage the trial would generate, only to infuriate the judge. Nordmann with Brunel, *Aux vents de l'histoire*, 199–201.

51. Léon Poliakov, *Mémoires* (Paris: Jacques Grancher Éditeur, 1999), 202. The Russian-born French scholar was one of the first historians of what was not yet called the Holocaust—his *Harvest of Hate: The Nazi Program for the Destruction of the Jews of Europe* (New York: Syracuse University Press, 1954) was published in French in 1951 a few months after the end of the trial.

52. Thomas Wieder, "L'affaire David Rousset et la figure du déporté: Les réscapés des camps nazis contre les camps soviétiques (1949–1959)," in *Qu'est-ce qu' un déporté? Histoires et mémoires des*

Rousset opened his side's case by posing the rhetorical question of whether we should at least consider whether "crimes against humanity" were being perpetrated in the Soviet Union. From this point on, the plaintiff side's rhetoric moved away from that of Kravchenko's suit. Rousset insisted that he had no desire to make assertions about camps in the Soviet Union until a commission could verify facts on the ground, thereby avoiding pressure on witnesses to prove conclusively that the camps were real and that prisoners had been sentenced arbitrarily and without trial (29). He remarked that the United Nations itself had taken up the question of such camps, though he offered no specifics, in order to demonstrate that the defense's libel charge against him was disingenuous. And he stated that his appeal to deportees of all political stripes to investigate the Soviet Union had been answered enthusiastically, alluding to his formation of the Commission Internationale Contre le Régime Concentrationnaire (CICRC). The group comprised former Resistance combatants who had survived Nazi camps (39–40), and it investigated camp systems in various countries based on its members' experiences as former inmates.[53] Rousset thus began his argument by discussing at length the camps whose existence he assured the court would not be debated at trial.

The witnesses called by Rousset's side were to testify to the validity of his appeal and thus to affirm, in essence, the *possibility* that there were hard labor camps in the Soviet Union. Documents already demonstrated that a camp system existed: the real question concerned their magnitude and the conditions under which workers labored (41–42). The witnesses included Buber-Neumann, now Buber Faust-Neumann, as well as others who had written memoirs about life in the camps, evidence that gave their testimonies particular credibility. Buber Faust-Neumann repeated the testimony she had given at Kravchenko's trial, and Nordmann once again insisted that she had *volunteered* to return from the Soviet Union to Germany—to "go to Ravensbrück!" as Rousset exclaimed facetiously—because she was sympathetic to the Nazis (185–86).

---

déportations de la Seconde Guerre Mondiale, ed. Tal Bruttmann, Laurent Joly, and Annette Wievi-orka (Paris: CNRS Éditions, 2009), 316–20. Anti-Communist elites in the United States believed that Rousset's trial, covered by the press heavily in France, was of such import that in a letter to the *New York Times* in 1951, Arthur Koestler, Arthur Schlesinger Jr., Reinhold Niebuhr, Norman Thomas, Roger Baldwin, George S. Counts, and Sidney Hook bemoaned the *Times*'s lack of coverage and listed all the prominent witnesses who testified. The Rousset trial, they wrote, "comparable in moral significance and surpassing in human scope the Dreyfus trial of half a century ago—has remained almost completely unknown to the American public." Arthur Koestler et al., "Coverage of Rousset Trial: Failure to Report Proceedings of Paris Libel Case Criticized," *New York Times*, February 15, 1951.

53. Kuby provides a comprehensive and insightful history of this commission in *Political Survivors*.

The Polish-born Jewish writer Jules Margoline (Julius Margolin), who was arrested in Soviet-occupied Poland while fleeing the 1939 German invasion, also testified. He had published two excerpts of his book about the Soviet camps in *Le Figaro* in October 1949 under the title *La condition inhumaine*, and claimed that when he appeared in court, Rousset and his lawyers had "not the least idea" what he was going to say.[54] On the witness stand, he declared: "I prefer to speak as little as possible about myself because this [testimony] is not about me, and it is not about my personal experience. What happened is that I have suffered with millions of others and it is in the name of the millions of detainees in Soviet prisons that I would like to address the Tribunal" (109).

Another witness, Elinor Lipper, was attacked by the defense during her less poignant testimony. She was Jewish and had written a book about her experience of eleven years imprisoned in Soviet camps. Born in Brussels of German-Jewish parents, she was in Berlin studying medicine when Hitler came to power. She joined the Communist Resistance, fled Germany for Switzerland, and then left for the Soviet Union in 1937, after trying to finish her medical degree in Italy. Instead of finding refuge in the Soviet Union, she was arrested and sent to forced labor camps, where she testified to being imprisoned for eleven years with thirty thousand other inmates. Lipper said she worked fourteen hours a day in temperatures of fifty degrees centigrade below zero, where the mortality rate, she claimed, was 30 percent a year because the prisoners received only one ration of bread a day (83–84).

Nordmann sought to portray Lipper as a fascist sympathizer. He claimed that her stay in fascist Italy was suspect, even though she had left for Turin in order to pass her medical exams: "I never said," she retorted, "that I went to Italy because I believed it was a free country" (84–85). Nordmann also insinuated that it was perfectly normal that, as a foreigner of German origin (she had become Swiss by marriage), she was held in the Soviet Union as an enemy alien even after the liberation. Since Lipper was Jewish, his interrogation smacked of desperation, even if he sincerely believed that she was lying. Lipper wilted in the face of the defense's sarcasm. She had memorized her testimony, which the defense insinuated was suspiciously rehearsed. She spoke good but not fluent French, and was interrupted repeatedly by defense lawyers.[55] She regained her footing in the end, replying indignantly to a comment by Nordmann, "But I was in a Soviet camp, sir, I was not in an internment

54. Julius Margolin, *Le procès Eichmann et autres essais*, trans. Luba Jurgenson (Paris: Le Bruit du Temps, 2016), 42. The original essay was published for the Russian émigré press in 1951. Jules Margoline, "La condition inhumaine," *Le Figaro littéraire*, October 17 and 27, 1949.

55. Margolin characterizes her testimony this way in *Le procès Eichmann*, 53.

camp; I worked as a forced laborer for six more years, and I was not alone. No one was liberated except for assassins, prostitutes, and thieves" (85).

When the judge questioned the relevance of Lipper's testimony to the libel case, Rousset insisted that his honor as well as the honor of all deportees on his side had been violated by Daix's libel. Her testimony's import, he said, was its moral significance, its role in restoring his honor, and, by implication, the honor of all deportees. To the judges' reasonable comment, seconded by the defense, that Lipper's detailed testimony about the Gulag exceeded the purpose of adjudicating the libel case, Rousset responded: "The questions I pose to the witness will not tend to recount the facts to demonstrate the truth, but the moral importance of these facts by virtue of their very magnitude [*grandeur*], if I can put it that way" (81). Lipper's response, he said, would "establish, as the others will establish, that this testimony is not just about an individual case but about a large number of cases. This affair thus has a considerable moral importance" (82). Rousset contended that if a sufficient number of witnesses could raise doubts about whether Soviet prisoners had been sentenced legitimately, Daix's attack on his appeal might constitute libel.[56]

By referring to the "moral importance" of facts, Rousset assured the court that "facts" about the Soviet camps were not meant to prove that such camps existed, but to uphold his honor, and were thus relevant to the libel case. Unlike Kravchenko, he did not expect testimonies to persuade skeptics to change their minds and argued instead that the defense's effort to preclude witness testimony on the grounds of factual irrelevance ignored the moral purpose of testimony—to restore human dignity and honor to all deportees. For the court not to hear such testimony amounted to a refusal to recognize the *grandeur* of what was at stake. He transformed witnesses into the guarantors of his honor and the honor of others not fortunate enough to return.

The judge insisted that Rousset's witnesses had to stick to the libel charges and not simply recount their suffering, but Rousset had made his point. Witnesses' testimonies were valuable evidence, but they were also "moral facts" that addressed not simply the offense caused by libel but also the offense against humanity caused by the camp system in the Soviet Union. According to Rousset, those who have suffered possess a particular expertise and are "specialists" (39) in the subject matter of suffering humanity. Rousset had stated in his appeal to former deportees that he envisioned them as veterans of camp life whose trials

---

56. On Rousset's reliance on testimonies when writing *Les jours de notre mort*, see Copfermann, *David Rousset*, 79–83, esp. 82. On victims' good conscience, see Rousset, "Rapport sur les camps de concentration soviétiques," in Rousset, *La fraternité de nos ruines*, 234. Rousset may have been alluding to Durkheim in his invocation of the "moral importance of facts." See Émile Durkheim, "Définition du fait moral [1873]," in Durkheim, *Textes 2: Religion, morale, anomie,* ed. Victor Karady (Paris: Éditions du minuit, 1975), 257–91. Durkheim used "moral fact" to reconcile abstract ethics and concrete morality according to scientific rules.

elevated them above the "poverty of imagination" to which those without such experience had been consigned.[57] He imagined a figure, the "man of the concentration camp system (40)," and a new form of expert knowledge—the ability to recognize and identify with suffering inflicted by camps—that is based on a specific experience of human suffering rather than on generic feelings of sympathy for the pain of others. These specialists were "irreproachable" and "indisputable," not only because of their exceptional reputations but because of the experience they had undergone (41).

In an extremely effective moment in his opening plea, Rousset turned Nordmann's words against him. In the previous court session, Nordmann had questioned Rousset's legal standing to bring the libel suit. Rousset proclaimed:

> I recall a phrase uttered by Mr. Nordmann during our last session, "these people without documents." But gentleman, this is characteristic of the man of the concentration camp system [*l'homme concentrationnaire*]. We have been men without documents for years, and this is what I believe a Nazi lawyer would have said to a foreign court in regard to any poor soul who had escaped from a camp: "This is a man without a document." It is our glory, and our only document is our experience of the concentrationary universe and the sufferings we have endured. (40)

His comparison of Nordmann to a "Nazi lawyer" was brilliant rhetoric. But Nordmann was merely a foil for Rousset's main aim, which was to enact performatively the camp witness's authority in his appearances before the judge, the public, and the defense lawyers. *L'homme concentrationnaire* and his camp experience—one Rousset had elaborated in his prize-winning book—was the dominant symbol of the libel trial and the ultimate representative of suffering humanity. Witnesses spoke on behalf of a symbolic *l'homme concentrationnaire*, and Rousset stood in for "him" in court, interpreting the meaning of witness testimony for the tribunal; the lawyers and judge tried to constrain witnesses to relevant legal facts, and Rousset emphasized the extralegal, moral dimension of their testimony, which otherwise would have had little if any role to play in court.

Rousset's positioning of camp witnesses as spokespeople for victims of "crimes against humanity" undermined witnesses for the defense, whom he portrayed as parochial no matter their own moral authority. Toward the end of the trial, Communist Party member Marie-Claude Vaillant-Couturier refused

---

57. "Au secours des déportés," reprinted in Copfermann, *David Rousset*, 208.

to acknowledge the existence of a camp system in the Soviet Union. As a former Resistance fighter and Auschwitz survivor who had testified movingly at Nuremberg, Vaillant-Couturier came to the witness stand with sterling credentials. But Rousset emphasized the particularity of her commitments. Would she really turn her back on the sufferings of her comrades in the Soviet Union rather than investigate whether or not concentration camps existed there? Vaillant-Couturier responded that "you can't ask me that question because I know that there are no concentration camps in the Soviet Union" (194). Rousset responded, "As former deportees, Madame, would you agree that we have only one allegiance [fidélité]? We do not have two loyalties. We do not have loyalty to a state, we do not have loyalty to a system of laws, but we have loyalty to men and to the sufferings they have endured" (195). By pitting loyalty to suffering humanity against loyalty to a state and its laws, Rousset transformed her loyalty to the party into a selfish refusal even to consider the pain of others when it challenged her belief system. From her point of view, he referred to different conceptions of human fulfillment, capitalist or communist, and it was necessary to choose. But Rousset's appeal to humanity above party rejected this political choice in the name of restoring human dignity wherever it was violated. As Sartre and Maurice Merleau-Ponty had pointed out in their criticism, Rousset mistook a moral commitment to human dignity for politics, divorcing the moral guarantee of human dignity from a specific political vision necessary to ensure it.

In his closing argument, Rousset's lawyer Bernard argued that it was important at least to consider the possibility that camps might exist. Like Rousset, he avoided making the argument on factual grounds, though the plaintiff's side had submitted many documents about Soviet camps to the court. Vaillant-Couturier's testimony, he declared, was evidence that she had an ideological commitment to a rosy vision of the Soviet Union for which she had no proof. He returned to a statement made by Communist Party member Jean Lafitte at the trial: you "can't ask me if my mother is an assassin, would you condemn her. I would tell you: sir, my mother is my mother and is not an assassin" (187). Rousset, Bernard implied, had turned the tables on the defense by arguing that, like Vaillant-Couturier, many people loyal to the Soviet Union simply refused to believe even the most incontrovertible evidence because of their fierce loyalty to the party (210–11).

In contrast to such closed-mindedness, argued Gérard Rosenthal in his own closing statement, Rousset wanted an "honest, impartial" investigation so that his conscience was clear (228). Like the general prosecutor at Nuremberg who said "that it was impossible to sleep soundly with a clear conscience" knowing what so many millions of deportees have suffered, Rosenthal declared that Rousset sought to live up to his "obligations" as a former deportee: "He appealed to the duty of the deportees. He appealed to the authority of the deportees. He appealed to the competence of the deportees. The court knows that he reached out to the group of those deported, to all those deported, with no bias, appealing to them and demanding their collective and communal presence in light of the duty to which, in some sense, their nobility, that is to say what they have suffered, obliged them" (227).[58] Rosenthal repeated in other terms Rousset's insistence that the trial was about "humanity" and even "humanism" (69), invoking humanity in the name of former camp detainees, whose experience imposed on them a set of obligations to suffering others regardless of where they might be found or what regime might have imprisoned them.

This time, when Rousset won, *Les Lettres françaises* had to pay real damages, although in an amount less than the original suit demanded because of Daix's status as a former Resistance fighter and deportee. The trial had a far more important impact in France than the one initiated by Kravchenko, even if many Communist Party members refused to take a stand against the Soviet Union during the Cold War. Most important, Rousset provided camp witnesses, absent any other forum and with incomplete forensic evidence for assessing or adjudicating "crimes against humanity," with a particularly important function. He attributed authority to witnesses not only because they had resisted the Nazis, but also because they had experienced an ostensibly new form of abjection, concentration camps, in which "everything is possible." These envoys from the "concentrationary universe" possessed deep and special knowledge of human suffering and revealed humanity to itself: "I came to feel for these men," Rousset wrote in reference to his German Communist companions in Buchenwald, "an affection founded on my discovery of Man, beyond all degradations, vile but magnificent, precious for his own sake and outside of all creeds and conventions."[59]

The source of the witness's moral fitness originates in the camp experience, which prepared him for future struggles. That experience is the sacred truth of human wretchedness known only to those who have lived in the depths of the "brotherhood of abjection."[60] As Rousset wrote to a friend about the impact of his camp experience:

---

58. The last section of the French reads: "Le Tribunal sait qu'il s'adressait sans aucune discrimination à l'ensemble des déportés, à tous les déportés, appellant et exigeant leur présence collective et commune, en vertu du devoir auquel, en quelque sorte, leur noblesse, c'est-à-dire leurs souffrances, les obligeaient."

59. Rousset, *Other Kingdom*, 168, 153.

60. Rousset, *Les jours de notre mort*, 742. Georges Bataille made much of Rousset's experience of abjection and cites this phrase in "Réflexions sur le bourreau et la victime: SS et déportés," *Critique* 17 (October 1947): 338.

Since I returned, with my abilities intact, I have not regretted this experience, to the contrary. I have the impression that, if I had not had
it, I would to a certain degree envy those who had. . . . But more profoundly, and although it remains extremely difficult to predict clearly
that which will survive, organically, as it were, from that experience—to
be sure a more robust clarity of mind [*décision*], a more tenacious will,
and some sort of purposefulness in struggle that allows us, today, to
use our weapons more resolutely. And thus, a more deliberate decisive-
ness that achieves all its goals. The feeling, also, that it is only within
somewhat exceptional conditions that it is possible to express oneself
wholeheartedly.[61]

His witness figure thus drew on the virility, commitment, and endurance Rousset
learned as a Resistance member, but his "clarity of mind" drew on his experience
of abjection in the camps.

In *L'univers concentrationnaire* too, Rousset used a metaphorical virility to
describe the insights of camp experience—now derived from special knowledge
of life and death, "a cool, sensual thrill of joy founded on the most complete
understanding of the wreckage, and consequently incisiveness in action and
firmness in decisions, in short, a broader and more intensely creative vigor."[62]
Rousset was the image of ravaged virility when he first returned from the camps.
He wore a black eye-patch because he had lost an eye in childhood, but after the
war many people assumed he had lost it in Buchenwald.[63]

Rousset claimed the camp experience imparted to him a new form of moral
insight shared by an elite of sufferers who had developed a special relationship
to death. The trial afforded him an opportunity to put witnesses, including himself, on stage as "specialists." Bearing witness was not only part of a moral and
politically salient duty to remember for the sake of humanity. It was also the
sacred mission of politically conscious former inmates who had participated in
the Resistance, and whose unexpected and "glorious" survival imposed on them
a duty to transmit their experience. Their knowledge and articulation of the
abyss were a means of struggling against the emergence of other camp systems;
they defined Nazi camps as a caesura between a world of violence and suffering, including warfare, and another entirely unfamiliar world of death. Bearing
witness by those whose experience allowed them to see deeper and further than

---

61. Rousset, "Lettre à Oscar Schoenfeld 1945," dated 1945, in Rousset, *La fraternité de nos ruines*,
45, 51. He had expressed these views in *Les jours de notre mort*, 959.

62. Rousset, *Other Kingdom*, 171.

63. Kuby, *Political Survivors*, 32.

FIGURE 2.1 / David Rousset and Jean-Paul Sartre, 1948.
Getty Images.

others constituted a form of politics by testimony, a means of achieving social solidarity. As Rousset wrote in his appeal, "We know that the gift we have been given, this permission to live (whereas logic would have had us in a mass grave), can only have one meaning: we are witnesses before other men to this warning about man and society represented by the Nazi camps."[64] Bearing witness was a dialogue between witnesses and spectators meant to forge and secure collective human bonds against camp systems everywhere, a celebration of humanity that demanded politics even as it transcended them; it was not only one important activity among others in the quest for justice, but also the form and content of the struggle for a camp-free world.

Rousset's concept of the witness's role turned the political struggle for social justice into an ethical imperative because he advocated bearing witness—the investigation of camps everywhere by former inmates—as its own struggle, and called on survivors to testify because the fact of having suffered compelled

---

64. "Au secours des déportés," reprinted in Copfermann, *David Rousset*, 208.

them to take up a political vocation.[65] In the last pages of *Les jours de notre mort*, Rousset refers to the inmates as having experienced the "extreme limits of ruins," an experience so abject that "it will never be spoken."[66] His moral vision cast no shadow between Nazism and Stalinism, dissolving the historical differences between them into an unprecedented destruction of the concept of humanity by the camp system.[67] Rousset did not merely compare Nazism and Stalinism, but defined the camp systems each built as utterly distinct from all other state-sponsored persecution and excluding, for example, victims of torture.[68] Nazi and Soviet camps or any camps that resembled them were unassimilable to or different from the suffering experienced by victims the world over. As he put it in *L'univers concentrationnaire*, the survivors of Nazi camps "weighed the ravages of starvation. For years on end they groped their way through the fantastic scene littered with the ruins of human dignities. They are set apart from the rest of the world by an experience impossible to communicate."[69]

Rousset's model of the witness also blurred boundaries between the treatment of Jews and other groups. He insisted that the difference between slave labor and extermination camps was a matter of degree, not of kind.[70] He recognized but downplayed the central role of antisemitism in Nazi ideology and

65. Emma Kuby offers this perspective in "In the Shadow of the Concentration Camp: David Rousset and the Limits of Apoliticism in Postwar French Thought," *Modern Intellectual History* 11, no. 1 (2014): 147–73.

66. David Rousset, *Les jours de notre mort*, 959.

67. This was not an unusual view at the time, especially on the political Right. A review of Buber-Neumann's *Under Two Dictators* in *Le Monde* notes that Nazi and Stalinist camps were equally terrible, and that the comparison was "not to the advantage of the U.R.S.S." Author listed as A.P., "Déportée en Sibérie par Margarete Buber-Neumann," *Le Monde*, May 9, 1949. This view resurged—if it had ever gone away—after the end of the Cold War and is especially apparent in the work of Tzvetan Todorov, *Facing the Extreme: Moral Life in the Concentration Camps*, trans. David Bellos (New York: Henry Holt, 1996).

68. David Rousset, "Le sens de notre combat," preface to Paul Barton, *L'institution concentrationnaire en Russie* (Paris: Plon, 1959), reprinted in Rousset, *La fraternité de nos ruines*, 328. Rousset conceives torture as less prevalent and less institutionalized than camp violence, a peculiar thing to say in the middle of the Algerian war. See also his statements in "Au secours des déportés," in Copfermann, *David Rousset*, 200–207. Kuby, "In the Shadow," esp. 157–59, argues that there were limits to Rousset's universalization of witnesses because he recognized only concentration camps as true loci of suffering, conflating the experience of Nazi and Soviet camps.

69. Rousset, *Other Kingdom*, 169.

70. Rousset, *Other Kingdom*, 61. See also Kuby, *Political Survivors*, 34, 60. Margarete Buber-Neumann argued that Nazism signified dead people, and Soviet communism signified dead people but also "dead souls." This view is often cited to explain the disillusionment of Communists because it betrayed true believers, and sometimes to argue problematically that communism was worse than Nazism. Cyrus Leo Sulzberger, "Prisoner Who Escaped Compares Nazi and Russian Labor Camps: Woman Says That Soviet Guards Never Had Sadistic Streak of Germans, Depended on Mental Threat to Bring Results," *New York Times*, March 12, 1949.

analyzed the camps primarily by reference to the injustice created by industrial capitalism.[71] Along with many others on the French Left like Germaine Tillion, he assimilated the particular victimization of Jews to a universal vision of victims modeled on the camp inmate who was worked to death.[72] Rousset was the architect of a specific and problematic version of the concentration camps that interprets dehumanization and death by forced labor rather than extermination as paradigmatic of the camp experience.[73]

Throughout his work and activism, Rousset pioneered a construction of politics by testimony, one that anticipated a more victim-centered concept of justice. In her work regarding the CICRC, the commission Rousset founded to investigate concentration camps, Emma Kuby demonstrates that its construction of camp witnesses marked a transition from the Nuremberg tribunal to later, more victim-centered testimony in the Eichmann trial. She shows that Rousset's effort to investigate camps in the Soviet Union was not merely Cold War propaganda derivative of human rights language, but "mobilized victims' memories of the Nazi camps." He placed witnesses center stage in an effort to rouse awareness of the failure of Western governments to demand accountability for the "crimes against humanity" in their midst, and turned bearing witness into a moral and political vocation that transformed abjection into glory and survivors into a new sort of "Man" born of the camps.

At the same time, Rousset's construction of witnesses and witnessing did more than shift a cultural focus from an abstract appeal to "humanity" to a victim-centered concept of justice and the politics of testimony that went with

---

71. See in particular his analysis of the causes of Nazism, which sidelined antisemitism, in Rousset, *Other Kingdom*, 114–15. He did not neglect the fate of Jews—he included it in his novel. But he linked witnessing to resistance and so conceived the camp experience through the eyes of resisters, not Jews. He thus participated in the general elision of the particularity of Jewish suffering during the postwar period.

72. On Rousset's apoliticism, see Kuby, "In the Shadow," 147–73. For an account of attitudes toward Jews by former partisans responsible, on a historical commission in 1951, for establishing the numbers of those deported, see Sylvie Lindeperg, "L'atelier d'Olga Wormser: De l'acceuil des déportés à l'écriture de l'histoire 1945–1979," in *Qu'est-ce qu' un déporté?*, 302–3. Also see Rousset, *Other Kingdom*, 61; Samuel Moyn, "From *L'Univers Concentrationnaire* to the Jewish Genocide: Pierre Vidal-Naquet and the Treblinka Controversy," in *After the Deluge: New Perspectives on the Intellectual and Cultural History of Postwar France*, ed. Julian Bourg (Oxford: Lexington Books, 2004), 277–300.

73. Kuby, "In the Shadow," 147–73. Many French commentators continue to resist this pertinent criticism of Rousset. Grégory Cingal heralds Rousset's sensitivity to Jewish persecution, arguing that suffering is suffering, and denouncing the notion of a "hierarchy of victims" in his preface to Rousset, *La fraternité de nos ruines*, 11–12. Olivier Le Cour Grandmaison, "Sur l'univers concentrationnaire: Remarques sur 'tout est possible,'" *Lignes* 2 (2000): 26–46, is less explicit, but takes the equivalence between Nazism and Stalinism for granted, relying on Rousset's influence on Arendt as if his impact on her thinking were a sufficient argument in favor of a universalist position.

it. He recast the Resistance fighter's survival as a novel form of heroism in keeping with the experience of penury and survival recounted by the witness that
emerged in the libel trial as well as in his portrayal of Nazi camps. His work
borrowed, as Kuby puts it, from "traditional narratives of *Bildung* and heroic
sacrifice," and reconfigured these narratives in keeping with his experience of
Nazism.[74] His transformation of combat into insight and moral obligation
recalls heroism on the battlefield and its mythic, redemptive dimension. But he
also reconceived heroism in the wake of his experience of the camp system. His
portrayal of abjection and nobility, though surely a Christian component in his
work that aligns it with the narrative of having sacrificed for a cause, pushed
the boundaries of traditional narratives to encompass the experience of Nazi
camps.[75] His depiction of the camp experience represented an effort to rise to
the challenge of explaining the advent of industrialized violence and in so doing
fashioned a symbol of suffering humanity that took the particular suffering of a
group of human beings to stand in for a potentially broader group of sufferers.

The purpose of bearing witness was to further commemorative and political
goals from the perspective of a camp survivor who had touched the abyss and
returned. Like combat veterans, former Resistance fighters who were camp survivors saw themselves, according to Olivier Lalieu, as combatants whose "moral
forces were augmented by the ordeal" they had undergone.[76] Former Resistance
members conceived the "duty to remember" as a moral obligation to future
generations and as a reminder that peace and democracy are fragile.[77] Rousset

74. Kuby, "In the Shadow," 153.

75. This conception of the witness owes less to Christian revival in France than to passionate
moral humanism acknowledging and yet resisting the wreckage of human dignity; it represents a
secular effort, with some displaced religious or sacralizing dimensions, to end camp suffering rather
than to redeem it in another world. Rousset demonstrated little interest in inter- and postwar Catholic efforts (he was a lapsed Protestant), led by Jacques Maritain, to explain antisemitism in Pauline/
Augustinian terms as revenge on a "witness people" who reminded Christians of their failure to live
in the image of Christ. On Jacques Maritain, but more specifically on his wife Raïssa Maritain, see
Brenna Moore, *Sacred Dread: Raïssa Maritain, the Allure of Suffering, and the French Catholic Revival,
1905–1944* (Notre Dame, IN: Notre Dame University Press, 2013). On the importance of political
Catholicism in the postwar legal order and its relationship to human rights (particularly on Catholic
constructions of "dignity"), see Samuel Moyn, *Christian Human Rights* (Philadelphia: University of
Pennsylvania Press, 2015).

76. Olivier Lalieu, *La déportation fragmentée: Les anciens déportés parlent de politique, 1945–1980*
(Paris: La Boutique de l'histoire éditions, 1994), 32.

77. Lalieu, *La déportation*, 32–34. For the self-perceptions of Holocaust survivors in Poland,
France, and the DP camps, in contrast to resisters, see Laura Jockusch, *Collect and Record! Holocaust Documentation in Early Postwar Europe* (Oxford: Oxford University Press, 2012). On France
and Italy, see Rebecca Clifford, *Commemorating the Holocaust: The Dilemmas of Remembrance in
France and Italy* (Oxford: Oxford University Press, 2013). Clifford notes that many Jews left the Amicale d'Auschwitz (an association of Auschwitz survivors and later their families) after the Rousset

believed that combat veterans and resisters had a moral obligation to remember, but he also conceived the camp survivor's experience of death and dying as unique:

> Normal men do not know that everything is possible. Even if the evidence forces their intelligence to admit it, their muscles do not believe it. The concentrationees do know. The solider who has spent months under fire has made the acquaintance of death. Death lived among the concentrationees at every hour of their existence. She showed them all her faces. They came to know all her exigencies. They lived dread as an ever-present obsession. They knew the humiliation of beatings, the weakness of the flesh under the lash. They weighed the ravages of starvation. For years on end they groped their way through the fantastic scene littered with the ruins of human dignities. They are set apart from the rest of the world by an experience impossible to communicate.[78]

If soldiers had made death's "acquaintance," the concentrationees had lived with "her."

Rousset rewrote the resister's endurance into the witness's special moral strength. The constitution of a cast of human beings whose glory is linked to their suffering surely builds in secular terms on the image of martyrdom. But the witness who emerged from the trial is not merely a hero whose suffering for an ideal redeems him, whose combat against the Nazis and endurance in the camps are of a piece.[79] The concentration camp survivor also represents an experience born of years of intimacy with dread, death, and the ruined landscape of human "dignities" that soldiers, who only make death's "acquaintance," do not develop. This experience, to which some of his comrades, he said, "refused to yield," is ubiquitous, inhuman, terrorizing, and forces its victims to fight not only with arms or "revolutionary faith," but also with "faith in life," that often

---

affair in order to escape the increasing domination of the Communist Party. Many had joined Resistance groups not associated with the Communist Party. The late Simone Weil said that the Amicale d'Auschwitz was "monopolized by the Communists" who "seemed unaware that there had been mostly Jews at Auschwitz." She had gone looking for fellowship and solace and never went back. Weil cited in Clifford, *Commemorating the Holocaust*, 40.

78. Rousset, *Other Kingdom*, 168–69.

79. Regarding this belief that resistance and deportation were of a piece, see Lalieu, *La déportation*, 33–35, esp. 35. He refers specially to Germaine Tillion. This attitude was the norm among French Resistance fighters. The Italian Resistance also shared this perception of continuity between resistance and deportation. See Robert S.C. Gordon, *The Holocaust in Italian Culture, 1944–2010* (Stanford, CA: Stanford University Press, 2012), 51–52.

could not save them.[80] The witness symbolizes an experience of dread proper to the camp system, and speaks for others dead and alive.

Rousset declared in a May 1951 address to the participants in a mock trial of the Soviet Union in Brussels,

> What I claim to be before you is merely the spokesman [*porte-parole*] of the victims, the millions of men who today live in conditions entirely similar, as I will demonstrate, to those we experienced. It is our duty to give them this chance to speak about their lives and their misfortune [*de dire leur vie et leur malheur*]. My role is confined to this. I bring before you the charge of the victims.[81]

Bearing witness was the vocation of a group of sufferers with a unique experience of abjection. Their experience conveyed a central truth about state power—the terror perpetrated by the Nazi and Soviet camp systems—and the human condition in the twentieth century. Rousset's witnesses symbolize the humanity-destroying violence of Nazi camps that had been insufficiently understood. He intuited that heroic narratives were important sources of resistance to camp systems: French Resistance fighters, unlike Jews and like soldiers, knew they could die and that deportation was inevitably a part of their choice. But those narratives were insufficient to transmit or account for the new forms of dehumanization the camps had created. By asserting that "the misfortune of having been in a concentration camp is without comparison" (244), Rousset conceived survival as a form of heroism shared by an international and exclusive "brotherhood" who continue their work as soldiers by other means.

Rousset surely conceived survival as a new and special form of moral strength continuous with the moral epiphanies of combat. Camp survival is a form of heroism willed from the depths of despair, and Rousset's witness is a combatant whose moral sense has grown stronger, who imagines his deportation as an extension of his resistance activities, persuaded that his political struggle helped him to endure the camps. Witnessing expressed the rightness of his decision to fight for social justice and the urgency of his struggle, as well as the combat soldier's mission to attest to the intolerable evil he had seen. But his concept of the witness also redefined the will to live in keeping with the realities of death in the camps. For Rousset, the "evil" of the camp, "like an ominous shadow threatening the entire planet with a fate in which all men must share," "far outweighs any

---

80. Rousset, *Other Kingdom*, 170.
81. Rousset, "Rapport sur les camps de concentration soviétiques," in *La fraternité de nos ruines*, 216.

military triumphs." From within the camp, the locus of "destroyed social values," it was possible to survive but nearly impossible to defy death.[82]

Survivors' unanticipated return to the world of the living invested them with the moral and political vocation of those who touched the abyss and understood the "wreckage." The mission of witnesses was to call attention to the new and radical forms of human subjection they experienced, the dissolution now not only of human dignity in the trenches, but also of the very concept of humanity. Rousset's trial stressed the distinctiveness of Nazi and Stalinist camps from all other experiences of atrocity and sought to redeem survivors as "witnesses" who "knew that everything is possible."[83] Survival was a form of "glory" not because the witnesses were heroes, not because they had managed to hold on to life against the odds, but because they devoted their lives entirely to the memory of a certain kind of death, the memory of having lived with death rather than merely having made "her" acquaintance. They had an experience of utter abjection whose deeper sense would remain elusive except to an elite resolved to bear witness, to save human beings from a fate they must share.

After the war, Jean-Marie Domenach, a French left-wing Catholic resister, asserted that "we weren't going to praise those deported on racial grounds: they were not among those whose deportation had a meaning in the struggle."[84] Domenach's assertion most obviously contrasts the meaning of resistance against the meaninglessness of dying without a redemptive struggle, and explains why Jews suffered the stigma of dying without a fight (chapter 3). Rousset did not dispute Domenach's views but nuanced them by rendering the former combatant camp survivor a symbolic stand-in for all the wounded humanity of the concentration camps. The "specialist" bears witness on humanity's behalf, and speaks for all victims and potential victims of camps. Jewish suffering is not meaningless, but is represented symbolically by camp laborers who, by virtue of their combatant experience, are imbued with distinctive insights and obligations into the suffering of the camps. Nazi crimes against humanity, to borrow a turn of phrase from Hannah Arendt, were committed most profoundly on the bodies of former Resistance members who labored in camps.[85]

---

82. Rousset, *Other Kingdom*, 169.
83. Rousset, *Other Kingdom*, 168.
84. Judt, *Past Imperfect*, 181. Judt takes the quotation from a French work that does not cite a reference about when Domenach said this, but the implication is that it was in the context of looking back on that period. Maurice Szafran, *Les juifs dans la politique française de 1945 à nos jours* (Paris: Flammarion, 1990), 35.
85. I paraphrase Arendt's comment that the Holocaust consisted of "crimes against mankind committed on the body of the Jewish people" in Arendt, *Eichmann in Jerusalem*, 7.

The labor camp witness reconciled the universal vision of Nazi violence as a "crime against humanity" with a particular experience of victimization conceived as the deep and incommunicable knowledge of life and death possessed by an elite brotherhood of "witnesses." Rousset's effort to describe Nazi violence in *L'univers concentrationnaire* was so powerful that his book was the most important account of the concentration camps in postwar Western Europe and inspired Arendt's own description of the destruction of the concept of humanity by "totalitarian" regimes.[86] The former combatant camp survivors who emerged in the course of Rousset's libel suit embodied the worst that has befallen humanity and were symbolic figures who represented an otherwise inarticulable experience of death and dying.

Like Tehlirian and Schwarzbard, Rousset's witnesses were heroes, but not in the conventional meaning of the term; the compulsion to bear witness was surely born of a moral epiphany, but it also rendered a new historical experience meaningful, replacing the tragic narrative of the soldier with another narrative of survival that accounted for and redeemed the humiliation and dread with which the survivor's camp years were saturated.

The witness symbol could not transcend the diverse politics and conditions of the survival of literal witnesses. Made up of former camp inmates, the CICRC, after securing politically difficult permissions, conducted investigations of prison camps in Tunisia, Spain, Greece, and Algeria to determine if they resembled the "concentrationary universe" the Nazis had created. Using Rousset's concept of politics by testimony, the CICRC issued white papers on what they found in Spain and elsewhere. They relied on a list of camp conditions to make the comparison, but their presumption was not only that Nazi camps were fundamentally different from other camps, but also that as former inmates, Rousset and his fellow commission members could best determine whether a particular system resembled that of the Nazis. Rousset believed that Soviet camps were akin to Nazi ones, but he was not about to find out by investigating on the ground, because the Soviet Union did not permit CICRC representatives to inspect prisons there. In response, in 1951 the commission held a mock trial in Brussels of Stalin's regime.[87]

The CICRC collapsed under the pressure of political realities that called into question its ability to represent all victims of camps and to define specifically the violations camp systems entailed. Once the commission had to report from Spain and especially Algeria, its insistence on drawing analogies between Franco's

---

86. Hannah Arendt, *The Origins of Totalitarianism* (1958; repr., New York: Penguin, 1976), 437–57.
87. For this paragraph and the next, see Kuby, *Political Survivors*, 193–222.

camps and those of Hitler's, between French detention camps for Algerian opponents and those of the Nazis, made little sense; commission members' experience was particular to what they had undergone in Nazi Germany. The collapse of the group spoke to the political limitations of a restricted ethical orientation, of a particular group speaking on behalf of humanity.

Whatever the political limits of bearing witness, Rousset made the concentration camp survivor an authoritative source of knowledge about an ostensibly new form of inhumanity, drawing on the postwar prestige of the Resistance movement in France. By the 1960s, yet another victim replaced the concentration camp survivor as the most authoritative of all: the Jewish Holocaust survivor. Rousset had ignored the particularity of the Jewish experience throughout his work, and no Jewish voices affirmed the virtue of having suffered. For Jews, whose worlds were shattered, this kind of redemptive interpretation made little sense. The Eichmann trial conceptualized the experience of Nazi violence by construing another haunted witness with a different experience of subjection. It focused not on Nazism's retaliation against its armed political opponents and their fate, but on imagining genocidal violence against a people who, with some astonishing exceptions, had been unable to fight back.

3

THE HOLOCAUST WITNESS /
The Eichmann Trial and Its Aftermath

We are often asked, as if our past conferred a prophetic ability upon us, whether Auschwitz will return.

—Primo Levi, *The Drowned and the Saved* (1986)

In 1965, the historian Fernand Braudel told his student Léon Poliakov, known today for his pioneering work on the history of the Holocaust, that his university career would be delayed: "As long as you work on antisemitism, you will not be promoted in my unit."[1] Braudel may have been declaring his own doubts about the topic or warning Poliakov to be realistic about his future in the academy. Whichever it was, the "frank" response, as Poliakov put it, by one of the greatest historians of the twentieth century at the peak of his influence, suggests how marginal the topic of antisemitism remained in the aftermath of World War Two.

Indeed, the postwar years in Western Europe are infamous for their celebration of Resistance movements and the marginalization of Jewish death.[2] In France, Switzerland, and West Germany, former partisans (as Resistance members were called) and ex-army officers received pensions, while Jewish victims struggled for recognition.[3] In both Western and Eastern Europe, others note,

---

1. "Tant que vous vous occuperez d'anti-sémitisme, vous n'avancerez pas chez moi." Léon Polia-kov, *Mémoires* (Paris: Grancher, 1999), 208, 257–58.

2. In an overview of the period, Tony Judt paints a bleak picture of how local populations treated returning Jews in Western Europe. Judt, *Postwar: A History of Europe since 1945* (New York: Penguin, 2005), 804–8, 816–20. This assessment is reiterated in the many studies devoted to this period, including work on DP camps.

3. Regula Ludi, *Reparations for Nazi Victims in Postwar Europe* (Cambridge: Cambridge University Press, 2012), 52–144. In France, under legislation passed in 1948, the term *déporté* applied only to men and women deported for political reasons. See also Judt, *Postwar*, 805.

for different reasons, democratic and Communist governments mostly lumped Jewish victims into the general category of victims of fascism.[4]

Studies of the immediate postwar period in Europe and the United States stress the multiple forms of public and especially private Jewish witnessing, but also acknowledge the silence with which European publics treated Jewish death unless it was rendered in universal terms of patriotism and bravery that emptied the Jewish experience of its specificity. Although Jewish victims spoke about their experiences in memoirs, formed survivor networks, and established memorials to their dead in New York and Paris, the public discussion about the war addressed less the fate of Jews than anti-fascism and anti-communism, collaboration, the heroism of former resisters, and Christian complicity in Nazi crimes.[5] When the US psychiatrist William Niederland used the diagnosis of "survivor syndrome" in 1960 to explain the symptoms of Jewish survivors, he recognized the particular impact of the war on Jewish victims in a profession still largely insistent on the somatic origins of trauma.[6] Moreover, as the Cold War loomed, governments

---

4. See especially Pieter Lagrou, *The Legacy of Nazi Occupation: Patriotic Memory and National Recovery in Western Europe, 1945–1965* (Cambridge: Cambridge University Press, 2000), and Judt, *Postwar*, 808–13. On East and West Germany, see Mary Fulbrook, *German National Identity after the Holocaust* (Cambridge: Polity, 1999); Jeffrey Herf, *Divided Memory: The Nazi Past in the Two Germanys* (Cambridge, MA: Harvard University Press, 1997); Robert G. Moeller, "The Politics of the Past in the 1950s: Rhetorics of Victimisation in East and West Germany," and Moeller, "Victims in Uniform: 1950 Combat Movies," in *Germans as Victims: Remembering the Past in Contemporary Germany*, ed. Bill Niven (New York: Palgrave Macmillan, 2006), 26–42 and 43–61, respectively. On Eastern Europe, see Timothy Snyder, *Bloodlands: Europe between Hitler and Stalin* (New York: Basic Books, 2010), 344–77.

5. General accounts of this period include François Azouvi, *Le mythe du grand silence: Auschwitz, les Français, la mémoire* (Paris: Fayard, 2012), who claims that debates about the Holocaust were widespread during the so-called silent period after the war; Rebecca Clifford, *Commemorating the Holocaust: The Dilemmas of Remembrance in France and Italy* (Oxford: Oxford University Press, 2013); Manuela Consonni, *L'eclisse dell'antifascismo: Resistenza, questione ebraica e cultura politica in Italia dal 1943 al 1989* (Bari: Laterza, 2015); Hasia R. Diner, *We Remember with Reverence and Love: American Jews and the Myth of Silence after the Holocaust, 1945–1962* (New York: NYU Press, 2010); Robert S.C. Gordon, *The Holocaust in Italian Culture, 1944–2010* (Stanford, CA: Stanford University Press, 2012); Laura Jockusch, *Collect and Record! Jewish Documentation in Early Postwar Europe* (New York: Oxford University Press, 2012), 391–411; Samuel Moyn, *A Holocaust Controversy: The Treblinka Affair in Postwar France* (Lebanon, NH: University Press of New England, for Brandeis University Press, 2005); Claudio Pavone, *A Civil War: A History of the Italian Resistance*, trans. Peter Levy (London: Verso, 2013), 669; Susan Rubin Suleiman, *Crises of Memory and the Second World War* (Cambridge, MA: Harvard University Press, 2006); Annette Wieviorka, *Déportation et génocide entre la mémoire et l'oubli* (Paris: Plon, 1992), esp. 162–90.

6. Ruth Leys, *From Guilt to Shame: Auschwitz and After* (Princeton, NJ: Princeton University Press, 2007), 27n18. For a broader history of the psychiatric treatment of Jewish Holocaust survivors, see Robert Krell and Mark I. Sherman, *Medical and Psychological Effects of Concentration Camps on Holocaust Survivors* (New Brunswick, NJ: Transaction, 1997), 12. Dagmar Herzog traces the history of psychiatric arguments for and against survivors requesting German reparations for psychological stress in *Cold War Freud: Psychoanalysis in an Age of Catastrophes* (Cambridge: Cambridge University Press, 2017), 89–122.

in Western Europe and the United States downscaled denazification efforts and softened once loudly proclaimed denunciations of Nazi crimes.[7]

In 1961–62, the trial of Adolf Eichmann in Jerusalem famously refocused public attention on the Jewish dimension of the Holocaust by putting Jewish suffering on display to a Western world still ignorant of the particularity of the Jewish experience of Nazism for reasons of guilt, indifference, denial, or political expediency.[8] Seats were reserved for almost five hundred journalists from around the world, and it was the first trial to be televised on home screens in Western Europe and the United States.[9] The US documentary maker Leo Hurwitz filmed the proceedings for broader television distribution using

7. Judt, *Postwar*, 52–61. Lawrence Douglas notes that by the time the last Nuremberg trials (the twelve US-led trials known as NMT) took place, the demands of politics and state sovereignty, particularly the United States' desire to guarantee the support of West Germany in the Cold War, led to the commutation of most sentences, including those of many of the *Einsatzgruppen* murderers. Douglas, "From IMT to NMT: The Emergence of a Jurisprudence of Atrocity," in *Reassessing the Nuremberg Military Tribunals: Transitional Justice, Trial Narratives, and Historiography*, ed. Kim C. Piemel and Alexa Stiller (New York: Berghahn Books, 2012), 276–95.

8. In *The Memory of Judgment: Making Law and History in the Trials of the Holocaust* (New Haven, CT: Yale University Press, 2001), 178, Lawrence Douglas writes, "As a triumph of didactic legality, the Eichmann Trial served to create the Holocaust in the popular imagination, transforming the destruction of European Jews into *the* emblematic event of the twentieth century." Deborah E. Lipstadt claims that the Eichmann trial gave survivors a "singular" moral authority, and adds, "Without the Eichmann trial, that may never have happened." Lipstadt, *The Eichmann Trial* (New York: Schocken Books, 2011), xi. Several critics remark on the significance of the Eichmann trial but see the turning point as 1978 and 1979, when the *Holocaust* miniseries appeared on German and US televisions. From among a vast literature, see Léon Poliakov, *Le procès de Jérusalem: Juger Adolf Eichmann* (Paris: Calman-Lévy, 1963), 22–26, which still provides one of the best summaries of the Western press coverage on both sides of the Atlantic; Hanna Yablonka, *The State of Israel vs. Adolf Eichmann*, trans. Ora Cummings with David Herman (New York: Schocken Books, 2004), for a full account of the background of the trial and its impact in Israel. Tom Segev, *The Seventh Million: The Israelis and the Holocaust*, trans. Haim Watzman (New York: Henry Holt, 1991), 323–84, calls the trial in Israel a form of "national group therapy" (351). In *Harnessing the Holocaust: The Politics of Memory in France* (Stanford, CA: Stanford University Press, 2004), 29–30, Joan Wolf writes that the French Jewish community interpreted the trial primarily as a legitimation of the State of Israel. See also Jeffrey Shandler, *While America Watches: Televising the Holocaust* (New York: Oxford University Press, 1999); Manuela Consonni, "The Impact of the Eichmann Event in Italy, 1961," *Journal of Israeli History* 23, no. 1 (2004): 91–99; Gordon, *Holocaust in Italian Culture*, 60–61; Annette Wieviorka and Sylvie Lindeperg, eds., *Le moment Eichmann* (Paris: Éditions Albin Michel, 2016). The German reception must be treated separately in the context of German denial and defeat. There is a general consensus that in spite of the coverage in Germany, the Frankfurt Auschwitz trials (1963–1965) had a greater if still muted impact, even though the Eichmann trial became the object of political tussles between Willy Brandt and Konrad Adenauer and the source of some soul-searching. See Peter Krause, *Der Eichmann-Prozess in der deutschen Presse* (Frankfurt am Main: Campus, 2002).

9. Yablonka, *State of Israel vs. Adolf Eichmann*, 56–57; Shandler, *While America Watches*, 90–92. Shandler emphasizes how much the English voice-over shaped the narrative of the trial and depicted Jewish suffering in universal terms of human psychology and morality (107). For a detailed account of the background to the trial's film production as well as the effects of the images, see Sylvie

hidden cameras in the courtroom, while in Israel the trial was broadcast on the radio because the population did not yet have television. The trial was conducted in Hebrew, and simultaneous translation was offered in French, German, and English. The judges as well as the defense and prosecuting attorneys all spoke native or fluent German, and some witnesses testified in Yiddish. Annette Wieviorka and Sylvie Lindeperg argue that the trial's influence was vast because of the TV coverage, and that many people still understand the Holocaust through its prism.[10]

Eichmann, kidnapped by Israeli agents in Argentina in May 1960, became head of the section of the Gestapo responsible for "Jewish Affairs" in 1941 and played an important role in organizing transports of Jews from Vienna, Berlin, and Budapest to death camps in the East. For thirteen months between April 1961 and May 1962, his trial competed for news coverage with dramatic developments in the US civil rights movement, Yuri Gagarin's first space mission, the Bay of Pigs invasion, and the French war in Algeria.

Scholars claim that the trial spurred the interest of a new generation in survivor testimony, and indeed the survivors' point of view offered a new narrative of the Holocaust in and outside of Israel that has largely displaced the previous twenty-year negligence of Jewish victims.[11] Initially, however, survivor testimony made the trial controversial because witnesses spoke about experiences of persecution often unrelated to Eichmann's specific crimes.[12] The Israeli prime minister David Ben-Gurion and the attorney general Gideon Hausner conceived the trial in both legal and pedagogical terms: the selection of 110 witnesses was determined by a variety of considerations, including their ability to supplement

Lindeperg and Annette Wieviorka, "Les deux scènes du procès Eichmann," *Annales: Histoire, Sciences Sociales* 63, no. 6 (2008): 1249–74.

10. Wieviorka and Lindeperg, *Le moment Eichmann*, 42. Wieviorka also made the latter point while speaking at the American University of Paris on October 21, 2016.

11. Donald L. Niewyk, *Fresh Wounds: Early Narratives of Holocaust Survival* (Chapel Hill: University of North Carolina Press, 1998), 12; Lipstadt, *Eichmann Trial*, xi, xx, 192–203.

12. Arendt famously protested that the trial had a primarily pedagogical rather than legal function because the outcome—Eichmann's condemnation—was known in advance. Hannah Arendt, *Eichmann in Jerusalem: A Report on the Banality of Evil* (1963; repr., New York: Penguin, 1994), 266. Moreover, the press focused on Eichmann's seemingly emotionless presence. Arendt's *Eichmann in Jerusalem* provoked and prolonged a debate about his character by challenging the demonic view of Eichmann and probably did as much to publicize the trial as press and television coverage itself. See also Richard I. Cohen, "Breaking the Code: Hannah Arendt's 'Eichmann in Jerusalem' and the Public Polemic; Myth, Memory, and Historical Imagination," *Michael: On the History of the Jews in the Diaspora* 13 (1991): 29–85; Valerie Hartouni, *Visualizing Atrocity: Arendt, Evil, and the Optics of Thoughtlessness* (New York: NYU Press, 2012). For an overall narrative of the trial and a reassessment of Arendt's account, see Lipstadt, *Eichmann Trial*, 148–87.

documentation of Eichmann's activities and to tell a "good story."[13] One hundred and one of the witnesses were Holocaust survivors, and of those, ninety-nine lived in Israel.[14] The Nuremberg tribunal had stressed documentation and downplayed witnesses; by contrast, the "representational paradigm at the Eichmann trial," as Lawrence Douglas argues, was "testimonial."[15] While Douglas defends the trial's legality, Hannah Arendt called the proceedings a "show trial."[16] Others are more ambivalent.[17] In any case, the trial's twin aims of judging Eichmann and making Israeli and Western audiences grasp the magnitude of Jewish suffering could be accomplished only with great difficulty. As Susan Sontag wrote, the trial "could not have conformed to legal standards" because "there was no strictly legal way of judging [Eichmann's crimes]." She called the suffering that permeated the trial its "tragic dimension," which took the form of a "collective dirge," a ritualized memorialization of Jewish death.[18]

The belief that the trial format was by definition inadequate to address victims' suffering is implicitly or explicitly the conceptual starting point of most work on survivor testimony at the Eichmann trial. Scholars have addressed how the trial brought Jewish death into public view and sought to make sense of the victims' experience. They have explored how the trial integrated Holocaust survivors into Israeli politics and society at that time, and how its redemptive Zionist narrative incorporated survivors into a heroic state.[19] They have also analyzed

---

13. Yablonka, *State of Israel vs. Adolf Eichmann*, 89. Yablonka provides a fascinating discussion of the witness selection process at 88–120.

14. Yablonka, *State of Israel vs. Adolf Eichmann*, 91, writes that many of those who might have testified were not selected, such as Léon Poliakov, who had hidden during the war rather than being deported. Primo Levi was not asked to testify, though he sent in a deposition. Levi, "Odissea Auschwitz," *L'Espresso*, September 27, 2007, 49–50. Presumably the investigators did not think him sufficiently representative of Italian Jewry—Yablonka does not mention him but implies as much—and selected instead an Italian living in Israel, Hulda Cassuto Campagnano (92).

15. Douglas, *Memory of Judgment*, 104. Douglas argues that the language of the law in the Eichmann trial was ultimately respected and produced a just verdict (173). Leora Bilsky claims that the trial used testimony systematically and soundly. Bilsky, "The Eichmann Trial: Toward a Jurisprudence of Eyewitness Testimony of Atrocities," *Journal of International Criminal Justice* 12, no. 1 (2014): 27–57.

16. Arendt, *Eichmann in Jerusalem*, 266.

17. Stephan Landsman, *Crimes of the Holocaust: The Law Confronts Hard Cases* (Philadelphia: University of Pennsylvania Press, 2013), 68–72.

18. Susan Sontag, *Against Interpretation and Other Essays* (New York: Doubleday, 1966), 125–26. Shoshana Felman adds nuance to Sontag's view of the trial as a work of art in *The Juridical Unconscious: Trials and Traumas in the Twentieth Century* (Cambridge, MA: Harvard University Press, 2002), 151–53.

19. The Zionist construction of "heroic memory," as Lawrence Douglas put it, is implicit or predominant in most accounts of the trial. Douglas, *Memory of Judgment*, 153–54. On the trial in Israel, see Yablonka, *State of Israel vs. Adolf Eichmann*; and Segev, *Seventh Million*, 323–84.

the trial's role in the emergence of Holocaust consciousness in Western Europe and the United States, its public validation of survivor stories, Arendt's controversial reporting for the *New Yorker*, and how, outside of Israel, the trial universalized Jewish suffering and made it accessible to non-Jews as a story about the human capacity for evil.[20] Volumes of work have appeared on survivor testimonies themselves.[21] Far less explored is how trial witnesses and observers shaped an alternative narrative about mass murder distinct from tales of tragic heroism like Hausner's Zionist account and the Warsaw ghetto uprising.

This alternative story figured survival not only in conventionally heroic terms, but also as a source of unfathomable vulnerability more in keeping with the events that witnesses relayed on the stand.[22] Like Rousset, who testified to the concentration camps' assault on the idea of dignified humanity, the Jewish witnesses transmitted their experience as a message to the world about a particular experience of human degradation. But unlike Rousset's resistance fighters, Jewish victims had to prove in the face of skepticism that they could not have resisted—they had to rebut insinuations that they had gone like sheep to the slaughter, a source of shame in Israel and of guilt and ambivalence toward Jewish victims elsewhere.

The Zionist narrative was the organizing framework for survivor testimony, recasting the victims' survival in redemptive, heroic terms. Prosecutor Hausner opened the trial by proclaiming that he would speak for the dead: "I am not standing alone. With me are six million accusers! . . . Their blood cries out, but their voice is not heard. Therefore I will be their spokesman and in their name I will unfold the awesome indictment."[23] He interpreted survivor testimony through

---

20. See the multiple works already cited in previous notes to this chapter. The argument about the universalization of Jewish suffering is not based on an account of trial testimony, but, in Devin O. Pendas's work, derives retrospectively from an important question regarding why the trial continues to draw so much interest more than five decades after it ended, especially because it had only a minimal impact on legal history. Pendas usefully historicizes what is implicit in other accounts about the "globalization" and "Americanization" of the Holocaust. Pendas, "The Eichmann Trial in Law and Memory," in *Political Trials in Theory and History*, ed. Jens Meierhenrich and Devin O. Pendas (Cambridge: Cambridge University Press, 2016), 226–28.

21. The literature on survivor testimony at the trial is extensive. Exemplary is Felman, *Juridical Unconscious*.

22. Yablonka, *State of Israel vs. Adolf Eichmann*, questions the evocation of conventional heroism in the trial. Legal theorist Stephan Landsman argues that the prosecutor used nationhood to evoke heroism because efforts to emphasize the brutality of the Nazis alone could not confer "pride and respect" on survivors. Landsman, "The Eichmann Case and the Invention of the Witness-Driven Atrocity Trial," *Columbia Journal of Transnational Law* 51, no. 1 (2012): 85. My argument differs from this assessment while not contesting the importance of heroism.

23. *The Trial of Adolf Eichmann: Record of Proceedings in the District Court of Jerusalem* (hereafter *TAE*), 9 vols. (Jerusalem: State of Israel, Ministry of Justice, 1992–95), 1:62.

the prism of six million accusers on whose behalf he was prosecuting Eichmann in Jerusalem. His statement invoked the "tears of the Jewish people," provided an overview of the history of Nazi antisemitism until and through the "final solution," and ended with rebirth, by "the mercy of Providence," of a "remnant" of Jews who thwarted Eichmann's design.[24] This narrative transformed the trial into the last stage of an epic struggle to defend the Jewish nation and redeemed victims' suffering by symbolically rectifying their statelessness. As Hausner asserted later, "Historic vengeance was Jewish survival itself."[25] This narrative proved successful in giving the suffering of survivors meaning, especially for those Israelis who held diaspora Jews and survivors in low esteem.[26]

But Jewish memory of Nazism was perhaps most dramatically embodied by the trial's most famous moment, the speech and subsequent collapse of witness Yehiel Dinur, known by his evocative pseudonym K-Zetnik, which signified the German initials KZ for *Konzentrationslager* (concentration camp).[27] Reluctant to appear in court, Dinur could not sleep and fasted for days before he was called to the stand—he told friends that the spirits who visited him at night had not eaten in Auschwitz.[28] When he testified, he referred to having lived on "Planet Auschwitz" and did not respond properly to questions. Dinur became so overcome with emotion that he collapsed in front of the stunned audience and was rushed to a hospital. After a long hospitalization, he recovered.

Assessments of his testimony intertwine the moral and juridical dimensions of witnessing. Wieviorka describes K-Zetnik as a typical Holocaust victim whose body endured while his psyche remained tormented; he was "annihilated by thinking about Auschwitz."[29] Hanna Yablonka writes that he "was destined," "not by his speech, but by his very being . . . to serve as spokesman for the hundreds

---

24. *TAE*, 1:116. "Remnant" is an allusion to the biblical "remaining survivors." See also Hanna Yablonka, *Survivors of the Holocaust: Israel after the War*, trans. Ora Cummings (London: Macmillan, 1999), 1. Arendt's conviction that the trial abandoned legalism in the interests of promoting nation building was largely based on Hausner's narrative of the Holocaust as the culmination of a long narrative of Jewish suffering. She believed that by making this argument, he neglected the historical distinctiveness of the Holocaust as a crime against humanity. Arendt, *Eichmann in Jerusalem*, 266–67.

25. Gideon Hausner, *Justice in Jerusalem* (New York: Harper & Row, 1963), 322–23.

26. Yablonka, *State of Israel vs. Adolf Eichmann*, 176, notes that after the trial, young Israelis no longer blamed the victims but the world that had abandoned the Jews to suffer. See also Idith Zertal, *Israel's Holocaust and the Politics of Nationhood*, trans. Chaya Galai (Cambridge: Cambridge University Press, 2005), 111.

27. Dinur used the pseudonym K-Zetnik 135633, but in his testimony insisted that it was not a pen name because he did not write "literary material." He was not permitted to use his pen name for purposes of identification at the trial. *TAE*, 3:1237. Because of the transliteration, he is referred to in secondary sources variously as Katzetnik and K-Zetnik.

28. Yablonka, *State of Israel vs. Adolf Eichmann*, 109.

29. Wieviorka, *Le procès Eichmann*, 90.

of thousands who died at Auschwitz"—he was their "symbol."[30] His testimony, Douglas claims, represented a "juridical failure," the point at which the crime was incommensurable with punishment.[31] Shoshana Felman argues instead that "confronted with K-Zetnik's testimony, *the law had a dialogue with its own limits.*" His collapse was not a juridical failure, she claims, but a "missed encounter" between the trauma intrinsic in survivor testimony and the cohesive language of legal interpretation, a moment that "*articulate[d] the difficulty of articulation* of the catastrophic story."[32] Arendt, an outlier, thought his performance was the nadir of the trial and played to the crowd, though this harsh response perhaps camouflaged her own sadness and unease.[33]

K-Zetnik's psychic and physical collapse stood in for the way in which all survivors' testimony pushed up against the limits of legal narrative, and the terrors the witnesses brought into the courtroom were as much a part of the trial's legacy as its Zionist nation building. This chapter argues that trial observers cast survivors as "witnesses" by capturing and condensing symbolically the "terrors of death" transmitted by the survivors on the stand.[34] The haunted figures conveyed their experiences by conjuring them up in the courtroom, bringing the dead to life and making present the torment that had rendered resistance mostly desperate and survival now a burden. Survivor testimony provided the first large public revelation, not only about the Holocaust's Jewish victims, but also of the psychological suffering endured by noncombatant victims targeted for extermination by mass killing and industrial murder. The witnesses undermined received wisdom about Jewish passivity in the face of Nazi terror; testimonies not only by K-Zetnik, but also by others, placed victims center stage, transforming them into human beings constrained by unimaginable terror and despised by an enemy determined to wipe them off the face of the earth.

This haunted Jewish witness lived on in another narrative that developed outside of Israel in the 1970s, when Jewish Holocaust survivors moved from the margins of the Holocaust to become its icons; as a new narrative of human and ecological survival developed in the 1960s and '70s, Holocaust survivors became quintessential witnesses to genocide, especially in the United States, and shorthand for the moral obligations of Western populations to remedy the suffering of others. A decade after the Eichmann trial, Jewish survivors, who had elicited

30. Yablonka, *State of Israel vs. Adolf Eichmann*, 109.
31. Douglas, *Memory of Judgment*, 149.
32. Felman, *Juridical Unconscious*, 144, 156, 159 (italics are in the original).
33. Arendt, *Eichmann in Jerusalem*, 223–24.
34. Segev, *Seventh Million*, 350.

sympathy because of what they endured, not only represented a broad and humanistic message about the consequences of tyranny, but also possessed dark knowledge capable of sparing other victims the agony they had lived.

After analyzing the trial testimony and observers' interpretations, I trace the emergence of this narrative of Jewish survival in the three stages in which it appeared, through three authors who responded explicitly or implicitly to the trial's narrative about victim blaming, filtered early on through the reception of Arendt's *Eichmann in Jerusalem*: the psychiatrist Bruno Bettelheim in the early 1960s, the psychiatrist Robert Jay Lifton in the late 1960s, and the scholar Terrence Des Pres in the 1970s. Each author condenses one segment of a narrative about survival in which Jewish Holocaust survivors, once blamed for not resisting their oppressors, became symbols of suffering humanity. The Eichmann trial considered deeply questions about victims' behavior and turned survivors into moral witnesses who testified to the triumph of Jewish life in unimaginable circumstances. Its most haunting legacy, the living dead figures of K-Zetnik and others who symbolized the experience of Jewish near-annihilation under Nazism, later became symbolic guarantors of human life after mass death, icons no longer only of Jewish redemption but also of universal suffering humanity.

Styles of Dying

As the Eichmann trial unfolded, the accounts of the torments to which survivors had been subjected contrasted with the solemnity of their demeanor.[35] Some witnesses were visibly shaken; many were not. Most spoke simply, in part because they were asked to limit their testimony for the sake of time and relevance. They often spoke in flat tones and with little flourish, in some instances becoming increasingly emotional and voluble as they continued.

Though Eichmann was under indictment, the witnesses were themselves forced into a defensive position from the outset. They had wrenching stories to tell and loved ones to honor, but the judges kept prompting them gently to restrict their testimonies. The survivors could finally set the record straight about the Jewish dimension of the Holocaust, but they also faced an attorney general

---

35. The expression "styles of dying" appears in Michal Glowiński, *The Black Seasons*, trans. Marci Shore (Evanston, IL: Northwestern University Press, 2005), 31. Robert Jay Lifton used it earlier in *History and Human Survival: Essays on the Young and Old, Survivors and the Dead, Peace and War, and on Contemporary Psychohistory* (New York: Random House, 1961), 152.

who asked them painful questions about why they had behaved passively in the face of the Nazi onslaught.

The contrast between the unembellished dryness of legal procedure and the horrific stories witnesses told amplified the accounts of suffering they had experienced.[36] *Le Monde*'s correspondent Jean-Marie Théollyre cited Frenchman Georges Wellers's testimony about children orphaned at Drancy and added, "The printed words do not suffice to translate the intonations and the realism of these precise evocations."[37] Hausner invoked the dissonance between Rivka Yoselewska's "quiet and restrained" tone and her testimony's "shattering" effects on observers, adopting the contrast to great effect in his own memoir of the trial.[38] The US writer Martha Gelhorn wrote about one witness: "The young man explained Treblinka in the voice we became used to: you could almost see muscles straining in the effort to speak clearly and calmly."[39] And in one of the earliest English-language books on Eichmann's capture and trial, Moshe Pearlman wrote that "the ability of most witnesses to report their story of suffering in calm and sober tones was a source of never-ending amazement to the public. Some, indeed, broke down, but resumed after brief intervals of sobbing."[40]

Witnesses' stories of their abandonment, isolation, and powerlessness conveyed their past suffering dramatically. Sometimes survivors explained how they summoned the will to live (though they never assumed that the will to live would guarantee life). Leon Wells said that his uncle told him not to commit suicide in order to tell the world "what happened here."[41] Avraham Lindwasser, a dentist working in the gas chambers in Treblinka, wanted to die but sought to stay alive in order to "relate what was happening here" and to "be of help to others."[42]

Others nearly violated courtroom procedures in order to honor their dead families. Judge Moshe Landau sought to wrap up the testimony of David Paul Meretz, who had been an official in a Czech Zionist organization, by saying to

36. There are myriad examples of the contrast between witness testimony and the necessarily neutral language of the law. In a matter-of-fact statement, a witness said that in Theresienstadt, the elderly sometimes became quiet and died as children were reading to them. His tone obviously contrasted with the content of his testimony so dramatically that the prosecutor asked the witness to repeat what he had said. *TAE*, 2:683.

37. Jean-Marie Théolleyre, "Le cauchemar des juifs français évoqué au procès Eichmann," *Le Monde*, May 11, 1961.

38. Hausner, *Justice in Jerusalem*, 74.

39. Martha Gelhorn, "Eichmann and the Private Conscience," *Atlantic Monthly*, February 2, 1962, 52–59, https://www.theatlantic.com/past/docs/issues/62feb/eichmann.htm

40. Moshe Pearlman, *The Capture and Trial of Adolf Eichmann* (New York: Simon & Schuster, 1963), 395.

41. *TAE*, 1:367.

42. *TAE*, 3:1217.

the witness that he was "certain that you still have much about which you wish to testify." Meretz did not take the hint: "Finally," he continued, "I only want to add that Franz Kahn, Edelstein, Zucker and my brother and his children—all of them were put to death; they died in October 1944, at the last moment."[43] The judge politely stopped him there. Meretz's tribute was all the more powerful because it hovered in the air, unmoored from the proceedings and yet integral to the trial's emerging portrayal of suffering and loss.

Hausner asked witnesses to recount as many instances of Jewish resistance as possible to demonstrate the exemplary courage of those who sought to die with dignity, in keeping with the emphasis on Jewish heroism. In his opening statement, he celebrated the Warsaw ghetto uprising. He admitted that it "was a desperate struggle without a shadow of hope, without prospects, without a chance of success," but he also argued that the uprising demonstrated that Jews "would no longer go as sheep to the slaughter—they would strike at the despicable killers."[44] Yet for all the moving accounts of Jewish resistance, the testimonies that recounted the pointlessness of resistance or escape were frequent in the trial and were among its most harrowing moments. They, too, were important to the pedagogical aims of the trial.

As is well known, Hausner elicited some of this testimony because he aimed to undermine then pervasive beliefs in Jewish cowardice and complicity, even at the risk of distressing witnesses.[45] He forced survivors to describe the effects of terror, imminent death, the price of resistance, and the power of hope, compelling young Israelis to grapple anew with their belief that Jews should have put up more of a fight. In Israel, where a half million survivors made up one-quarter of the total population, the murder of Europe's Jews was a source of rage but also embarrassment, supposed proof that living in the diaspora rendered Jews

---

43. *TAE*, 1:296.

44. Though Hausner defines the uprising as heroic, he acknowledges that once the youth had lost hope, their only motive was the desire "to cost the enemy an ocean of blood." The uprising thus demonstrated bravery in the face of impossible odds, but was also further evidence of the absolutely hopeless situation in which Jews found themselves. *TAE*, 1:91.

45. In his memoir, Hausner describes the "flower of Allied youth" who behaved "exactly like . . . millions of . . . Jews," who did not protest, hoping for another end. But it never occurred to anyone, he said, "to suggest that the prisoners of war died like cowards and went 'like sheep to the slaughter.' Nor did anybody speculate on the 'innate desire for death' that 'must' have animated the Jews and led them subconsciously to cooperate in their own destruction." Hausner, *Justice in Jerusalem*, 183. Arendt, who has a notorious reputation for victim blaming, actually stated that she did not believe that Jews, who were like any other group, could have put up resistance. And in spite of some of her comments about witnesses, she was deeply moved by the testimony of others, like Zyndel Grynszpan. Arendt, *Eichmann in Jerusalem*, 11, 229–30. Her comments on the Jewish Councils were far less nuanced.

compliant and weak.[46] Covering the trial for the *New York Times,* one correspondent commented on the "rustle of uneasiness" among younger Israelis who wanted to know why "the Jews didn't fight back."[47]

Hausner's questions were also meant for a wider Western audience who presumed that Jews had been weak or that survivors had done unsavory things to remain alive. He sought to provoke answers that would combat stigmas about Jewish parasitism, which the outcome of the war had done little to alleviate. In a statement that suggests how pervasive victim blaming and indifference to the Holocaust was in the early 1960s, Pearlman told his English-language readers that the subject of why Jews did not resist "is the key question asked by most people interested enough to hear or read of the Nazi slaughter of six million Jews."[48]

Hausner's own inquiries about resistance were sometimes indirect, as when he asked why Jews continued to believe they would live in spite of what they knew about extermination camps after 1942. Hausner raised a widespread question: If the Jews knew the Nazis' murderous intentions, why did they go to the gas chambers without protest? In response, the Czech Auschwitz survivor and artist Yehuda Bakon testified about a plan to "set Auschwitz on fire" on the Sabbath. Some inmates planned to set the "huts alight" and escape. Both Judge Landau and Hausner asked for clarification about why the plan failed, to which Bakon answered,

> A[NSWER]. [WITNESS BAKON]: Most of the older people did not want to believe.
>
> PRESIDING JUDGE: What did they not want to believe?
>
> WITNESS BAKON: That they would be sent to the gas chambers. Only the younger ones believed it.
>
> ATTORNEY GENERAL: Inside Auschwitz, they did not want to believe? Why? You saw the crematoria, you saw the fire rising from them, why did you not believe?

46. Yablonka, *State of Israel vs. Adolf Eichmann,* 36.

47. Flora Lewis, "Israel on the Eve of Eichmann's Trial," *New York Times,* April 9, 1961. *Le Monde*'s correspondent Jean-Marie Théollyre wrote an article focused on why the victims did not revolt, and stated that when the survivors were on the stand in Jerusalem, their "burning breath [*souffle brûlant*] passes through the courtroom, [which was] frozen until then." Théolleyre, "Les témoins s'efforcent d'expliquer pourquoi ils ne se sont pas révolté contre la barbarie nazie," *Le Monde,* May 3, 1961.

48. Pearlman, *Capture and Trial of Adolf Eichmann,* 273. See also Lord Russell of Liverpool, *The Trial of Adolf Eichmann* (1962; repr., London: Pimlico, 2002), esp. 254. In spite of the trial, these questions were still being denounced in the 1970s as if they remained relevant. Dorothy Rabinowitz, *New Lives: Survivors of the Holocaust Living in America* (New York: Knopf, 1976), 218.

WITNESS BAKON: They received this special treatment, so to speak, by
    which they arrived with the children and the old people, and with all of
    them, and they refused to believe. It is the nature of man to believe.[49]

The testimony of Abba Kovner, leader of the Vilna (Vilnius) ghetto Resistance,
also characterized the situation as one in which the illusion of hope prevailed
and sealed the Jews' fate. Kovner spoke at length and was often reprimanded by a
judge for his lengthy and sometimes off-topic answers. Arendt said sardonically
that he was used to being center stage.[50] When he recounted how the Resistance
operated and what it knew, and Hausner and Landau sought to keep him on
track, he moved unexpectedly in another direction:

ATTORNEY GENERAL: You learned that in Ponary [a mass execution site
    just outside Vilnius, Lithuania] they were simply murdering Jews?
WITNESS KOVNER: If you will allow me, I shall describe the thing which
    is engraved in my memory most of all.
Q[UESTION]: What was engraved in your memory most of all?

Kovner recounted what he heard from Sara Menkes, who survived a mass execution in the forest in Ponary in October 1941. Kovner described what this woman
told him about how a Nazi tricked a woman who had once been, "you could say, . . .
a pupil of mine," and part of a group destined for slaughter:

A. [WITNESS KOVNER]: Her name was Tsherna Morgenstern. . . . . After
    they had waited at some point, a group of them was taken and lined
    up in a row. They were told to undress. They undressed down to
    their shirts. A line of men out of the Einsatzgruppen stood facing
    them. . . . He looked at her [Tsherna Morgenstern] for a long time,
    smiled and said: "Take one step forward." She was terrified as all of
    them were. At that moment nobody spoke, nobody asked anything.
    She remained where she was, evidently panic-stricken, and did not
    step forward. He ordered her, asking: "Hey—don't you want to
    live—you are so beautiful—I say to you: 'Take one step forward.'"
    Then she took a step forward. He said to her: "It would be a pity to
    bury such beauty in the ground. Walk, but don't look backwards.

49. *TAE*, 3:1247. Bakon refers here to the German euphemism for extermination, "special treatment" (*Sonderbehandlung*).
50. Arendt, *Eichmann in Jerusalem*, 230.

There is a path here, you know this path, walk along it." For a moment she hesitated and then she began walking. The rest of us—Sara Menkes told me—gazed at her with a look in our eyes, I don't know whether it was only of fear and also of envy. She walked forward weakly. And then he, the officer, drew his revolver and shot her, as the first, in her back. Why should I tell more?[51]

The attorney general immediately went back to his prior line of questioning about the resistance, ignoring, for the sake of legal procedure, the seemingly irrelevant testimony, which Kovner reckoned to be his most important memory. He also ignored Kovner's speaking as if he were present at the scene he described—Kovner said "the rest of us" before he added that of course Menkes had told him what had happened.

At the end of his testimony Kovner also remarked vaguely, "Between us and the enemy there was something more." This prompted Judge Halevi to ask him what he was referring to, and Kovner explained what he called the "illusion that we did not all share the same fate." He continued by saying:

> WITNESS KOVNER: That until the last moment, even if one knew that
> there was a Ponary, they always gave us a spark, this distorted hope,
> that possibly you would be exempt. The frightful illusion produced
> frightful results of people wanting to prolong the life of some at the
> expense of others.[52]

Kovner distinguished a "minority" among the Jews, whom he characterized as "possibly less stricken, less misled, less under shock, due to its past, its education and its adherence to certain movements which trained people to give a personal example, perhaps only they could cope with it." These were his comrades in the Vilna ghetto who resisted, "who formed the fighting nucleus." He suggested that they "experienced less degradation, that they were less panic-stricken, and they knew better how to live in the ghetto as free men in every respect."[53]

For Kovner, hope impeded resistance, especially in the face of the terror induced by the *Einsatzgruppen*. He speculated about the type of people who retained their inner freedom. They were a small minority, likely Zionists with training, who knew how to manage the degradation and panic from which even they were not immune, as suggested by his use of the conditional "possibility"

---

51. *TAE*, 1:460.
52. *TAE*, 1:466.
53. *TAE*, 1:466.

and "perhaps" in reference to them. Whatever his debt to Zionism, for which he was a fervent advocate, the memory of those too weak to fight, like Tsherna Morgenstern, was most engraved in Kovner's mind. The hero and avenger remembered most acutely not the uprising, but the terrified young woman as she was shot, a scene at which he had not even been present.

In his memoir of the trial, Hausner wrote that Jewish passivity in the face of the Nazi onslaught was no mystery to him, but that it remained so for a large portion of the audience. He sought to disabuse that public of its preconceptions. Moshe Beisky, who survived the Kraków ghetto, Płaszów, Gross Rosen, and a death march, "was the right man to explain the relative passivity of the prisoners, if it is possible to give any explanation of human behavior in hell."[54] In a famous moment at the trial, Beisky recounted a brutal public hanging he witnessed at Płaszów. At the end of his description, he commented: "one had to stand there and look on. It was a sight."[55] Hausner jumped in:

> Q. 15,000 people stood there—and opposite them hundreds of guards. Why didn't you attack then, why didn't you revolt?
>
> A. I believe that this thing cannot be explained—it cannot be answered. To this there is no single reply. What I can talk of is the general situation.

Beisky was clearly taken aback, and he asked to sit down. After being given permission, he continued.

> A. First of all, I can no longer—and I acknowledge this—after eighteen years I cannot describe the sensation of fear. This feeling of fear, today when I stand before Your Honours, does not exist any longer and I do not suppose that it is possible to define it for anyone. After all, this thing is ultimately a terror-inspiring fear. . . . One could ask something else: If we did [try to revolt], where could we go?[56]

Beisky's response in the end was moving and persuasive: not only were they paralyzed by terror, but if the men had revolted, they would also have risked the lives of fifteen thousand people who had nowhere to go, dressed as they were in camp uniforms in a hostile environment where they would find no shelter and were

54. Hausner, *Justice in Jerusalem*, 176.
55. *TAE*, 1:349.
56. *TAE*, 1:349.

likely to die anyway. Attempting to survive within a system of extermination, Beisky implied, was the only response to terror.

In an interview conducted almost thirty years after the trial, Beisky, who had been part of a *Sonderkommando* (a special squad of Jews whom the Nazis forced to burn dead bodies and extract items of value, like gold teeth, from corpses), said he was "completely unprepared" for Hausner's question and could barely answer. He added that "the prosecutor didn't understand the situation, he couldn't imagine it."[57] Hausner said that Beisky reproached him later for having asked the question, which struck Beisky "like a blow between the eyes." Hausner concluded, however, that Beisky's "reply . . . was the most convincing piece of human truth I have ever heard on the subject."[58] Another witness for the prosecution, Leon Wells, who wrote a memoir about his experience, said in his 1986 video testimony that it was "immoral" to ask whether victims had "fought back."[59]

Victim testimony led to increased empathy and an outpouring of grief for Holocaust survivors, not least for those who had been abandoned to their fate by an indifferent world or had been unable to mourn their loved ones. The Israeli journalist Haim Gouri, who covered the trial for the paper *Lamerhav*, said the proceedings prompted Israelis to interpret the Holocaust in its "wholeness" rather than by making a distinction between the "Holocaust and heroism."[60] In Gouri's account, the courtroom gave survivors back their voices and provided a forum in which to challenge all those in Israel or anywhere who were dubious about how they survived; their cries for dignity were an "angry heartrending chorus."[61]

---

57. Testimony of Moshe B., interviewed February 1, 1990, Fortunoff Video Archive for Holocaust Testimonies, Yale University Library, New Haven, CT (hereafter Fortunoff), HVT-1832.

58. Hausner, *Justice in Jerusalem*, 176, 177.

59. Testimony of Leon W., interviewed November 15, 1986, Fortunoff, HVT-788; Leon W. Wells, *The Death Brigade (The Janowska Road)* (New York: Holocaust Library, 1978). Wells also reported that the trial helped because, in a dramatic reversal of power, the "SS were in pajamas," and added that he didn't "want to be a martyr." Leon W., Fortunoff, HVT-788. Other victims who testified mostly reported a negative response to Eichmann's presence or satisfaction at seeing him on trial. Ada Lichtman said that she "didn't recognize him so well" and that the trial felt like "someone sticking me with a hot iron." Testimony of Ada Lichtman, interviewed May 22, 1992, Fortunoff, HVT-3345. A survivor who was not called to testify but attended the trial echoed Wells, noting that Eichmann was "a little piece of nothing." Testimony of William P., interviewed January 24, 1984, Fortunoff, HVT-231.

60. Haim Gouri, *Facing the Glass Booth: The Jerusalem Trial of Adolf Eichmann*, trans. Michael Swirsky (Detroit: Wayne State University Press, 2004), 325–26. In *State of Israel vs. Adolf Eichmann*, Yablonka argues that the Eichmann trial transformed Holocaust memory in Israel, replacing "Why didn't you revolt?" with "Why didn't the Yishuv rise up against the nations who might have been able to help [but did not]?" (233).

61. Gouri, *Facing the Glass Booth*, 268. Elie Wiesel, who met Gouri at the trial, said that the Israeli journalist was outraged by Israeli Jews' indifference to the destruction of their brethren and, after the trial, felt deep sorrow and a sense of complicity. Wiesel, "Eichmann's Victims and the Unheard Testi-

Hanna Yablonka echoes these comments about understanding the Holocaust in its "wholeness," arguing that survivor testimony called into question familiar cultural categories for conceiving human behavior in extreme circumstances and that it generated an alternative narrative to the heroism of tragic gestures into which Jewish death could only rarely be incorporated.[62] She suggests that survivor testimony might be interpreted in terms of a "new kind of heroism," manifested, among others, by the testimony of the Hungarian Zionist Hansi Brand, who devoted herself to saving Jews from deportation. She was married to Joel Brand, who, toward the end of the war, went on a brave but failed mission abroad at Eichmann's behest in order to provide the SS with ten thousand trucks in exchange for a million Hungarian Jews. Hansi Brand would remain Eichmann's hostage in Budapest to guarantee her husband's return and also continued other negotiations on her own, saving many Jewish lives. She was tortured by the Hungarian secret police, who wanted details that the SS had not shared with them. She gave them no information. In response to questions at the trial, Brand insisted that she was not a hero but a rescue worker, and that shooting Eichmann would have achieved little.[63]

The "new kind of heroism" that Brand embodies reveals heroic gestures to have been useless under the circumstances, in which dying was easier than living and maintaining rescue activities. This heroism, Yablonka suggests, is "perhaps in line with the rabbis' definition of a hero as one who conquers his desire."[64] "New heroism" surely represents the refashioning of heroism suited to dire times, and Yablonka sensitively draws our attention to an important undertone of the testimonies. But "new heroism" as she envisions it also arguably expands heroism to cover not only its masculine but also its feminized forms—care for others and endurance rather than death with dignity.[65] Thus "new heroism" demonstrates

mony," *Commentary* 32, no. 2 (1961): 513. This essay was republished in 1968 in a slightly revised and expanded form in Elie Wiesel, *Legends of Our Time* (New York: Holt, Rinehart, and Winston, 1968), 161–97, in two segments, "The Guilt We Share" (161–73) and "A Plea for the Dead" (174–97). The reference cited here is on 167–68. Further references from this text will be given from the version in *Legends*, with any revisions noted.

62. Hanna Yablonka, "Three Variations on the Testimony in the Eichmann Trial," in *Holocaust Historiography in Context: Emergences, Challenges, Polemics, Achievements*, ed. David Bankier and Dan Michman (New York: Berghahn Books; Jerusalem: Yad Vashem, 2008), 577. She also argues that the judges in the trial were often insensitive and not nearly as affected by the commentary as the audience and other Israelis (571). One might counter that even within the constraints of the trial they let witnesses testify for long periods of time about extraneous matters and often assured them that they could sit down or take their time.

63. *TAE*, 3:1060–61. This story is multilayered, but in brief, Brand was arrested by the British authorities on his way to Istanbul, where he was to negotiate with Jewish authorities. He was sent to Cairo and held there. Joel Brand also testified at the trial.

64. Yablonka, "Three Variations," 577.

65. *TAE*, 3:1060. Judge Halevi, commenting on Brand's assertion that "we were not heroes," referred to her "personal courage" through rescue work. Yet to exemplify her "bravery" he chose not

how inadequate more conventional understandings of heroism have been in interpreting an important dimension of the Eichmann trial as well as the experience of Jews under Nazism. Witness testimony, however, revised such constructions of heroism—however inspiring and important—in line with the realities of victims' powerlessness. Trial observers shaped an image of dignified death, dying, and survival adapted to those realities.

On Behalf of the Dead

The contrast between received ideas about how human beings might fight and defeat their persecutors and the terror that discouraged all but the most desperate acts of resistance or escape best describes the incommensurable gap between cultural presumptions about heroic resistance and survivors' experience. Jewish commentators often called Holocaust survivors martyrs in spite of the senselessness of their suffering, suggesting how difficult it was to represent its extremity otherwise. Julius Margolin, who wrote on the Eichmann trial for the Russian émigré press and had testified at David Rousset's libel proceedings, claimed that when silent, witnesses often appeared "as though they were dead while still alive" (*comme s'ils étaient morts de leur vivant*), and noted that their survival was "miraculous"; they had been "elected by fate."[66] Hausner, Gouri, and other writers described the inconceivable suffering that haunted most of the witness testimonies by invoking the deathly atmosphere they brought into being. In so doing, they did not imagine survivors as conventional heroes but as emissaries of the dead.

Elie Wiesel, who resented Hausner's questions about why Jews did not resist, wrote in a 1961 essay on the Eichmann trial that the real explanation for those questions was the truncated understanding of existential choices in Europe: "the hero of the modern novel, absorbed in his protests, overlooks the nuances." The hero sees only "a man good or bad, a resister or a collaborator or indifferent."[67] Audiences, Wiesel implied, were not equipped to understand the novel circumstances under which Jews died and survived, and therefore blamed them for their own deaths.[68]

---

an episode of self-abnegating care for others (though it involved her willingness to die). Instead, he pointed to her silence when tortured, a more conventional and manly form of martyrdom. The Eichmann trial testimony was important because of how it so dramatically undermined this powerful construction of heroism even while drawing on it, especially by reference to the Zionist narrative.

66. Julius Margolin, *Le procès Eichmann et autres essais*, trans. Luba Jurgenson (Paris: Le Bruit du Temps, 2016), 18, 25.

67. Wiesel, "Eichmann's Victims," in *Legends*, 169.

68. Wiesel, "Eichmann's Victims," in *Legends*, 179.

Wiesel claimed that the witnesses in the Eichmann trial were "afraid of their own voices" because of the guilt they felt toward their dead. Speaking from the perspective of a survivor who wanted the lawyers and the spectators to "leave [the dead] alone," he insisted that survivors were members of a secret society of "initiates," who spoke of the "sacred meaning" of the Holocaust "with hesitation and fear, always lowering their eyes and always trembling with humility, knowing themselves unworthy."[69] Hausner could not conceive the torment his questions must have inflicted on the witnesses, who now had to defend those who died not only from the usual suspects, but also from an Israeli prosecutor:

> It is by a strange irony of fate that the only ones who were, who still are, fully conscious of their share of responsibility for the dead are those who were saved, the ghosts who returned from the dead. They do not feel this through any concept of original sin; they are Jews, they do not believe in original sin. The idea that rules them is more immediate, more agonizing, a part of their very being.
>
> Why did you not revolt? Why did you not resist? You were a thousand against ten, against one. Why did you let yourselves, like cattle, be led to the slaughter?[70]

Angry at Hausner's provocation, Wiesel argued that Jews died with dignity. "Knowing themselves abandoned, excluded, rejected by the rest of humanity, their walk to death, as haughty as it was submissive, became an act of lucidity, of protest, and not of acceptance and weakness." Survivors preferred, he wrote, "not to hurl their defiance at men" but to "keep silent" in a monologue "which only the dead deserve to hear."[71] He continued:

> Let me reveal a secret, one among a thousand, about why Jews did not resist: to punish us, to prepare a vengeance for us later. We were not worth their sacrifice. If, in every town and in every village . . . Jews formed endless nightly processions and marched on to eternity as if carrying within themselves a pure joy, one which heralds the approach of ecstasy, it is precisely to reveal to us the ultimate truth about those who sacrificed on the margins of history. In staying alive, at that price,

---

69. Wiesel, "Eichmann's Victims," in *Legends*, 173, 179, 193, 178. Elsewhere, Wiesel referred to survivors who speak "in code," a language that "cannot be deciphered." Elie Wiesel, "The Holocaust as Literary Inspiration," in Wiesel, Lucy S. Dawidowicz, Dorothy Rabinowitz, and Robert McAfee Brown, *Dimensions of the Holocaust: Lectures at Northwestern University* (Evanston, IL: Northwestern University Press, 1977), 7.

70. Wiesel, "Eichmann's Victims," in *Legends*, 170.

71. Wiesel, "Eichmann's Victims," in *Legends*, 187, 173.

we deserve neither salvation nor atonement. Nor do we even deserve that lesson of solemn dignity and lofty courage which, in spite of everything, in their own way, they gave us by making their way toward death, staring it full in the face, point blank, their heads high in the joy of bearing this strength, this pride within themselves.[72]

Wiesel recasts Jewish "resistance" in keeping with the realities of death camps, and he portrays the burdens of Jewish survival in a new light. The dead now set an example for those still alive, demonstrate their courage in the face of abandonment by the world, and show lucidity in the face of certain death. In this passage, Jewish pride and protest are not intrinsic in resistance, but in consciously chosen martyrdom, in setting an example of dying with dignity. His interpretation transformed behavior that the world stigmatized as weakness into a source of unheralded and magnificent strength. The example set by the dead was a "punishment" for the survivors who did not pay the ultimate price and had to live forever tormented by guilt, knowing that they were not as good, that they were not worth the lesson, because they were still alive.[73]

Wiesel's evocation of a suffering beyond words inhabited by "initiates" was thematized by many other trial observers, although without the sacred overtones. Survivors' experience took the form of an inscrutable and yet seemingly intimate bond with death that, as Gouri wrote, "hovers ghostlike over the trial."[74] The Dutch writer and survivor Harry Mulisch, who had hidden during the war, protected by his prominent gentile father, said little about the survivors' testimony in his own account of the trial, but noted that the pain expressed by the face of Ruzka Korshak, a leader of the Vilna ghetto uprising he met in Jerusalem, left him shaken because he could not attach it to anything with which he was familiar. "I will never forget her face. While she is telling us that they did not fight for their lives, but to determine their own way of dying, a pain appears in her face that I would not have thought possible in a human being, miles away from crying, a memory of despair and death, and she is still alive; a pain that is indescribable, at least with my pen."[75] The writer's vision of Korshak's face leaves us with a sense of unresolved and enduring suffering, a glimpse of a life irretrievably and unbearably marked by death.

---

72. Wiesel, "Eichmann's Victims," in *Legends*, 193.

73. Wiesel, "Eichmann's Victims," in *Legends*, 173, the reference to being "punished" on 193.

74. Gouri, *Facing the Glass Booth*, 271.

75. Harry Mulisch, *Criminal Case 40/61: The Trial of Adolf Eichmann*, trans. Robert Naborn (Philadelphia: University of Pennsylvania Press, 2005), 40–41. The original Dutch version appeared in 1961.

Survivors' intimate relationship with death appeared again and again throughout the trial. Asked by the attorney general and the judge if he had worked in a *Sonderkommando* until July 1944, witness Avraham Karasik replied: "On 13 July 1944 they liquidated us."[76] Another witness, Dov Frieberg, ordered to carry corpses, described how someone he thought was dead "sat up and asked me: 'Is it still far to go?'"[77] Leon Wells recounted how an SS man had listed him as among those shot so he would not have to admit he let a sick prisoner escape. As Wells testified, "I was dead. I knew that I am on the death list."[78] Gouri dubbed Wells, who had survived a *Sonderkommando* in Janowska, "living corpse number 182."[79] The Israeli journalist wrote that "his speech was monotonous and unadorned as if he were creating an abstraction of himself, as if he were actually somewhere else and the person speaking only a stand in."[80]

Gouri figures the witnesses as living dead whether or not this kind of experience was part of their testimony because the image best conveyed not only what they said, but also how they appeared and told their stories. Neither Gouri nor other commenters conceived the testimony in the martyrological mode of Wiesel, but they all repeatedly invoked images of the living dead to interpret survivor testimony. Gouri described Itzchak Nechama, a Greek Jew who testified about the deportation from Salonika to Auschwitz in 1942, as having hollow cheeks, speaking in a heavily accented Hebrew, and standing throughout his testimony. Nechama looked at photographs, including one of himself, which showed Jews tormented and beaten. At the very end of his testimony, the judge asked him:

[PRESIDING JUDGE] Q. Did you know the people who came with you
    from Salonika to Auschwitz?

A. Certainly.

Q. As far as you know, are there others still alive, and how many?

Nechama looked down at his fingers and appeared to count.

A. I'll tell you, 56,000 Jews left Salonika on the transports and only
    1,950 of them returned.

---

76. *TAE*, 1:474.

77. *TAE*, 3:1177.

78. Cited in Douglas, *Memory of Judgment*, 125. Douglas refers to Wells as "Lazarus." He also refers to Yoselewska as the "image of the survivor as an undead" (171). He notes generally that the survivor "occupies a liminal position between the living and the dead" (103–4).

79. Gouri, *Facing the Glass Booth*, 40.

80. Gouri, *Facing the Glass Booth*, 38.

PRESIDING JUDGE: How many of those who went with you and whom you knew returned?

WITNESS NECHAMA: I can tell you exactly: Four live here.

Q. In Israel?

A. Yes. Three live in America. Altogether there must be ten.

Q. Out of the 78 whom you mentioned [in prior testimony]?

A. In our transport there were 2,700.

STATE ATTORNEY BAR-OR: What does the figure 78 you mentioned—persons in one carriage?

WITNESS NECHAMA: Yes. On the whole transport there were 2,700.

PRESIDING JUDGE: And out of these, out of those who went with you, only 10 are alive today?

WITNESS NECHAMA: I am talking of the whole train.[81]

In the video of the trial, we see Nechama speaking quickly and uneasily. To capture his demeanor, Gouri wrote, "The witness came back from the railway platform at Auschwitz to answer the question."[82]

Witnesses did not simply honor an oath to the dead: they also brought that bond into being. Ghostly survivors took courtroom observers on a journey to hell, plunging them into flames, smoke, gas, death, and dying. Gouri proclaimed: "You saw the fire that lit up the faces of the murderers and their innumerable victims alike." "One hundred eleven witnesses, an endless procession now receding from view, sinking and rising in a miasma of blood and smoke. One hundred and eleven proxies, each taking his or her turn on the witness stand, and leading us across the desolate landscape."[83] Hausner said he could smell "lethal gas" in the courtroom.[84] The courtroom was "engulfed in poisonous vapors of the crematorium," as the witnesses "tirelessly gave their testimony." The testimony about extermination was as "vivid as a scream in the night."[85] Mulisch, who went to

81. *TAE*, 2:856.
82. Gouri, *Facing the Glass Booth*, 79.
83. Gouri, *Facing the Glass Booth*, 140.
84. Hausner, *Justice in Jerusalem*, 346. Hausner's account of the trial is dramatic. Others have called attention to his grandstanding. David Cesarani, *Eichmann: His Life and Crimes* (London: William Heinemann, 2004), 282; Arendt, *Eichmann in Jerusalem*, 8. Accounts like Cesarani's claim that Hausner was out of his depth when he cross-examined Eichmann, whom he underestimated, and accuse him of bullying. Lipstadt, *Eichmann Trial*, 121, 130, calls him "overwrought" and cites an article in the *New York Times* that called him "shrill and positioning."
85. Hausner, *Justice in Jerusalem*, 346, 328.

Independence Day celebrations while in Jerusalem for the trial, wrote that noise outside the courtroom on that day momentarily drowned out the "rattling of the death train and the howling of the crematoriums—tears filled my eyes."[86]

Witness Yoselewska's otherwise flatly delivered testimony brought back the dead and dying so dramatically that Wiesel imagined her as an otherworldly presence, a symbolic repository of cries from the mass grave. She gave her testimony only one court session after Hausner announced that she had suffered a heart attack and might not be able to appear. Brought to a mass grave with her family and village, she was shot along with all of them. As she put it: "The four whom we likened to Angels of Death shot each one of us separately."[87] Left for dead, she crawled out of the mass grave covered by blood, with nowhere to go. In despair, she sought to dig her way back into the grave, but it rebuffed her efforts. She slept on the grave for three nights and wandered around it for several weeks, surviving because a sympathetic peasant took pity on her and gave her food, after which she joined a group of Jews in the forest.

Her survival, Wiesel wrote, was a miracle: "That woman returned to the ditch after a little while to rejoin the phantasmagoric community of corpses. Miraculously saved, she still could not accept a life which in her eyes had become impure."[88] He meant that her life was "impure" because the dead were pure and she was alive.[89] Pearlman expressed a similar sentiment: "She remarried, has two children, and now lives in the Ramat Gan garden suburb close to Tel Aviv. But you can tell from her face and the way she speaks that she relives her living death in the bloody pit every moment she is awake."[90] On a more hopeful note, Pearlman wrote that Ada Lichtman, another witness, with a similarly horrific story, "stepped down from the witness box, out of the horror of Nazi Poland, and walked into the 1961 sunshine of Jerusalem."[91]

The witnesses spoke, the audience listened, and the room was transformed into an enormous meeting of the living and dead in which it was hard to distinguish between the two. For many observers—and before the vocabulary of trauma, with its emphasis on reliving the past in the present, was widespread—the

---

86. Mulisch, *Criminal Case 40/61*, 57. Mulisch quite deliberately juxtaposes the founding of the state with images of the Holocaust.

87. *TAE*, 1:516.

88. Wiesel, *Legends*, 173.

89. Robert Jay Lifton, *Death in Life: Survivors of Hiroshima* (New York: Random House, 1967), 504, speaks about an "image of purity modeled on the dead" in reference to survivors of both Hiroshima and Nazi camps.

90. Pearlman, *Capture and Trial of Adolf Eichmann*, 311. Interviewed in David Perlov's 1979 Israeli film *Memories of the Eichmann Trial*, Yoselewska repeated much the same thing about how she felt on a daily basis, but also remarked that many other people went through the same experience.

91. Pearlman, *Capture and Trial of Adolf Eichmann*, 270.

FIGURE 3.1 / Rivka Yoselewska on the witness stand in Jerusalem.
Israeli Government Press Office, Photography Department.

FIGURE 3.2 / Ada Lichtman on the witness stand in Jerusalem.
Israeli Government Press Office, Photography Department.

past came alive in the courtroom.[92] Gouri, in a biblical allusion, noted: "We felt as though we had come to console each of them under the same sky filled with the souls of the dead, and like a silent honor guard, we heard someone say, You see that pillar of fire? My wife and daughters are now part of it."[93] Gouri believed he understood more clearly why Jews did not resist as if they had been in an ordinary war with ordinary enemies.

Gouri added that "the Holocaust is taking place now and not at any other time between those years [when it actually happened] and the beginning of the trial."[94] Mulisch wrote in his own account: "Only in times of the plague or during the invasion of the Huns have horror stories been told on such a scale as in the past few weeks. . . . The blow hit exactly as hard as Hausner had intended. Because the witnesses talked about past experiences, which will never truly be 'past' because they will always remain present to them, as if happening today, and maybe even closer—that is why this 'today' created itself for those who did listen. The things heard in the past few weeks happened only the moment the world heard them: in the Spring of 1961."[95] And in her 1965 novel featuring the Eichmann trial, *Mandelbaum Gate*, Muriel Spark exclaimed that "the massacre was living."[96]

Gouri, we recall, referred to Wells's "monotonous and unadorned speech," which erased the witness's presence and allowed another to appear in his place.[97] In so doing, he suggested that the witness was a medium for someone else's speech. Survivors not only testified about their experiences, they also appeared to observers as oracles from another world: some transmitted the voices of the dead in a flat, constrained, and humble delivery, as if self-abnegation would allow their agonized bond with the dead to surface.[98] Critics interpreted survivors' testimony as free of sentimentality, let alone self-indulgence, and rather as a form of

---

92. Here one might thus speak of secondary trauma. The image of survivors as haunted by ghosts or as ghostlike brings to mind Nicolas Abraham's and Maria Torok's use of the ghost symbol to describe the transmission of trauma as a "transgenerational phantom" in *The Shell and the Kernel: Renewals of Psychoanalysis*, vol. 1, ed. and trans. Nicholas Rand (Chicago: University of Chicago Press, 1994), 171–86. My interest, as should be clear, is to understand the cultural role the figure of "living death" played in refashioning ideas about survival rather than in interpreting trauma as it appears in the trial testimony more specifically.

93. Gouri, *Facing the Glass Booth*, 268. In Exodus, God takes the form of a pillar of fire to ensure the safety of the Jews as they cross Egypt. Thanks to Bruno Chaouat for pointing this out.

94. Gouri, *Facing the Glass Booth*, 270.

95. Mulisch, *Criminal Case 40/61*, 87.

96. Muriel Spark, *Mandelbaum Gate: A Novel* (1965; repr., New York: Welcome Rain, 2001), 187.

97. Gouri, *Facing the Glass Booth*, 38.

98. *TAE*, 1:324. Douglas, *Memory of Judgment*, 104, casts Ada Lichtman as Tiresias because she wore enormous sunglasses (figure 3.2.). She was also asked by the judge if she saw "all this with [her] own eyes." This tone of testimony is now most often equated with traumatized witnesses who narrate flatly what they feel in excess.

self-surrender and an exercise in humility. Martha Gelhorn wrote that "all of the witnesses were humble; none had anything much to say about his own life or acts. They were only reporting what they knew because they had seen and heard it, lived through it. . . . . They spoke of others."[99]

The "living dead" describes the survivor who returned from the massacres and camps miraculously intact but still among the dead. Indeed, the symbol of the Holocaust survivor is a pervasive image of clinical trauma in which people are alive but feel dead or deeply tied to the dead, and the image of ghostly possession is an important theme now in the work of some psychoanalysts and literary theorists who work on survivors' trauma. Right before he collapsed, K-Zetnik exclaimed, "they [the dead] are staring at me."[100] The Chelmo survivor Simon Srebnik said, "No, I don't sleep at night, I cannot sleep at night. I am constantly being haunted."[101] As Henry Greenspan notes, the image of death in life or the experience of feeling one's own death is a powerful motif in survivor testimony, from Wiesel to Charlotte Delbo, who, in her memoir about life in Auschwitz wrote, "I feel myself die."[102]

Gouri's image of the witness who returned from the railway platform at Auschwitz during the trial is a ghostlike appearance of death in life, a phantom who inhabits both the world of the dead and the living, who transmits messages to the living while commiserating with the dead. It was as if the witness had survived only on a superficial level at best or even in name only. Wiesel excepted, observers did not transfigure survival into a higher state of being—that happened later—but construed survivors as beings who walked in the shoes of the dead and spoke on their behalf, shouldering responsibilities to the dead that drained them of emotional and bodily strength. This image conveyed "*the difficulty of articulation* of the catastrophic story" of K-Zetnik's collapse on the stand.[103]

Toward the Holocaust Survivor Witness: Bruno Bettelheim

The survivor as a witness figure emerged in a Western and especially US cultural field that sought above all—in a replay of the Eichmann trial—to reevaluate the

---

99. Gelhorn, "Eichmann and the Private Conscience."

100. *TAE*, 3:1237.

101. *TAE*, 3:1201.

102. Cited in Henry Greenspan, "Imagining Survivors: Testimony and the Rise of Holocaust Consciousness" in *The Americanization of the Holocaust*, ed. Hilene Flanzbaum (Baltimore: Johns Hopkins University Press), 48.

103. Felman, *Juridical Unconscious*, 159 (italics in the original).

meaning of survival in the context not only of industrialized genocide and murder, but also of the victim blaming that was pervasive in the 1960s, and against which the witness testimony so forcefully protested.[104] At that time, Wiesel was not yet the consummate public Holocaust witness, but he was sounding the themes in his work that I have already discussed.[105] In the rest of the chapter, I trace the transformation of the survivor into a witness in the United States, where the icon of the witness to genocide emerged as a powerful antidote to victim blaming, in particular as a rejoinder against Bettelheim's then popular work on concentration camps and Arendt's 1963 *Eichmann in Jerusalem*, in which she famously claimed that Jewish Councils had been complicit with the Nazis.[106]

Bettelheim's were the terms in which the general public initially understood survivors in the 1960s. An Austrian-Jewish refugee, Bettelheim had been imprisoned in Dachau and Buchenwald in 1938–39, paid bribes to secure his release, and never experienced death camps.[107] He was interested in how the Nazis

---

104. See Leys, *From Guilt to Shame*, 17–55, for the emergence of the psychology and psychiatry of survival. For the US origins of Holocaust memory culture in the 1970s and '80s, see Alina Both and Markus Nesselrodt, "Survivor: Towards a Conceptual History," *Leo Baeck Institute Year Book* 61, no. 1 (2016): 60, 66–67.

105. As Alvin H. Rosenfeld and Irving Greenberg wrote in their introduction to a volume in Wiesel's honor, "More than any other single writer of the postwar years, [he] educated this generation to the absolute need not only to remember but continually to confront the anguish and mystery of the Holocaust. His writings have come to embody the witness and the crisis of facing this event." Rosenfeld and Greenberg, eds., *Confronting the Holocaust: The Impact of Elie Wiesel* (Bloomington: Indiana University Press, 1978), xii. David G. Roskies underlines Wiesel's public importance in a compilation of Yiddish writers responding to Jewish destruction. Wiesel, Roskies notes, "became different things for different people." He carried "the normative Jewish response to catastrophe one crucial step further: He turned the internal dialogue outward." Roskies, *The Literature of Destruction: Jewish Responses to Catastrophe* (New York: Jewish Publication Society, 1988), 10–11.

106. Arendt's work was complex, and this claim, plus the general tone of her account, overwhelmed the book's reception, and gives us a sense of how important the question of whether Jews resisted or not was at the time. She defends herself aggressively in the postscript to *Eichmann in Jerusalem*, 283–84, where she notes that "the controversy [over the book] began by calling attention to the conduct of the Jewish people during the Final Solution, thus following up the question, first raised by the Israeli prosecutor, of whether the Jews could or should have defended themselves. I had dismissed that question as silly and cruel, since it testified to a fatal ignorance of the conditions at the time." As early as *The Origins of Totalitarianism* (New York: 1951 repr. 1976), Arendt, following Rousset, argued that the totalitarian state rendered its imprisoned subjects incapable of resisting by murdering the "moral person in man" (451).

107. See Richard Pollack, *The Creation of Dr. B.: A Biography of Bruno Bettelheim* (New York: Simon & Schuster, 1997), 107–13. This very critical biography by a former student in Bettelheim's Chicago Orthogenic School for autistic children goes further than most in discussing Bettelheim's manufacturing of his degrees, his alleged cure for autism, and his cruelty. Indeed, Bettelheim's account of autistic children not only blamed mothers for autism in a trope about overbearing women common at that time, but likely used camp survivors as models for these children. These facts about Bettelheim are documented, but interpretations of his legacy are diverse. In spite of Bettelheim's dishonesty, cru-

destroyed moral character. In his first essay, "Individual and Mass Behavior in Extreme Situations," published in 1943, he stressed how camp victims became docile and obedient, an allusion to the psychoanalytic concept of identification with the aggressor, which diagnosed unconscious identification with perpetrators as a form of defense against external threats. This identification, itself a mode of self-preservation, led survivors later to feel guilty for not having done more to help those who perished, even if there was nothing they might have done.

Bettelheim thus linked guilt to a will to survive turned against the ego. In the same essay, however, Bettelheim exempted himself from the psychic fate of other victims, claiming that he developed a different, carefully honed self-defense in the camps by conducting an informal psychological inquiry into the effects of camp conditions on prisoners.[108] Though he was interested in why some prisoners succumbed psychologically and others did not, he implied that his survival strategy, which he claimed protected him from psychic disintegration, originated in his quick mind and professional training. He did not entirely single himself out: Bettelheim implied much later that all survivors' experiences might add depth to their characters—"understanding, compassion, the ability to feel guilty."[109]

Often attacked for applying reductively a Freudian paradigm of guilt and regression to Holocaust victims, Bettelheim did blame them for their complicity, however unconscious, with perpetrators.[110] In so doing, he was instrumental in shaping a widely accepted view regardless of the nuances of his own contributions to understanding survivors' trauma.[111] In *The Informed Heart*, published in 1960, he insisted that Anne Frank's family might have bought "a gun or two" to kill their tormentors rather than "walking to their death." He claimed that Jews who understood that the Nazis were not "business as usual" could have survived, and insisted

elty, and problematic suppositions, his work is worth examining, given its real contribution to the discussion about survivors and its influence on Lifton and others.

108. Bettelheim, "Individual and Mass Behavior in Extreme Situations," *Journal of Abnormal and Social Psychology* 38, no. 4 (1943): 417–52, reprinted in his *Surviving and Other Essays* (New York: Knopf, 1979), 81, 51.

109. Bruno Bettelheim, "Surviving," *New Yorker*, August 2, 1976, 31–52, reprinted in *Surviving*, 274–314. This essay criticizes Lina Wertmüller's film *Seven Beauties* and Des Pres's *Survivor*. He attacks Des Pres for making heroes out of survivors and takes Wertmüller to task for her farcical representation of a survivor, which, he argued, "robs survivorship of all meaning" (282).

110. Many critics interpreted Bettelheim's harsh moral judgment as intrinsic in Freud's thought, an entirely contestable view. Ruth Leys gives Bettelheim his due, noting also that all the psychiatrists trying to come to terms with survivor guilt expressed what Dr. William Niederland called "'tremendous difficulty' in formulating and reducing the survivor experience into words, and other analysts, such as Bettelheim and Krystal, voiced the same frustration." Leys, *From Guilt to Shame*, 48.

111. Kirsten Fermaglich, *American Dreams and Nazi Nightmares: Early Holocaust Consciousness and Liberal America, 1957–65* (Waltham, MA: Brandeis University Press, 2006), 27, 71, for his influence on Stanley Elkins and on Betty Friedan.

that some of his Jewish acquaintances were still alive because of their foresight. In one characteristic passage, Bettelheim speculated about whether the Nazis decided to exterminate Jews only once they saw how easily Jews accepted their degradation: "One wonders," he remarked, "if the notion that millions of Jews (and later foreign nationals) would submit to extermination did not also result from seeing how much degradation they would accept without fighting back. . . . It may have been Jewish acceptance, without a fight, of ever harsher discrimination and degradation that first gave the SS the idea that they could be gotten to the point where they would walk to the gas chambers on their own." He also referred to a "death instinct running rampant" among Jewish camp populations.[112]

In the wake of the trial, Bettelheim agreed with Arendt's contention that Hausner's questions about resistance were misplaced. In "Eichmann: The System, the Victims," his favorable 1963 review of *Eichmann in Jerusalem*, Bettelheim claimed that the absence of resistance among most of the Third Reich's victims was "an empirical finding of history."[113] Like Arendt, who criticized *his* work for victim blaming, he never confused perpetrators and victims, but blamed the Jewish Councils for assisting the Nazis to murder the Jews in their communities more easily.[114] He also agreed with Arendt that the Eichmann trial's focus on witnesses was misguided—though he did not object to Israel's trying Eichmann. Mostly, Bettelheim shared Arendt's preference for a legally defensible condemnation of the transport minister over the emotion-laden drama of the Jerusalem court. To this end he picked up on Arendt's reference to the interwar trials, saying that he would have preferred "the solution Arendt suggests, that Eichmann should have been killed by a Jew, as the Armenian Tindelian [*sic*] killed Talaat Bey . . . and the Jew Schwartzbard killed Simon Petlyura . . . If such an executioner of Eichmann had then been tried, through that trial all the crimes of Eichmann could have been forced on the conscience of the world without extraneous questions such as the kidnapping and the legality of the trial interfering with the clear message of the murderous nature of totalitarianism."[115] Tehlirian's and Schwarzbard's assassinations

---

112. Bruno Bettelheim, *The Informed Heart: Autonomy in a Mass Age* (Glencoe, IL: Glencoe Free Press, 1960), 254, 259, 258–59, 260–61. Dorothy Rabinowitz took issue with his characterization in her *New Lives*, 177–79. Lawrence Langer accused Bettelheim and Austrian-Jewish psychiatrist Viktor Frankl of a "stance of moral superiority" over the victims. Langer, *Versions of Survival: The Holocaust and the Human Spirit* (Albany: SUNY Press, 1982), 52–53.

113. Bruno Bettelheim, "Eichmann: The System, the Victims," *New Republic*, June 15, 1963, 22–33, reprinted in *Surviving*, 258–73, at 269.

114. Peter Novick cites a 1962 letter Arendt wrote blaming Bettelheim for "inverted chauvinism," and arguing that he "looks for a Jewish problem where it does not exist." Arendt cited in Novick, *The Holocaust in American Life* (New York: Houghton Mifflin, 2000), 139.

115. Bettelheim, "Eichmann: The System, the Victims," in *Surviving*, 273.

preserved the focus on the perpetrators' crimes by virtue of the great risk, as Arendt put it, that the victims were willing to take to avenge their dead. Their deeds also testified to Bettelheim's hope that some victims would prove resilient.

In line with Arendt's own focus, Bettelheim was most interested in how "the obedient servant of Hitler and the prisoner who walked to the gas chambers became alike as true symbols of the total state. The rewarded servant and the prisoner to be murdered, each had lost his free will, his ability to act out of personal conviction." They were different sides of the same coin because the Nazi camp system turned them both into "living corpse[s]."[116] He warned that those victims who "roll with the punches dealt not by the vagaries of life, but by one's eventual executioner" might not have the power to resist "when death becomes imminent," particularly if "yielding to the enemy is accompanied not by a commensurate strengthening of the personality but an inner disintegration."[117] When Hausner and Wiesel made their dismissive comments about writers who imagined a Jewish death wish, they were both referring to Bettelheim's conflicted account of concentration camps peopled with automatons and hapless victims whom he condemned by contrast with his own self-preservation.[118] In his 1961 essay on "Eichmann's Victims," Wiesel chided Bettelheim for having attributed to victims a "death wish" and disintegrated personalities: "Why did the Jews in the camps not choose a death with honor, knife in hand and hate on their lips? It is understandable," Wiesel noted facetiously, "that Bruno Bettelheim should wonder why."[119]

Robert Jay Lifton

Brooklyn-born psychiatrist Robert Jay Lifton, though relying on some of Bettelheim's insights about survivor guilt, eventually transformed all survivors into epitomes of moral conscience born of trauma and specific to twentieth-century

---

116. Bettelheim, "Eichmann: The System, the Victims," in *Surviving*, 267. Bettelheim's focus on the numbness of inmates may have been a reference to Freud's discussion of the absence of a readiness to feel anxiety as an aspect of traumatization.

117. Bruno Bettelheim, "The Ignored Lesson of Anne Frank," *Harper's Magazine*, November 1960, 45–50, reprinted in *Surviving*, 246–57, at 252.

118. Hausner, *Justice in Jerusalem*, 183; Wiesel, *Legends*, 170.

119. Wiesel, "Eichmann's Victims," 514, 516. In the 1968 reprint of this essay in *Legends*, Wiesel wrote "well-known psychiatrists" (170) in place of Bettelheim and Viktor Frankl in the original (he had also mentioned Austrian-Jewish psychiatrist Frankl), and replaced Bettelheim's name ("Bettelheim should wonder why") with a now non-facetiously rendered "all of us" (172). The 1968 essay was aimed at a larger audience who might not be familiar with the specific references to Bettelheim and Frankl.

catastrophes. Bettelheim imagined some survivors as paragons of moral fitness, but developed no vocabulary beyond heroism to explain the survivor's suffering in affirmative terms—he said merely that some survivors were braver, more ingenious, and more perceptive than others. Lifton abandoned victim blaming both by developing a symptomatology of survival and by universalizing trauma. He erased divisions between different kinds of victims in favor of a generalized conception of survivors that extended from survivors of Hiroshima to the Holocaust and eventually also to traumatized war veterans.[120]

A Jewish intellectual involved with the antiwar movement but never with its most radical wing, Lifton was instrumental in overturning a 1950s and 1960s US liberal consensus about victim blaming based on Bettelheim's presumptions about the effects of camps on victims.[121] Sent by the air force to Japan as a war psychiatrist, he had developed an interest in the victims of the atomic bomb. According to Ruth Leys, Lifton attended workshops on trauma during the 1960s in which participants discussed Arendt's criticism of the Jewish Councils' ostensible complicity in the fate of the Jews.[122] In his 1969 National Book Award–winning *Death in Life*, he compared Hiroshima and Holocaust victims. Basing his analysis of Jewish survivors on works by Levi, Wiesel, Bettelheim, Jorge Semprun, and others, Lifton saw more similarities than differences between the two groups. The shock of unprecedented mass destruction, Lifton argued, left victims no escape from death even after they survived. Plague survivors moved on because they were "released from the encounter with death," but the atomic bomb or camp survivors' recovery was "the beginning of a lifelong sense of vulnerability to the same grotesque death."[123] He defined the concept of survival accordingly as a relationship to death that persisted in life: "We may define the survivor as one who has come into contact with death in some bodily or psychic fashion and has himself remained alive."[124]

According to Lifton, mass killing entailed a breakdown in "faith in the larger human matrix supporting each individual life." He maintained that "however

120. Robert Jay Lifton, *Home from the War: Learning from Vietnam Veterans; Neither Victims nor Executioners* (New York: Simon & Schuster, 1973).

121. See the discussion of Lifton in Fermaglich, *American Dreams*, 124–58, esp. 143. Dagmar Herzog notes the importance of the excesses of the Vietnam War in making Americans receptive to hearing about the Holocaust in *Cold War Freud*, 110–11.

122. Leys, *From Guilt to Shame*, 53. See also Lifton, *History and Human Survival*, 172. She argues that "concern about the ways in which theories about the survivor's identification with the aggressor could be seen as 'blaming the victim' surfaced in psychoanalytic circles even before Des Pres and other made it the center of their critique" (53).

123. Robert Jay Lifton, *Death in Life: Survivors of Hiroshima* (New York: Random House, 1968), 481.

124. Lifton, *Death in Life*, 479.

philosophically they [the survivors of Hiroshima] accept the horrors of war, they had an underlying sense of having been victimized and experimented upon by a horrible device, all to no avail in a world which has derived no profit from their sufferings."[125] Survivors who feel invulnerable after having confronted death and returned conceal their deeper "death anxiety," and are in reality extremely fragile.[126]

Lifton used other analysts' emphases on the death drive and other psychoanalytic constructs to reshape conventional ideas of heroism in such circumstances. Victims cannot fully escape psychically catastrophes of such magnitude and trauma cannot be character forming.[127] Instead, survivors identify so dramatically with the dead that they can only make survival meaningful by bearing witness to the suffering of those who died:

> As in other mourning experiences, survivors have identified themselves with and incorporated the dead (both as specific people and as an anonymous concept). But they have found no adequate ideological interpretation—no spiritual explanation, no "reason" for the disaster—that might release them from this identification, and have instead felt permanently bound by it. They have felt compelled virtually to merge with the dead and to behave, in a great variety of ways, *as if* they too were dead. In judging all behavior by the degree of respect it demonstrates toward the dead, they must condemn any effort which suggests too much self-assertion or vitality—that is, which suggests life.[128]

For Lifton's survivors—he worked with multiple Japanese victims who had lived through the dropping of the atom bombs—there was no release from death other than by "render[ing] significant the deaths they have seen."[129]

Lifton referenced a controversial French debate that occurred in 1966 regarding Jean-François Steiner's *Treblinka: The Revolt of an Extermination Camp*.[130] The book

---

125. Lifton, *History and Human Survival*, 153. See also Lifton, *Death in Life*, 491. On Lifton's challenge to the Freudian concept of "identification with the aggressor," see Leys, *From Guilt to Shame*, 53–54.

126. Lifton, *Death in Life*, 482.

127. Leys, *From Guilt to Shame*, 47–55, criticizes Lifton, among others, for jettisoning subtle accounts of unconscious motivation, emphasizing shame rather than guilt. Her own analysis underestimates the power of victim blaming to distort even sophisticated views of psychic functioning and does not address the noxious cultural role of Bettelheim's work, with which she assumes readers will be familiar.

128. Lifton, *History and Human Survival*, 170.

129. Lifton, *History and Human Survival*, 204.

130. Lifton, *History and Human Survival*, 204. In *A Holocaust Controversy*, Samuel Moyn has reconstituted the French debate around the novel, which Steiner wrote to redeem the Jewish dead from shame. Steiner's book shaped the reception of Arendt's *Eichmann in Jerusalem* in France.

sought to remind readers that not all Jews refused to fight, affirming the stereotype of Jewish passivity while seeking to downplay it. Lifton's essay refuted reviewers who had argued that the book's rebels were merely vengeful or desperate by insisting that they rebelled in order to bear witness. In so doing, he defined the driving force of resistance not as an assertion of courage, rage, or desperation against all odds, but as an inescapable struggle to ensure the dignity of the dead. Survivors' ability to honor the dead justified their existence and gave them a reason to live.

In Lifton's view the reverence for the dead was a symptom of trauma. But his was also a decidedly novel conception of events to which there is no heroic response and in which survivors are tormented by memories of the dying and dead. By insisting that bearing witness was a response to the breakdown in trust engendered by the camps and the nuclear bomb, Lifton conceived the solidarity performed by witnessing as the resurrection of a sundered social bond. The relationship between psychiatrist and patient—the psychiatrist bearing witness to the patient's own witnessing—modeled the meaning of responsibility for others in human community. *Death in Life* moved survivors into public consciousness as symbols of a catastrophic breakdown in the wake of the Holocaust and the nuclear bombing of Hiroshima; they were witnesses who served the cause of peace and humanity. Regarding our responses to Hiroshima or to Nazi persecution, Lifton wrote, "As we examine these categories we find ourselves dealing with universal psychological tendencies; the survivor becomes Everyman. But the holocausts of the twentieth century have thrust the survivor ethos into special prominence, and imposed upon us all a series of immersions into death which mark our existence."[131]

This rather extraordinary assertion rendered all of us potential survivors and the witness an emblem of our time. If, as Lifton wrote, the death imprint was most strongly imposed on actual survivors, no human beings could escape the ubiquity of industrial or technologically induced death, and he called on all survivors and potential survivors to bear witness.

Terrence Des Pres

This revaluation of the survivor's cultural role is most dramatic in Des Pres's 1976 work, *The Survivor: An Anatomy of Life in the Death Camps*.[132] As Leys notes, "With few exceptions, critics now applauded Des Pres's work in such

---

131. Lifton, *Death in Life*, 479.
132. Terrence Des Pres, *The Survivor: An Anatomy of Life in the Death Camps* (Oxford: Oxford University Press, 1976).

glowing terms as to suggest that a fundamental paradigm shift was in the air."[133] According to the writer and his once-colleague Frederick Busch, Des Pres, an English professor who died young, was a tormented soul, and his work, Busch speculates, was a quest for goodness in other fragile people. Des Pres imagined that he could find "what he needed . . . in the lives of strangers in other kinds of hell."[134] Busch speaks of Des Pres's gestures one night as they were discussing his work on survivors. His colleague was moved by his sources, wanting to be worthy of them, and began to "flick empty glasses on the kitchen table," which he eventually threw, "one after the other, until they flew and shattered, and the tabletop was clear. Terrence was in tears." Busch recounts that Des Pres also suffered from stress whose symptoms landed him in the emergency room, where he told the doctor, "I'm writing a book about survivors of the Nazi camps." Once the book met acclaim, Busch says, their friendship grew strained as Des Pres let the fame go to his head and became "demagogic"; he "traded on his celebrity" and "began to trivialize the subject on which he had written so powerfully."[135]

In spite of the gentle mockery implicit in Busch's account of Des Pres, it captures the latter's passion, the newfound recognition achieved by survivors, and the enthusiasm with which *The Survivor* was received. Des Pres's book condemned psychoanalytically inspired arguments according to which Jews did not resist because they had regressed psychically and, if they survived, did so as damaged people.[136] Survivors, Des Pres argued, were special witnesses and a new "moral type." Their survival augmented rather than diminished their humanity because "the survivor-as-witness . . . embodies a socio-historical project founded not upon the desire for justice (what can justice mean when genocide is the issue?), but upon the involvement of all human beings in common care for life and the future." "Faith in humanity," he insisted, "came to its end in Auschwitz, in Hiroshima, in the forests of Vorkuta. What remains to us now is simple care, a care biologically inspired and made active through mutual need." To this end Des Pres cited Rousset's *The Other Kingdom*, which, he insisted, expressed the "'positive side' to the experience of survival."[137]

133. Leys, *From Guilt to Shame*, 56.

134. Frederick Busch, *A Dangerous Profession: A Book about the Writing Life* (New York: St. Martin's, 1998), 180.

135. Busch, *Dangerous Profession*, 178–79.

136. Des Pres is still invoked as having created a "resilient" and thus problematic model of survival. Arguably that was not Des Pres's intention, though it is implicit in his work. See David Weinberg, "Dealing with Survivor Youth in West European Jewish Communities after the War," in *Survivors of Nazi Persecution in Europe after the Second World War*, ed. David Cesarani, Suzanne Bardgett, Jessica Reinisch, and Johannes-Dieter Steinert (London: Vallentine Mitchell, 2011), 196n1.

137. Des Pres, *Survivor*, 47, 209, 167.

Des Pres's work dramatically reworked the survivor figure for general consumption. He not only developed themes that emerged during the Eichmann trial, but also conceived the task of bearing witness as a project affirming human solidarity after the collapse of "faith in humanity." Des Pres criticized Lifton's alleged emphasis on survivors' "neurosis" and praised his emphasis on bearing witness. He wrote that in Lifton, at least, guilt becomes an affirmative form of moral conscience rather than mere neurosis: "the idea of guilt transcends itself."[138] He conceived the psychiatrist's views as sympathetic and engaged him briefly to repudiate Lifton's view of survivors as damaged by their experience. His real target was Bettelheim, whose influence he wanted to undercut, and with whom he had a famous feud. Bettelheim, he said, spoke with the authority of someone who had been in the camps, which gave "the weight of precedence to a [psychoanalytic] position which has never been challenged and which has influenced all subsequent study. Even among laymen his ideas are known and accepted. His version is *the* version."[139]

In other references to Bettelheim, Des Pres described ideas about Jews going to their death like sheep as a projection of our own fear and terror onto a form of absolute powerlessness that those who have not been in concentration camps cannot understand or imagine. He argued that blaming victims for their own demise displaces spectators' guilt about doing nothing for victims onto the victims themselves. He went after Bettelheim for his criticism of Anne Frank's family, for not understanding the desperation of life in the camps, and for making a distinction between prisoners' loss of autonomy and Bettelheim's own seeming self-possession in the same circumstances. Bettelheim celebrated those prisoners who defied their guards, risked their own lives, and thereby achieved "autonomy" because his concept of heroism was, according to Des Pres, "an isolated act of defiance."[140]

---

138. Des Pres, *Survivor*, 40.

139. Des Pres, *Survivor*, 157. I discuss Des Pres's criticism not in order to reexamine the debate between the two of them or to bemoan Des Pres's part in celebrating the survivor, but to assess instead how Des Pres rendered survivors iconic figures across a new memory-scape by extending motifs that first emerged in the Eichmann trial, particularly his own dramatic effort to cleanse the taint associated with survival. Roger Luckhurst addresses the debate between Bettelheim and Des Pres in *The Trauma Question* (New York: Routledge, 2008), 68–69. As Henry Greenspan argues, Lifton and Des Pres represented a division of the survivor discourse into psychiatric and heroic accounts of survival, by which he means a model of the traumatized survivor and another that "romances" survival. Greenspan, "Imagining Survivors," 59, 62.

140. Des Pres, *Survivor*, 89–90, 4, 161. Des Pres's argument also resonates with the recent assertion by two psychiatrists specializing in the treatment of survivors that Bettelheim's argument "maligned survivors for two generations." Robert Krell and Mark I. Sherman, eds., *Medical and Psychological Effects of Concentration Camps on Holocaust Survivors* (New Brunswick, NJ: Transaction Publishers, 1997), 5–6. They underline their assessment by arguing that "a long list of credible critics challenged

In an echo of Hansi Brand's testimony during the Eichmann trial about the uselessness of heroic gestures in a camp environment, Des Pres fulminates over Bettelheim's words about a prisoner who refused to dance for an SS guard, grabbed his gun, shot him, and was then killed herself: "It is heroic, but it is still suicide. What can 'autonomy' at the cost of personal destruction amount to? How effective would underground activities, or any of the forms of resistance, have been on such a principle?"[141] Des Pres discounts the uplifting impact of stories of resistance on camp inmates because they were so rare—the famous story of the suicide to which Bettelheim referred—in order to cast the very act of survival alone in affirmative terms.

His criticism of Bettelheim's harshness toward victims' alleged passivity brings us to Des Pres's most important claim about the difference between conventional forms of heroism and "heroism commensurate with the sweep of ruin in our time."[142] He argues that Bettelheim's work assumes that "human bondage can be transcended only in death. Death is at once the entrance to a world of fulfillment unobtainable on earth and the proof of a spirit unvanquished by fear or compromise." This attachment to tragic heroism forced Holocaust and Gulag survivors into a meaning system their experiences challenged: "the real behavior of survivors goes unobserved because it was covert, undramatic, not at all in accord with our expectations of heroism. And so it happens that we do not see them as *survivors*. They belong to that world [of our own "worst fears"], and in Hell there are none but the damned, none but the spiritually maimed unto death." Survival, the simple fact of enduring, he argued, was the new heroism of our time. Bettelheim's approach, indeed that of psychoanalysis, he insisted, ascribes meaning to those lives sacrificed for some higher ideal and not "disgraced by [their] own gross will to persist. Survival in itself, not dedicated to something *else,* has never been held in high esteem and often has been viewed with contempt."[143]

Des Pres attributed survival to a biological life force that preserved human qualities in the most extreme conditions, and in this way affirmed the mere fact of survival as having preserved a place for human dignity in the most undignified circumstances.[144] Those who survived developed a "capacity for realism,

---

his incredible writings. He [Bettelheim] continued undaunted for decades despite ample evidence that his initial psychologic observations of inmates in the concentration camps Dachau in 1938 and Buchenwald in 1939 were in any case not relevant to inmates who survived the death camps of 1942–1945" (6).

141. Des Pres, *Survivor,* 161.

142. Des Pres, *Survivor,* 6.

143. Des Pres, *Survivor,* 163, 172, 163–64 (italics in the original).

144. Ruth Leys's focus on Des Pres's "literalism" is a welcome discussion of this dimension of Des Pres's work. Leys notes that Des Pres was a member of the Harvard Society of Fellows for three

impersonal and without the least illusion" because the body's resilience sustained their skills in the worst of circumstances.[145] The question is whether this updated vitalism, a biological drive infused with a special life force, can serve as a foundation for human dignity, let alone a "capacity for realism," since survival on these terms is hard to attribute to anything distinctively moral or psychological at all. In this tautological argument, survival, not luck, one's past, or particular skills, accounts for the qualities Des Pres attributes to survival. His concept of psychoanalysis, moreover, is oversimplified in part because the book is a critique of Bettelheim's Freudian concept of survivor guilt that addresses psychoanalysis on moral rather than theoretical terms.

Des Pres sought to undermine Bettelheim's view that camp inmates regressed to a childlike state. Nonetheless, his insistence on the limits of familiar concepts of heroism in extreme circumstances took up a central theme first made relevant by the Eichmann trial: questions posed to witnesses about the ostensible lack of resistance among Jewish captives gave way to observers' recognition that tragic heroism was inadequate to describe the camp experience. In Des Pres's account, survivor guilt derived not from a psychoanalytic "identification with the aggressor" or from a melancholic attachment to the dead of the sort Lifton described, but from survivors' transgression of the "blockade men erect against knowledge of 'unspeakable' things." The "world" silences survivors, and they begin to doubt themselves.[146]

Des Pres replaced heroic resistance with the concept of heroic survival and provided a uniformly positive view of the victims, repudiating the victim blaming that had become so predominant and was closely associated with psychoanalysis. Bettelheim's attack on *Survivor* was no match for the warm reception his somewhat tortured argument generally received.[147] Survivors, Des Pres argued, are the origin of "conscience in its social form, something we would not normally attribute to animal behavior." "Wisdom depends on knowledge and it comes at a terrible price." He describes bearing witness as a "warning call" to other humans much like those generated by animals in distress, situating the survivor's cry as central to the survival of human community. "The will to bear witness is a typical and in some sense necessary response to extremity. Confronting radical evil, men and women instinctively feel the desire to call, to warn, to communicate their shock."

years, where he came into contact with the sociobiologist Edward O. Wilson. Leys, *From Guilt to Shame*, 56–92.

145. Des Pres, *Survivor*, 87.
146. Des Pres, *Survivor*, 42–43.
147. Bettelheim, "Surviving," in *Surviving*, 274–314.

Even Wiesel's protagonists, he argued, "desire a silence they cannot keep." For this reason, too, the animal scream replaces political analysis, the scream "begins to be our own," and by absorbing this lesson from those who have suffered, we pursue "common care for life and for the future" in place of justice—not because we do not believe in justice, but because bearing witness is the only form of social solidarity conceivable once "faith in humanity" has collapsed.[148]

The Eichmann trial recast the Jewish survivor as free of shame or culpability, relieving the public of its suspicions about what victims might have done to survive. It showed the world that the conditions of Nazi camps made any resistance at all a miracle and turned survival into national redemption. The trial narrated witnesses' survival not only as the glory of statehood after near annihilation, not only in terms of a redemption of the Jewish people, but also as a particular kind of tormented life bound to death. Survivors' fealty to the dead was proof of suffering beyond words, evidence of the otherwise unimaginable experience of genocidal violence, and symbolized the particularity of their despair.

By transforming survivors into symbols of living death, trial observers imagined them as victims who relive an unbearable past and whose haunted presence was central to understanding the violence perpetrated by genocidal regimes. Primo Levi, writing about the Eichmann trial, heralded the witness of "massacres of women and children, by the hand of whomever, in whatever country, in the name of whatever ideology" as a central vehicle for the construction of human moral conscience.[149] Like Rousset, who took up bearing witness as his life's calling, Levi asserted that the experience of deportation "conferred a purpose on my life, that of bearing witness so that nothing of the sort would ever happen again."[150] Arendt famously remarked, reconciling the universalizing concept of the *univers concentrationnaire* with the specific violence the Nazis perpetrated against European Jewry, that the Holocaust represented "crimes against mankind committed on the body of the Jewish people."[151]

A decade after the Eichmann trial, Jewish survivors, who now elicited sympathy because of what they endured, not only represented a broad and humanistic message about the consequences of tyranny, but also possessed special knowledge capable of sparing other victims the agony they had lived. By the 1970s, the

---

148. Des Pres, *Survivor*, 46–47, 33, 36, 49.
149. Primo Levi, "Testimonianza per Eichmann," *Il Ponte* 17, no. 4 (1961): 647. Reprinted in *Così fu Auschwitz: Testimonianze 1945–1986 con Leonardo De Benedetti*, ed. Fabio Levi and Domenico Scarpa (Turin: Einaudi, 2015), 70.
150. Primo Levi, *Così fu Auschwitz*, 129.
151. Arendt, *Eichmann in Jerusalem*, 7.

survivor symbolized an affirmative and universal message about human survival and its moral purpose, as if the fact of surviving genocide, stripped of having chosen one's fate, and enduring, by chance, provided survivors with authority and their lives with meaning. Bearing witness transformed survivors' survival into an identity; they were not merely victims of genocidal violence, but living reminders that they had been slated to die and that millions of others were dead. The figure of the Jewish Holocaust survivor became a metaphor of all genocidal suffering and formed the basis for social solidarity based on a burning address to the world in which the once-victim demanded that no one be abandoned to such a terrible fate. As Lifton and Des Pres conceived this vision of survival and its moral imperatives, however differently, the need to bear witness was now a psychic or bodily symptom, an expression of the guilt-ridden bond with the dead, and a compulsion that drove survivors to speak; it was a sign of both inescapable death and the resilience of life, as well as an assertion of the value of sustained moral engagement. To bear witness required no grand, heroic gestures, but an obligation to transmit the powerlessness and terror that ordinary people could not conceive of or did not want to acknowledge.

The witness to genocide was a reminder of Western murderousness and at the same time an image of Western soul-searching; it represented a legacy of violence against European Jews and the triumph of human conscience, however fragile. The symbol of the witness transformed the most extreme suffering into survival on behalf of a greater good. After the late 1970s the Holocaust witness continued to embody Western moral conscience, but the logic by which survival conferred on individual victims a special moral role already had its detractors. In a 1977 essay, the US journalist and writer Dorothy Rabinowitz bemoaned what were by then widespread assumptions about Holocaust survivors: that they possessed both deep knowledge of things human and a special concern for others.[152] Most of them were just ordinary people, she insisted, an assertion that did not go without saying at that time, when Americans began to speak and write about Holocaust survivors in the way Des Pres had characterized them. Rabinowitz wrote regarding Holocaust memory that neither the Holocaust revisionists nor the "up to date clichés" of the political Left would remain. Instead, "what will remain will be the imperishable eloquence of numbers tattooed on an arm."[153] Her protective criticism of assumptions about

---

152. Dorothy Rabinowitz, "The Holocaust as Living Memory," in Wiesel, Dawidowicz, Rabinowitz, and Brown, *Dimensions of the Holocaust*, 39. See also her remarks on the Eichmann trial in Rabinowitz, *New Lives: Survivors of the Holocaust Living in America* (New York: Knopf, 1976), 177, 197.
153. Rabinowitz, "Holocaust as Living Memory," 45.

survivors' specialness was in keeping with her conservative posture against liberals whom she believed failed to understand the difference between the Vietnam War and the Holocaust. By asserting that the numbers on survivors' arms were eloquent, she made a claim about the quiet and painful work of memory.

In 1982, the Holocaust scholar Lawrence Langer also rejected the redemption inherent in the narratives about survivors: "The Nazis left no room for the *exemplary* value of human behavior; the authentic martyrs in the deathcamps, who voluntarily chose death when through some compromise they might meaningfully have chosen life, may be counted on the fingers of two hands. This is not to denigrate the victims, but to describe accurately their moral situation, which was not of their own making." Langer's antiredemptive stance rejects even Lifton's perceptions of survivors as damaged witnesses who might heal as far too optimistic, as if any acknowledgment of healing might stigmatize those who never recover, and as if recovery could not be accompanied by some feelings of guilt.[154]

These more realistic conceptions of survival, including Langer's rather extreme views, demonstrate above all the extent to which survivors had been sanctified. As we will see, and as Lifton already insinuated, the normalization of mass and genocidal violence—the recognition that such violence was not limited to the Holocaust but was a feature of modern geopolitics and imperial conquest—transformed all survivors into symbols of human conscience, into representatives of the consequences of extreme violence. Auschwitz nonetheless remained a central reference point.[155] By 1983, Wiesel, in reference to a movie about nuclear catastrophe, stated: "I had a strange feeling that I had seen it before. Except that once upon a time it happened to my people—and now it happened to all people. And suddenly I said to myself, maybe the whole world, strangely, has turned Jewish."[156]

---

154. Langer, *Versions of Survival*, x, 14 (italics in the original). Dominick LaCapra makes a similar argument about Langer in *Representing the Holocaust: History, Theory, Trauma* (Ithaca, NY: Cornell University Press, 1994), 194–200.

155. The cultural importance of survivors was institutionalized in the video archives of their testimony, which got off the ground at Yale University in 1981—as a community-inspired project. The literature on video testimony is now widespread, including the impact of the institutional context in which the tapes are made (and now digitized). Such discussion is beyond the scope of this chapter, though it is worth analyzing for current conceptions of witnessing. On testimony in videos and film, see Dominick LaCapra, *Writing History, Writing Trauma* (Baltimore: Johns Hopkins University Press, 2001), 86–113.

156. Wiesel cited in Shandler, *While America Watches*, 204–5.

4

THE GLOBAL VICTIM AND THE COUNTERWITNESS

What is this humanity? It is a quality things have in common when they are viewed as photographs.

—Susan Sontag, *On Photography* (1973)

In 1995, the ad hoc International Criminal Tribunal for the former Yugoslavia (ICTY) indicted the Bosnian Serb leader Radovan Karadžić on eleven counts in absentia, including the massacre of seventy-five hundred Bosnian Muslim men at Srebrenica. Lawyers also brought charges against the Bosnian Serb army commander Ratko Mladić. A few months before the indictment, prosecutors argued in favor of international rather than national trials on the grounds that local memories were powerful and that victims and perpetrators often still resided in close proximity: "This burden on witnesses who are interviewed on multiple occasions is particularly relevant to witnesses who have suffered trauma and who may be at physical risk as a result of their co-operation. Witnesses faced with these burdens could, in fact, refuse to co-operate with any investigating body at all."[1]

A year later, Elisabeth Rehn, the undersecretary general of the United Nations who had worked in the former Yugoslavia, also invoked this concern for witnesses when she appeared before the tribunal. She stressed not only the impediments to prosecution posed by victims' traumas, but also the important role of witness testimony in alleviating that trauma by restoring victims' dignity and providing the foundation for reconciliation between victims and perpetrators. She made several points when the judge pressed her on the matter of victim

---

1. International Criminal Tribunal for the Former Yugoslavia (hereafter ICTY), request for referral, prosecutor vs. Karadžić, May 15, 1995, no. IT-95-5-D, 24, p. 398.

testimony, all of which have become truisms in discussions of the psychological role of bearing witness and the pursuit of restorative justice.

In line with increasingly prominent concepts of the role played by testimony in working through victims' trauma, not to mention the tribunal's obligation to facilitate this process, Rehn linked survivor testimony to the establishment of "truth" for the benefit of the victims.

> It has been crystal clear to me that for those who are the victims of the conflict, whatever side they are on and whoever have [sic] made the abuses, it is so important for them to get the truth and to get justice because, and I should say that they are not asking for revenge, like the women from Srebrenica and Tuzla [cities where there were massacres of Bosnian Muslims by Serbs in 1995], or those who are just looking for their own relatives in the surroundings of Banja Luka, Serbs who are missing about 2,000 killed loved ones or not knowing about their fate, for them it is very important to know exactly the truth.[2]

Referring to the interethnic hatred that had survived the conflict, she hoped the trial might lead to reconciliation among those "still alive" by focusing on the guilt of individual perpetrators instead of on the collective group to which they belonged. Rehn also stated that she was "furious" that politicians wanted to pass on indictments in the name of the peace process, when the only realistic means of making peace was to guarantee truth and justice for the victims by punishing their tormentors:

> Therefore, as I have said several times, that there seem [sic] to be a collective guilt, that like all Serbs have been accused to be murderers or in some cases all Croats or all Muslims. It is very important to have this individual guilt stated. So that we can free the majority of the people who are absolutely innocent from the collective guilt. That is why I find the work of the Tribunal so extremely important because I really believe that those people who are alive and who are still in very bad circumstances, they should be taken really care of.[3]

---

2. ICTY, Radovan Karadžić, July 5, 1996, case no. IT-95–18-R61, 809–10, http://www.icty.org/x/cases/karadzic/trans/en/960705it.htm.

3. ICTY, Radovan Karadžić, July 5, 1996, case no. IT-95–18-R61, 809–10, http://www.icty.org/x/cases/karadzic/trans/en/960705it.htm.

Finally, Rehn insisted that victim testimony restores "dignity" to the living and the dead, whose identities would no longer be of a piece with their dying or degradation. In short, convicting the perpetrator would facilitate mourning:

> I think it is very much a question of human dignity and it is a human right, even for a dead young man, to have some kind of dignity. So this is something that is very much making me furious, that there is no real dignity with those who suffered, who died. They should, at least, have a decent burial by their families, by their own. That is something that I have been very much involved with trying to make this possible. That is the wish of the Tuzla women too.[4]

Thirty-some years after the Eichmann trial, bearing witness had clearly become essential to promoting peace and dignity: by establishing the truth, victims' testimony would help to punish the real perpetrators; it would make reconciliation among former enemies possible; and the truth would heal the living and allow them to bury their dead with dignity. The seeming self-evidence of these presumptions is stunning in light of the obstacles to the Eichmann trial's recognition of survivors and their sufferings. In 1998, 120 countries adopted a treaty in Rome for the creation of the International Criminal Court (ICC) on the heels of ad hoc tribunals established by the UN Security Council to try instigators of ethnic cleansing and genocide in the former Yugoslavia (1993) and Rwanda (1994).[5] In 2002, when the ICC commenced its operations, the state signatories added special provisions for victims to rectify problems regarding their treatment in the ad hoc trials. The Rome Statute article 43 (6) instituted a "Victim and Witnesses Unit" that included "staff with expertise in trauma, including trauma related to crimes of sexual violence."[6] By then, what had formerly been known as "survivor syndrome" had evolved into "post-traumatic stress disorder" (PTSD), and trauma had emerged as a recognizable and pervasive framework within which to understand the impact of extreme violence.[7]

How did the institutionalization of care for the suffering victim in courts and by humanitarian organizations, as well as the popular mobilization of concern

---

4. ICTY, Radovan Karadžić, July 5, 1996, case no. IT-95-18-R61, 809–10, http://www.icty.org/x/cases/karadzic/trans/en/960705it.htm.

5. Eric Stover, *The Witnesses: War Crimes and the Promise of Justice in The Hague* (Philadelphia: University of Pennsylvania Press, 2005), 12–13.

6. Stover, *Witnesses*, 174.

7. See, among others, Didier Fassin and Richard Rechtman, *The Empire of Trauma: An Inquiry into the Condition of Victimhood*, trans. Rachel Gomme (Princeton, NJ: Princeton University Press, 2009); Ruth Leys, *Trauma: A Genealogy* (Chicago: University of Chicago Press, 2000); Leys, *From Guilt to Shame: Auschwitz and After* (Princeton, NJ: Princeton University Press, 2007).

for victims of mass atrocities or genocide, transform the meaning of witnessing and recast the moral witness at the beginning of the twenty-first century? Rehn's faith in the healing properties of testimony and its capacity to restore survivor witnesses' dignity has become an axiom not only in the courtroom but also in the struggle for global human rights. Although there are many arguments about whether truth commissions or criminal trials most effectively facilitate survivors' healing, as well as about the strengths and weaknesses of different trial formats, the ICC, humanitarian organizations, and human rights activists take for granted their obligation to restore dignity to survivors of crimes against humanity and genocide.

In order to address the cultural role accorded to victim testimony, I move out of the courtroom; the ICC is only one of a broad array of global humanitarian organizations and institutions that place victims' sufferings center stage as the moral challenge of our time. Politicians, lawyers, policy makers, and human rights activists celebrate the internationally sanctioned pursuit of perpetrators across national borders in spite of obstacles posed by often inadequate funding, uncooperative governments, and red tape.[8] The imperative not only to seek justice for victims but also to remedy their suffering often overrides even the seemingly inviolable principle of state sovereignty, as humanitarian intervention becomes increasingly a justification for military intervention, and caring for victims is more than ever inextricable from international security, crisis management, and global governance.[9]

Humanitarian organizations have existed since the nineteenth century to attend to victims of catastrophe and war, and humanitarian workers in the field have long used the term "witness" to describe not only those who survive mass atrocities and genocide but also those who observe them. Henry Dunant founded the International Committee of the Red Cross in 1863 after having come across the Battle of Solferino. But in contrast to his religiously inflected and apolitical concept of witness, the French humanitarian medical

---

8. Karen Engle argues that in contrast to the earlier goals of an organization like Amnesty International, which sought the release of prisoners of conscience, activists since the 1990s increasingly identify the goals of human rights with the hunt for perpetrators of war crimes, genocide, and crimes against humanity by the International Criminal Court. Engle, "A Genealogy of the Criminal Turn in Human Rights," in *Anti-Impunity and the Human Rights Agenda*, ed. Karen Engle, Zinaida Miller, and D.M. Davis (Cambridge: Cambridge University Press, 2016), 18–20.

9. Of course, whose sovereignty can be overridden is a highly political question. As Richard Ashby Wilson demonstrates, because the ICC was created by international treaty rather than established by the UN Security Council (as were the ad hoc tribunals), it has broader jurisdiction than the ad hocs and yet is far more vulnerable to the interference of nation-states. Wilson, *Writing History in International Criminal Trials* (New York: Cambridge University Press, 2011), 193.

organization Doctors Without Borders (Médecins Sans Frontières) defined their activism as a form of witnessing in 1971, breaking with the Red Cross's policy of neutrality toward all parties in conflict. Doctors Without Borders' activist usage of the term has become increasingly common over the past fifty years: exhibit-goers "bear witness" to photographs, spectators become "witnesses" of human rights violations from a distance, journalists "bear witness," and the press refers to people in proximity to acts of violence as "bearing witness."[10] By the mid-1970s, the post-Holocaust discourse of "never again" had rendered the prevention of suffering a moral goal not only of human rights institutions but also of activists and concerned citizens. In order to prevent suffering, activists ask us to bear witness by organizing exhibits about crimes against humanity, write books from the field, and create Internet sites about the pedagogical potential of atrocity photographs. They are all part of a global commitment, within the parameters of geopolitical power balances, to repairing the seemingly endless injuries inflicted by war crimes, crimes against humanity, and genocide.

This chapter distills three accounts of the moral and political challenges represented by the ubiquity of traumatized victims and reinterprets them within a genealogy of the moral witness: literature critical of the ICC and other courts' treatment of victims; sociologist and anthropologist Didier Fassin's influential criticism of humanitarian witnessing; and debates about the political and moral efficacy of atrocity photographs. All three accounts question whether putting traumatized victims rhetorically front and center actually remedies their injuries, and all map the dispersion of the witness's testimonial role among lawyers, humanitarians, journalists, and spectators of atrocity who were not victims and were not, in many cases, even present at the scene of the crime. These accounts chart two mutually constitutive developments: second- and third-party witnesses' complicity in suffering they wish to alleviate; and activists' own fashioning of another moral witness.

Using these arguments as my primary sources, I trace in a condensed and suggestive fashion a genealogy of the moral witness of which these arguments are a part. Rather than taking the self-evident centrality of victim testimony in twenty-first-century moral culture as my point of departure and analyzing its uses and abuses, my broader approach asks how the global victim, bearing

---

10. The journalist Mark Leibovich argues that "bearing witness" has become "a mass market trope available to anyone who wants to weigh in, or show up," including politicians, journalists, bystanders, protesters, even the "American people." Leibovich, "How Many Outsiders Does It Take to 'Bear Witness' in Ferguson?," *New York Times Magazine*, September 3, 2014.

witness, and the counterwitness emerged and with what consequences.[11] How does the global victim fit into the longer process by which second- and third-party witnesses replaced the Holocaust survivor, and how fully have they done so? How did the global victim represent all survivors as the symbolic mainstays of a Western global discourse of human rights? Why are victims often not referred to as witnesses unless they testify, while those who work on their behalf are called "witnesses"? How has bearing witness become a central moral activity of contemporary Western culture?

The narrative that follows moves into a more abstract register than the one I adopted in the previous three chapters and brings the story into the present. It evaluates criticisms of the ICC that illuminate the role of global legal justice in promoting a vision of the victim for our time. It then outlines another witness figure that appears in Fassin's work and in the discussion about atrocity photography: the counterwitness. It suggests that the moral witness now represents a new global responsibility for healing victims' wounds rather than victims' unfathomable experience, and signifies the ubiquity and self-evidence of trauma rather than the shock of mass graves. This symbol no longer of justice belatedly delivered but of justice failed appears as a diminished but stubborn remainder of the Holocaust survivor's imputed agency; it represents betrayed political and ethical commitments in a world suffused with suffering.[12] Since critics have long interpreted the Holocaust as ground zero of twentieth-century human rights (and thus of the contemporary witness to genocide), there are resemblances between the iconic Holocaust witness and the counterwitness.[13] But these symbols, while related, are not twins, and emerge in vastly different political and cultural landscapes. Indeed, the appearance of the counterwitness suggests that when activists supplement the testimonial roles of witnesses, they

11. For a balanced and insightful account of the role played by historical narratives about the causes of mass violence in international criminal trials, see Wilson's *Writing History*.

12. The figure I am calling the "counterwitness" also appears in myriad other accounts on the political Left that I cannot discuss here. Robert Meister's *After Evil: A Politics of Human Rights* (New York: Columbia University Press, 2011), develops a powerful image of the counterwitness.

13. This argument about the Holocaust and human rights is pervasive and covers how the Holocaust became a point of reference for other wars (Vietnam, Bosnia) as well as establishes a line from Nuremberg to the ICC that has only recently been questioned. See the introduction to this book. Meister, *After Evil*, 16, sums it up: "The late twentieth-century paradigm of universal *human* rights ... was self-consciously developed to prevent what happened to Jews in the Holocaust from happening again, to anyone." See also Paul Gordon Lauren, *The Evolution of International Human Rights: Visions Seen* (Philadelphia: University of Pennsylvania Press, 2003), 204–7. G. Daniel Cohen contests this view in "The Holocaust and the 'Human Rights Revolution': A Reassessment," in *The Human Rights Revolution: An International History*, ed. Akira Iriye, Petra Goedde, and William I. Hitchcock (Oxford: Oxford University Press, 2012), 53–72.

recast the symbolic power once possessed by the Holocaust survivor. The coun-terwitness, a marginal cultural figure, emerges as a symbol of frustration with uneven global justice and the strain injustice places on the governance systems it has created and sustained.

The Traumatized Victim and the International Criminal Court

Eric Stover's 2005 book *The Witnesses* examines the attitudes toward the ICTY among Bosnian, Croatian, and Serbian victims of ethnic cleansing and other atrocities, many of whom testified. Stover notes how widespread recognition of victims' trauma and a heightened awareness of their plight resulted in bet-ter treatment of witnesses. He points out, for example, that recent findings on memory processing made it harder for the defense to attack the reliability of witnesses who forgot details. In the trial brought against the Serb leader Radislav Krstić, the court accepted a witness's claim that whether he saw forty or twenty murdered bodies was less relevant than the fact that he saw a number of bodies and described those consistently.[14] Moreover, the court was not surprised by such testimony, suggesting that an account of dead bodies stacked like cordwood no longer had the shock value it generated in the years after World War Two.

Stover's work recommends changes in the court's treatment of witnesses. He reveals how they were disappointed with the court's proceedings and under-scores other logistical failures: administrative overload for already overwhelmed victims, who had to fill out complicated forms to have their day in court, and underfunding for travel to and from The Hague and for witness protection in Bosnia, Croatia, and Serbia. For all his concern for victims, Stover criticizes legal scholarship that envisions trials as restorers of dignity, enablers of community reconciliation, and providers of lessons that might prevent future crimes. Trials too focused on healing victims risk compromising their fairness, he notes, by allowing victims to testify anonymously or to provide minimally relevant tes-timony for the sake of dramatizing the injuries suffered. Positioning himself between "legal purists" who minimize the theatrical dimensions intrinsic in trials and those who emphasize courts' expressive potential, Stover advocates changes to facilitate victims' testimony but wants the courts to stick to their

---

14. Stover, *Witnesses*, 8.

obligation to provide the accused a fair trial, even if fairness imposes limits on victim testimony.[15]

Other critics writing more recently are less sanguine about the possibilities of reforming the court to better accommodate survivor testimony. Barrie Sander, who synthesizes a vast array of work on victim participation in international courts, argues not only that realities on the ground shape how violence-torn communities interpret trials, but also that "expressive limits" constrain the court's construction of trials' messages in the first place.[16] These limits run counter to the expansive role of the victim in the courts' political and moral life: "Typically invoked in the abstract," he argues, "the imagined victim of mass atrocities has become the raison d'être of international criminal justice, the absent sovereign of international criminal law, and the mark of moral legitimacy for international criminal courts."[17] Sander's synthesis of multiple trials demonstrates that the tenets of a fair trial are fundamentally at odds with restorative justice, and that the wholesale cultural and legal embrace of victims has not led to substantial shifts in trial proceedings.

International courts, Sander argues, subordinate victims' interests "to the adjudicative needs of tribunals": judges discourage victims from offering emotional testimony in favor of condensed narratives that focus on precise recollections, often interrupting witnesses whose testimony veers away from the case at hand. In spite of courts' rhetoric about their commitment to victims, victims' healing is secondary to a trial's determination of whether the accused is guilty. Moreover, victims must be selected to testify—not everyone who was injured can appear on the witness stand. Judges who prefer, for the sake of time, breadth of testimony to overlapping accounts of one incident, compound the harm done to those who are not chosen to appear on the stand. Sander notes that in the ICC trial of Congolese commander Jean-Pierre Bemba Gombo for crimes against humanity, only three victims were permitted to testify in person.[18]

In yet another impediment to a focus on witness testimony, the ad hoc tribunal established to prosecute Rwandan *génocidaires* illuminated the cultural gaps between judges and those witnesses who reported events as if they were eyewitnesses when they were not. In Rwanda, Sander writes, relaying information as if you were there when you were not was customary, but this cultural norm raised

---

15. Stover, *Witnesses*, 22–23.

16. Barrie Sander, "The Expressive Limits of International Criminal Justice: Victim Trauma and Local Culture in the Iron Cage of the Law," iCourts Working Paper Series, no. 38 January 2016, 7.

17. Sander, "Expressive Limits," 8.

18. Sander, "Expressive Limits," 8, 9, 11–12.

questions about how to impose a consistent set of evidentiary standards across cultures. The practice also raised questions about whether such cultural explanations might be exploited by defendants trying to pull the wool over some judges' eyes.[19]

Victims' marginalization by courts that seek to give them a voice is a significant problem for all critics, whether they embrace or eye warily courts' promises to restore victims' dignity. In contemporary legal discourse about international law, Stover's argument exemplifies the perspective of critics who focus on how courts might more effectively provide protection and aid for victims, while Sander's analysis represents a more skeptical view of international courts' ability to deliver on such promises. The advocates of an even more forceful treatment of victims' marginality call into question those promises, criticizing lawyers' and activists' invocation of the traumatized victim *tout court*. They argue that such rhetoric sets in motion an agenda more beneficial to the perpetuation of the ICC's particular ideological biases than to the victims in whose name the ICC purports to exist. Many claim that the recent attachment of human rights to criminal prosecutions represents a dramatic shift in the human rights agenda toward the "anti-impunity" of perpetrators undertaken in the name of the victim. They also underscore the novelty of this turn to prosecution and away from amnesty, peace and reconciliation, forgiveness, and truth seeking.[20]

Sara Kendall and Sarah Nouwen claim that "The Victim" emerges as a "deity-like and seemingly sovereign entity" in ICC proceedings; "as abstraction," they argue, "'The Victim' acts in some ways as the absent 'sovereign' of international criminal law"; "'Victim'" works as a "placeholder for the agency of others."[21] They cite the 1998 comments of the United Nations secretary-general Kofi Annan speaking in Rome during negotiations on the statute that created the ICC: "'The overriding interest must be that of the victims, and of the international community as a whole.'" And they point to the ICC website: "For the first time in the history of international criminal justice, victims have the possibility . . . to present their views and observations before the Court." The "dead" are an "exhaustive source of justification for trials," they argue; they are appropriated by the court as a rationale for its proceedings. Even surviving victims often have

19. Sander, "Expressive Limits," 11–15.

20. In a nutshell, this is the argument of the essays in Engle, Miller, and Davis, *Anti-Impunity*, though Karen Engle writes most extensively about the history of the "criminal turn in human rights," 15–67.

21. Sara Kendall and Sarah Nouwen, "Representational Practices at the International Criminal Court: The Gap between Juridified and Abstract Victimhood," *Law and Contemporary Problems* 76, no. 3–4 (2014): 241, 254, 255.

little actual power and may be "victimized again" by legal procedures that cannot account for their trauma and the difficulty of testifying.[22]

Kendall and Nouwen do not dispute the trauma diagnosis or the victim's credibility but question how the ICC mobilizes the figure of the victim and with what consequences. Like Sander, they argue that repeated references to the victim mask a discrepancy between the court's promises and its real treatment of witnesses; but unlike him, they frame this discrepancy not only as intrinsic in the court's "expressive limits," but also by reference to what Karen Engle, Zinaida Miller, and D.M. Davis term the very "conceptualization" of the ICC's focus on criminal prosecution and the practice of international law.[23] The ICC, they argue, is circumscribed politically, and its approach to justice is determined by legal liberalism, its commitment to restraining politics by law. Geopolitical considerations mean that the court cannot call to account bad actors whose governments are not signatories; it has no "constabulary," as Samuel Moyn puts it, to charge in and make arrests when states refuse to do so.[24] Crimes perpetrated by the US government, which is not a signatory, are beyond its jurisdiction, and other political leaders are punishable only when criminal instigators lose their political stature at home.

The court's legal liberalism, moreover, is not commensurate with its expansive rhetoric about victims. The ICC invokes a capacious concept of victims that includes persons who have suffered harms that are not even actionable under international law: "The rhetoric of the role of the victim in the ICC transcends legally recognized victims. Indeed, it transcends *actual* victims with their individuated harms and suffering. The 'victims'—whom the court's first prosecutor referred to when he said that his mandate was 'justice for the victims' . . . are not specific individuals. Instead, in these contexts, 'the victims' is a reference to an abstraction—'The Victims'—which is based on the *idea* of victims." Kendall and Nouwen add: "[That idea] stands for the collective suffering produced through international crimes without containing the particular suffering of wronged individuals."[25]

All injured people are victims, though only some are legally victims, restricting criminal liability to the physical violence the law condemns and the crimes it charges, and letting perpetrators of economic injustice and also murder, if such

---

22. Kendall and Nouwen, "Representational Practices," 240, 237, 255.

23. Engle, Miller, and Davis, *Anti-Impunity*, 1.

24. Samuel Moyn, "Anti-Impunity as Deflection of Argument," in Engle, Miller, and Davis, *Anti-Impunity*, 73.

25. Kendall and Nouwen, "Representational Practices," 253–54. Italics in the original.

violations are not properly part of the indictment, off the hook. The court's procedural logic even turns some victims into perpetrators. Since all legally defined physical violence is a crime, international law, notes Karen Engle, held victims of apartheid and its enforcers equally culpable for atrocities.[26] This logic cannot address historical grievances or be part of a political solution because it perpetuates rather than undoes what Mahmood Mamdani calls the "cycle of violence" that leads to conflicts in the first place.[27] The court ignores, erases, and at worst reinforces political and economic inequities while proclaiming a neutral, apolitical pursuit of all criminals in the name of the victims who are the court's raison d'être.

The abstract designation of "The Victims" reduces the tension between the court's dual aims of judging perpetrators and repairing victims. "The Victims" serve as the "telos" of the court, as if a commitment to anti-impunity could itself heal them.[28] Nouwen and Kendall refer to Pierre Bourdieu's concept of "usurpatory ventriloquism" to describe the phenomenon by which the victim, or, as Bourdieu put it, "the represented entity," "relies upon the representative to make [the represented entity] present." A "spokesperson gives voice to the group in whose name he speaks, thereby speaking with all the authority of that elusive, absent phenomenon."[29] The demand for dignity is not articulated by victims but by well-meaning advocates who speak in their stead. As Kamari M. Clarke writes, "Institutions such as the International Criminal Court actually draw their power from the imaginary of the victim, whose liberation is possible only through suffering; the victim figure thus remains both central and marginal to the process."[30] Kendall and Nouwen conclude that the court's invocation of victims does not restore agency to them but uses them as "placeholders"; the symbolic victim provides a rationale for the usurpation of victims' voices by lawyers, human rights' proponents, and politicians, and is thus also an alibi for the empowerment of voices other than those of the victims.[31]

These critics believe that the focus on anti-impunity in criminal law strips victims of agency, reduces them to objects of moral concern whose suffering is their capital, and presumes to know what victims want—legal prosecution—even

---

26. Engle, Miller, and Davis, *Anti-Impunity*, 8.

27. Mahmood Mamdani, "Beyond Nuremberg: The Historical Significance of the Post-Apartheid Transition in South Africa," in Engle, Miller, and Davis, *Anti-Impunity*, 352.

28. Kendall and Nouwen, "Representational Practices," 239.

29. Pierre Bourdieu, *Language and Symbolic Power*, ed. John B. Thompson, trans. Gino Raymond and Matthew Adamson (Cambridge, MA: Harvard University Press, 1991), cited in Kendall and Nouwen, "Representational Practices," 255–59.

30. Kamari M. Clarke, "Fictions of Justice: The ICC and the Challenge of Legal Pluralism in Sub-Saharan Africa," cited in Kendall and Nouwen, "Representational Practices," 262.

31. Kendall and Nouwen, "Representational Practices," 237, 235, 239.

when, as Stover writes, he was "flabbergasted" to find that many survivors had little faith in the ICTY and preferred to settle their own scores.[32] Victims are not permitted truly to witness in the context of the "expressive constraints" implicit in court proceedings and in keeping with the invocation of victims as passive if symbolically authoritative sufferers. Instead, the court most often places the anguished survivors' demands that the dead be buried with dignity into the mouths of lawyers who speak in their name. Moyn asserts: "Today victims mutely serve international criminal justice as tools of rhetorical evasion while being denied the opportunity to voice their entire set of aspirations, as if the role of 'bearing witness to atrocity' now widely supplied in judicial proceedings exhausted their use."[33]

The international court's dismay before all the suffering in the world thus comes not with a rush of humanitarian sympathy for distant others, not with the belated recognition of victims' profound dignity, but with a commitment to alleviate and remedy their pain. According to these scholars, the ICC's reduction of survivors largely to symbolic victims who authorize its proceedings allows the tribunal to transcend the politics in which it is mired; the court is a stage on which a commitment to victims' dignity is symbolized over and over through the dogged pursuit of perpetrators, and on which actors dramatize the power of human solidarity.

The activists who represent the court's work do not redeem myriad victims or even a group of victims, as did the Eichmann trial, but a symbolic global victim who represents all victims being violated somewhere at some time and thus whose suffering never ends.[34] ICC rhetoric transcends victims' differing needs now in the name of a universal suffering victim, abstracted from the bodies of real victims, who has no distinct features that communicate what, how, or where he or she has suffered. The public is presumed to be familiar with the crimes to which victims have been subjected and is told what they want by others: they want "justice" and "to be less of victims and more of citizens."[35]

32. Stover, *Witnesses*, x.

33. Moyn, "Anti-Impunity as Deflection of Argument," 86.

34. The symbolic victim may be a metaphor not only for the endlessness of catastrophe but also for real victims' ongoing trauma when courts fail to deliver. See Valerie Hébert's analysis of the International Criminal Tribunal for Rwanda's failure to produce reconciliation in Rwanda and the subsequent failure of community Gacaca courts in Rwanda: "'Truth Heals' and Other Myths," in *Revenge, Retribution, Reconciliation: Justice and Emotions between Conflict and Mediation; A Cross-Disciplinary Anthology*, ed. Laura Jockusch, Andreas Kraft, and Kim Wünschmann (Jerusalem: Hebrew University Magnes Press, 2016), 264–65.

35. United Nations Secretary-General Kofi Annan and prosecutor Luis Ocampo cited in Kendall and Nouwen, "Representational Practices," 254 and 257.

This generic victim has displaced Holocaust witnesses. It should also be clear by now that this "Victim," this "sovereign entity," is more precisely a moral witness drained of its history and identity. The global victim that critics identify represents an abstraction not only from the bodies of real victims, but also from the symbolic body of the Holocaust survivor whose distinct characteristics have been blurred almost beyond recognition and whose authoritativeness is diminished. Victims' haunting presence is now conjured by second and third parties who declare what victims want, and their tormented bond with the dead is emptied of content in favor of a nonspecific and timeless suffering already implicit in Robert Jay Lifton's more historically bound but universalized trauma victims. In these critical accounts of the ICC, victims' suffering is no longer the source of an imagined insight into genocidal violence; their trauma is no longer a symbol of their fealty to the dead. The global victim is thus no longer a form of (culturally bound) recognition, but is an alibi for the moral activity of others and a source of activists' motivation. The global victim is a haunting and at times luminous presence. And yet it is also a false idol whose authority is dependent on and outsourced to others.

This analysis of the court's elevation and emptying out of victims' experiences provides no easy remedies to what by consensus is a general problem. It is, however, consistent historically and structurally with the making of a generic global victim whose features are no longer specific to a particular event like the Holocaust. Didier Fassin's work makes the loosening connection between the global victim and the Holocaust witness more explicit by fashioning a counterwitness who knows better than anyone else what he has suffered and demands the right to speak on his own behalf.

The Traumatized Victim and Humanitarian Reason

New symbolic iterations of the moral witness are arguably now all expressions and symptoms of the following dilemma: How can we preserve the dignity of the witness after the 1990s, now that we know that institutions designed to remedy violations of human dignity paradoxically sideline victims and in some instances even cause them harm? Proponents and detractors of humanitarianism's large organizational and fund-raising apparatus question its infrastructure and accomplishments even when they laud its purpose. Humanitarian workers often involuntarily harm the very people in whose name they undertake their missions. Their missions have become a legitimate reason for invasion or intervention in the name of combating human rights violations, generating more fluid forms of state power, and aligning humanitarians with oppressive states. In Kosovo in 1996 or Afghanistan in 2001, humanitarians were already on the ground and served as an implicit demand for more aid. Humanitarian operations could also help states rationalize nonintervention because aid workers were providing care with which military intervention might interfere, as happened in Rwanda in 1994.[36] Humanitarian aid likely prolonged the 1987 Ethiopian famine by providing warlords with foodstuffs to use as bargaining chips in the conflict.[37] One scholar argues that activists on behalf of human rights as well as humanitarians in Gaza treat the murder of civilians as acceptable below certain thresholds and collude with US and Israeli power.[38]

Like nineteenth-century humanitarianism so often satirized as the pleasure of being moved by all the suffering in the world, contemporary humanitarianism also turns the recipients of care into objects of philanthropic condescension.[39] Spectators, Robert Meister claims, enjoy the spectacle of their own charity.[40] Contemporary humanitarian consumerism—feeling good about feeling bad—generates either a new philanthropy that neglects the structural causes of oppression or a politics that eschews resistance in favor of proclamations of injury.[41]

---

36. David Rieff, *A Bed for the Night: Humanitarianism in Crisis* (New York: Simon & Schuster, 2002), 273–74, 281, 323.

37. Michael N. Barnett, *Empire of Humanity: A History of Humanitarianism* (Ithaca, NY: Cornell University Press, 2011), 155–58. For particular discussions of this dilemma and for trenchant criticism of the history of humanitarianism and human rights, see Stephen Hopgood, *The Endtimes of Human Rights* (Ithaca, NY: Cornell University Press, 2013); Samuel Moyn, *The Last Utopia: Human Rights in History* (Cambridge, MA: Harvard University Press, 2010); Stefan-Ludwig Hoffmann, ed., *Human Rights in the Twentieth Century* (Cambridge: Cambridge University Press, 2011); Sharon Hutchison, "Perilous Outcomes: International Monitoring and the Perpetuation of Violence in the Sudan," in *Genocide: Truth, Memory, Representation*, ed. Alexander Laban Hinton and Kevin Lewis O'Neill (Durham, NC: Duke University Press, 2009), 54–79; Eric A. Posner, *The Twilight of Human Rights Law* (Oxford: Oxford University Press, 2014).

38. Eyal Weizman, *The Least of All Possible Evils: Humanitarian Violence from Arendt to Gaza* (London: Verso, 2011).

39. A paradigmatic example of philanthropic condescension is Mrs. Jellyby in Charles Dickens's *Bleak House*. Karen Haltunnen argues that there was a prurient underside of abolitionist tracts against slavery in "Humanitarianism and the Pornography of Pain in Anglo-American Culture," *American Historical Review* 100, no. 2 (1995): 303–32. In an increasingly common argument about global philanthropy, Keith David Watenpaugh demonstrates how the terms of humanitarian aid to Armenians after the 1915 genocide imposed Western morality on non-Western cultures in the name of helping the victims, reshaping existing customary norms. See "The League of Nations' Rescue of Armenian Genocide Survivors and the Making of Modern Humanitarianism," *American Historical Review* 115, no. 5 (2010): 1315–19.

40. Meister, *After Evil*. For historical approaches, see Heide Fehrenbach and Davide Rodogno, eds., *Humanitarian Photography: A History* (Cambridge: Cambridge University Press, 2016).

41. Meister, *After Evil*; Hopgood, *Endtimes of Human Rights*. On human rights and humanitarianism as forms of consumer culture, see, among others, Lecia Rosenthal, *Mourning Modernism: Literature,*

None of this is surprising, since there is always bound to be a discrepancy between theory and practice. The deeper concern is that the invocation of victims rationalizes all sorts of humanitarian operations that seem to make victims suffer more. Didier Fassin's writing on "humanitarian reason" and (with Richard Rechtman) on trauma stand out among this literature by addressing the structural and historical contexts in which victims' needs are ostensibly met, even emphasized, but in reality encourage new forms of subjugation. In particular their work combines an analysis of humanitarian politics on the ground with one that addresses the changing relationship between moral sentiment and politics.[42] Fassin and Rechtman also rectify the absence of a historicized discussion of the diffusion of trauma discourse outside of psychiatry (*ET*).[43]

Catastrophe, and the Politics of Consolation (New York: Fordham University Press, 2011); Keith Tester, *Humanitarianism and Modern Culture* (University Park: Pennsylvania State University Press, 2010); Mary Mostafanezhad, *Volunteer Tourism: Popular Humanitarianism in Neoliberal Times* (Farnham, UK: Ashgate, 2014).

42. Their point of departure remains the discipline of psychiatric medicine, its theoreticians and practitioners. Fassin and Rechtman, *Empire of Trauma*; Didier Fassin, *Humanitarian Reason: A Moral History of the Present*, trans. Rachel Gomme (Berkeley: University of California Press, 2012). Both works are hereafter cited in parentheses in the text as *ET* and *HR*, respectively.

43. The investigation of the relationship between moral sentiments and politics (or the affective forms of economic relationships) now underscores a vast array of work about humanitarianism and is the central question posed by cultural critics concerned with its contemporary iteration. Fassin does not engage this narrative because his methodological approach is so radically different, but it is important to underline its existence. The historian Thomas L. Haskell argued three decades ago that the rise of impersonal capital markets in the late eighteenth and early nineteenth centuries corresponded with the emergence of humanitarianism. He meant that impersonal markets and the requirements of property holding demanded not only new forms of propriety—self-discipline, long-term goals, promise keeping—but also new feelings for distant others commensurate with the abstract equality of all people that market expansion and the dominance of contract over status introduced. Early capitalist expansion created the possibility of abstractly equal subjects while naturalizing the subordination of labor in new terms that included the language of freedom: hence slavery became increasingly implausible as wage labor triumphed. His work has been long criticized for idealizing humanitarianism. Haskell sought to counter prominent interpretations of humanitarianism's emergence as an expression of bourgeois class interest. He does not take fully into account either the illusory freedom of choice that contractual relationships presume or the imperialist rhetoric of the civilizing mission. But by historicizing the relationship between politics, economics, and affective regimes, historians now ensure that moral recognition of suffering is not reduced merely to a capitalist or imperialist venture but represents a new and particular iteration of "humanity." Haskell, "Capitalism and the Origins of Humanitarian Sensibility: Part 1," and "Capitalism and the Origins of Humanitarian Sensibility: Part 2," *American Historical Review* 90, nos. 2 and 3 (1985): 339–61 and 547–66, respectively.

For a helpful overview of the history and meaning of humanitarianism, including the critique that it is a reformulation of the white man's burden, see Richard Ashby Wilson's and Richard D. Brown's introduction to *Humanitarianism and Suffering: The Mobilization of Empathy*, ed. Richard Ashby Wilson and Richard D. Brown (Cambridge: Cambridge University Press, 2009), 1–28. Trauma discourse was developed outside of psychiatry by literary theorists, who focus on the healing function of bearing witness. In particular I am thinking of the work of Cathy Caruth, for whom trauma is a missed experience; trauma can only be experienced belatedly and is not a form of affect. Shoshana Felman calls great

In Fassin and Rechtman's *The Empire of Trauma* and in Fassin's *Humanitarian Reason*, the authors address our attachment to the recent cultural importance conferred on victims' suffering with unparalleled depth. They do so by articulating humanitarian moralism as a complex political form rather than only as a type of updated nineteenth-century philanthropy. They make a counterintuitive argument only implicit in other accounts and explicit in work about the ICC: the more the language of trauma and the practice of humanitarianism drew attention to global suffering, the more state power took on the fluid form of humanitarian intervention, the more victims were subjected and silenced. Human rights, they argue, became part of a bureaucratic, administrative, and judicial apparatus whose mandate to care for traumatized victims also controlled them by regulating their needs and demands.

Together—for the texts overlap in important ways—*The Empire of Trauma* and *Humanitarian Reason* claim that sometime after the 1960s, when Holocaust survivors first became sympathetic victims, psychiatrists began to take their symptoms seriously. Doctors since the nineteenth century long believed that people feigned trauma symptoms to claim insurance fraudulently, and that soldiers during the Great War mimicked "shell shock" to evade combat. Holocaust survivors, however, had very little to gain from reliving their catastrophic experiences of suffering and loss, and doctors for the most part believed them.[44] By the 1990s, the increased diffusion of the PTSD diagnosis accorded new social value to victims' claims and expanded the number of victims. It also supported humanitarians' mandate to heal global suffering in the name of alleviating trauma.

According to Fassin and Rechtman, the ubiquity of trauma can be traced to a moment when it became unmoored from those who suffered its ravages:

> The persistence of the psychic scar guaranteed that the memory of the intolerable would never be erased. But the meaning of that trace was still inextricably linked to the moral qualities ascribed to survivors—their

---

writers "precocious witnesses" because they make palpable an experience whose traumatic content cannot be clearly articulated. Caruth, *Unclaimed Experience: Trauma, Narrative, and History* (Baltimore: Johns Hopkins University Press, 1996); Felman, *The Juridical Unconscious: Trials and Traumas in the Twentieth Century* (Cambridge, MA: Harvard University Press, 2002), 97. Karyn Ball offers a sustained critique of trauma discourse in *Disciplining the Holocaust* (Albany: SUNY Press, 2007).

44. This account restores Bettelheim's important role in developing the concept of survivor guilt, but also underplays, by skipping over, the ambivalence about Holocaust survivors that characterized Cold War discourse until the 1960s and explains the cultural importance of the Eichmann trial. German reparations were extremely hard to argue for on the grounds of mental health precisely because many German physicians did not or did not want to believe victims. Fassin and Rechtman, *Empire of Trauma*, 70–76. On German reparations, see Dagmar Herzog, *Cold War Freud: Psychoanalysis in an Age of Catastrophes* (Cambridge: Cambridge University Press, 2017), 89–122.

innocence and their weakness in the face of the brutal forces that overwhelmed them—and to the empathy they inspired. Now [after the Ho-
locaust], through this encounter between conceptions of memory and
clinical practice, trauma was seen as the locus of an essential truth about
humanity that stood apart from the moral qualities of the victim. (*ET*, 95)

In this passage, Fassin and Rechtman trace a historical shift away from the experience of survivors to "humanitarian psychiatry." Trauma is no longer a medical diagnosis but transforms particular experiences of suffering into a generic
truth about humanity. Trauma now represents the "common understanding of
suffering" (*HR*, 222), as well as a medical diagnosis, and testimony is the moral
account that emerges as often in the words of humanitarians as it is intrinsic in
the "innocence" and "weakness" of survivors.[45]

In an argument that overlaps with criticism of the ICC's invocation of victims by judges and lawyers, Fassin asserts that trauma "indicates more about
the moral sentiment of the [second- or third-party humanitarian] witness than
about the experience of the victim" (*HR*, 222). Primo Levi, for example, was a
survivor, but he also claimed that the dead were the true witnesses; he might
speak on their behalf, but Levi never claimed to speak as an omniscient authority
(*HR*, 205). In contrast to Levi's humility, humanitarians speak volubly on behalf
of victims. Fassin argues that "in the contemporary era, the prolixity of humanitarian workers stands against the silence of survivors. The voice of the former is
substituted for the voice of the latter" (*HR*, 206). By his reckoning, "the second
age of humanitarianism . . . corresponds to the emergence of the witness—not
the witness who has experienced the tragedy, but the one who has brought aid to
its victims" (*HR*, 207).

Fassin attributes victims' silencing to "humanitarian government," or the
"deployment of moral sentiments in contemporary politics," and "humanitarian reason," a late modern iteration of political morality that emerged with
abolitionism and provides the genealogical framework for humanitarian government.[46] The focus on suffering and trauma in political discourse, the social
sciences, and the growing human rights infrastructure does not simply reflect

45. Fassin's and Rechtman's insight that there is an important relationship between Holocaust
survivor trauma and its recent emergence, abstracted from real survivors, traces how "traumatic
experience became a testament to the unspeakable" (*Empire of Trauma*, 72).

46. Fassin, *Humanitarian Reason*, 1, 3. Fassin's reference to "government" is also an allusion to the
concepts of "governmentality" and "biopower" that Michel Foucault developed in his lectures at the
Collège de France in the 1970s and 1980s and incorporated into his work beginning with *The History
of Sexuality*, vol. 1: *An Introduction*, trans. Robert Hurley (New York: Vintage, 1990).

moral progress, but also constitutes an entirely new way of interpreting how we define social problems and their solutions:

> Inequality is replaced by exclusion, domination is transformed into misfortune, injustice is articulated as suffering, violence is expressed in terms of trauma. While the old vocabulary of social critique has certainly not entirely disappeared, the new lexicon of moral sentiments tends to mask it in a process of semantic sedimentation that has perceptible effects both in public action and in individual practices. . . . The translation of social reality into the new language of compassion is thus mirrored by a sort of epistemological, but also emotional, conversion of researchers and intellectuals to this approach to society. (*HR*, 6)

Moral sentiments now drive political action on a broad scale, from the welfare state to humanitarian crises and interventions (*HR*, 4–5). Sentimentality saturates the language of social critique so thoroughly that its vocabulary of exclusion, misfortune, and trauma replaces the structural forces acting on vulnerable populations—inequality, domination, injustice. Thus we "invoke trauma rather than recognizing violence" (*HR*, 8) and give permanent immigration status to those who have health problems rather than offer political asylum to others fleeing persecution.[47] Humanitarian reason conceals and naturalizes the structural causes of injustice, but also regulates injustice through the language of psychic and physical suffering; troubled youth and poverty-stricken immigrants are no longer conceived as social problems to be addressed by government agencies but as traumatized bodies in pain whose potential discontent is regulated by government's compassion for their woes.

Fassin offers as an example among others the "listening centers" introduced in France during the 1990s. They replaced social and political solutions to the problem of marginalized youth, drug addiction, and crime with psychological regulation. He notes that "a consultation with a psychologist became part of recipients' 'job-seeking project,' and refusal to attend could theoretically result in their monthly income being reduced or withdrawn" (*HR*, 39). Of course, people need psychological assistance. His argument is rather that suffering has become yet another diagnostic tool and category by which modern governments regulate subjectivity and thus shape individuals. Why are we so attached both to showing and talking about suffering today? Fassin answers, "In an era in which social

---

47. For a similar argument and probing work on this subject, see Miriam Ticktin, *Casualties of Care: Immigration and the Politics of Humanitarianism in France* (Berkeley: University of California Press, 2011).

inequalities have continued to deepen, the normalization of social suffering in the public arena and the institutionalization of a national policy of listening do not derive only from new forms of subjectivization resulting in the manifestation of a concern for the misfortune of others; they are also modes of government that strive to make precarious lives livable and elude the social causes of their condition" (*HR*, 42). "Humanitarian reason" is the expression not only of an institutionalized mandate to care for suffering others, but also of a newly fluid form of power that constitutes them as traumatized subjects.

Pain, to summarize, is a form of social capital that replaces social critique as a means of expressing injustice. Medical experts and state bureaucrats must verify its past or current intensity to establish the legitimacy of immigration or asylum cases, among other social expressions of trauma. Political demands take the form of tear-drenched clamors for recognition in which political subjects are encouraged to embrace their loss of agency as a condition of possibility for selfhood. The language of suffering not only describes defenseless people but also transforms vulnerable humanity into precarious beings who must be spoken for. Victims who speak about their pain thus participate in self-erasure rather than possess special knowledge or heal, and their narratives become a source of illusory agency. The "truth" of humanity is no longer possessed by the witness, but belongs to the humanitarian state that defines the victim's needs and turns the humanitarian into its representative.

Fassin argues that humanitarians transform the desperate acts of male Palestinian suicide bombers into symptoms of young men's helplessness, ignoring the bombers' message of protest. He defines a difference between "neurotic" despair and politicized despair that defies oppression. From some Palestinians' point of view, those who die in the service of combating Israeli occupation serve God by dying rather than "betraying their faith" (*HR*, 206). But the "discourse of mental health," Fassin insists, "replaces the martyr subject with a neurotic subject, substituting the politics of justice proclaimed by the martyr with a politics of compassion, which has the sufferer as its object" (*HR*, 211). He maintains that suicide bombers style themselves as combatants, while humanitarians, moved by and angry about Palestinians' everyday living conditions, interpret their self-styled martyrdom as pathetic acts of desperation. In so doing, humanitarians subordinate the suicide bombers' carefully constructed self-image to their own vision of helpless victims: "Humanitarian subjectivization blurs the image of violence—or rather, through the offices of psychiatrists and psychologists, it requalifies it as trauma" (*HR*, 211).

Fassin's work is a piercing interpretation of our contemporary moment. In his account, victims are a product of humanitarian government that is symbolized and enabled by the humanitarian witness. Humanitarians have abstracted trauma from the "moral qualities" of Holocaust survivors and turned trauma into the universal truth of humanity. Humanitarian government strips victims of agency by making their weakness and innocence the condition of making claims for recognition *tout court*. The regulation of victims takes the form of a warm and compassionate embrace that transforms them into supplicants rather than subjects in their own right. Sympathy for survivors "makes precarious lives livable" (*HR*, 42).

And yet Fassin also counters the sweeping regulatory powers of humanitarian reason by recasting victims in the image of quiet humility and dignity, of hope betrayed. As the Holocaust witness rendered survivors symbolically blameless and dignified, Fassin renders victims of humanitarian government quiet and insightful: survivors gaze wearily at everyone around them—at humanitarians' efforts to re-create survivors' experience, speak for them, and commemorate their suffering. Victims, Fassin writes, "distance themselves from affect . . . because they need the facts to be established and because they are aware of the risk of not being believed. The aid workers, conversely, because they seek primarily to move their audience . . . engage affects" (*HR*, 207). Victims also prefer minimalist memorials to grandiose commemoration: "For example, we could contrast the striving to eliminate all affect in the walls of names of the dead in the Holocaust memorials with the attempt to sensitize the public to the violence of the world" undertaken by humanitarians (207). He illustrates the difference between the victims' "silence" and the humanitarians' "prolixity" by contrasting the reduced affect in minimalist Holocaust memorials—though there are many memorials that are not minimalist at all—with Doctors Without Borders' sensationalized efforts to help nonvictims imagine how victims feel.[48] The organization invites people to staged checkpoints and camps in order to help them imagine what it is like to pass through a checkpoint or enter a refugee camp (*HR*, 206–7).[49]

Fassin contrasts survivors who bow their heads in deference to victims—Primo Levi, for example—with humanitarians in thrall to their own compassion (*HR*, 208). By contrasting the suicide bomber's self-image as a combatant with

---

48. See, for example, the famous work of realism in Warsaw, the 1948 Warsaw Ghetto Heroes Monument by Nathan Rapoport, commemorating the 1943 Warsaw ghetto uprising.

49. This kind of activity has become a common pedagogical practice and has been celebrated as well as criticized for fostering a kitschy form of commemoration. See, for a positive approach, Alison Landsberg, *Prosthetic Memory: The Transformation of American Remembrance in an Age of Mass Culture* (New York: Columbia University Press, 2004); and for a more skeptical view, Marita Sturken, *Tourists of History: Memory, Kitsch, and Consumerism from Oklahoma City to Ground Zero* (Durham, NC: Duke University Press, 2007).

humanitarians' diagnosis of him as a neurotic, Fassin reminds us of the willful and disciplined comportment of the martyr that humanitarians erase. At the same time, he also tends to distinguish between dignified restraint and affect, aligning victims symbolically with the muted tone of dignified restraint and associating humanitarians with the "prolixity" of affect.

Fassin argues that victims' identities are now commensurate with their subjection, but also implies by this portrayal of dignified victims that they are not. In so doing he suggests that victims may not be able to evade humanitarian government, but also that they are more than its residual effect. The contrast he draws between victims and humanitarians restores victims' dignity in spite of humanitarian government's relentless efforts to strip them of it. He rescues victims from the light of compassion by providing them with a positive cultural valence, a humble, masculine comportment—it is hard to ignore the implicit if inadvertent gendering of the contrast between the constrained self and the "neurotic" one, between minimalist taste and overwrought affect. Observers at the Eichmann trial and later fashioned the iconic Holocaust witness to figure their redeemed dignity. Fassin casts survivors as counterwitnesses who are at once the perfect products of humanitarian government and its wary, quietly dignified survivors.

Atrocity Photos and the Counterwitness

Atrocity images are now a staple of human rights activism: they come by mail from humanitarian organizations seeking donations, are displayed in exhibits and public conferences, and are often posted on social media.[50] In the late

---

50. Jonathan Benthall, *Disasters, Relief and the Media* (London: I.B. Tauris, 1993), 103. For reasons of conceptual coherence, I address only images of suffering and persecuted humanity. Photographs of tormented animals (in war or in other contexts) as well as pictures of sites where capital punishment is administered may be conceived as atrocity photographs but tend not to be assimilated into arguments about them. See Wendy Lesser, *Pictures at an Execution: An Inquiry into the Subject of Murder* (Cambridge, MA: Harvard University Press, 1993); Maria Pia Di Bella, "Observing Executions: From Spectator to Witness," in *Representations of Pain in Art and Visual Culture*, ed. Di Bella and James Elkins (New York: Routledge, 2013), 170–85. Extant categories of interpretation, like human dignity, still do not apply in any systematic fashion to animal life, and thus not to images of animals' pain. I also do not discuss social media, which often allow victims to "speak" if they have a camera. Social media offer spectators the opportunity to intervene, whether by sharing an image or becoming involved in the tracking of images for the purposes of developing charges about the violation of human rights. Moreover, videos are widespread on social media but revitalize the image and are closer to film than photography. Michal Givoni speaks about the humanitarian organization Witness, which is a platform for activists. The differences between photography and digital media require a separate treatment. Givoni, *The Care of the Witness: A Contemporary History of Testimony in Crisis* (Cambridge: Cambridge University Press, 2016), 210–16.

1970s through the 1990s, after the haunting images from the Nazi concentration camps had become a familiar emblem of suffering in the world, atrocity images, which activists had long used to mobilize against social injustice, became part of an expansive moral imperative to picture the consequences of state violence, including famine, war, and genocide. Debates about atrocity photography now raise an old ethical question in terms consistent with the dilemma proper to humanitarian and human rights ventures: ending violence depends on photographs of injured humanity to move publics, but those images may also exploit suffering for the benefit of voyeuristic audiences or, if the photographer is gifted, even make suffering beautiful.[51] The limited body of critical work about atrocity photography foregrounds this ethical and political question about spectators' responses to such images, and is often as concerned with their political efficacy as their aesthetic value.[52]

Some work addresses victims who want to be photographed in order to bring attention to their plight. It examines photographs taken by victims—four famous images of crematoria in Auschwitz, for example—whose impact may be tempered by empathy for the photographers and admiration of their determination to bear witness under extreme duress.[53] But most debates ask curatorial

---

51. Critics of photography often repeat Platonic worries about the substitution of false idols for essences as well as Christian iconoclasts' recurrent anxieties about the representation of Christ's suffering (whose representation could also motivate good works). An eighth-century iconoclast once protested against reproducing Christ's "humiliation." Arnold Hauser, *The Social History of Art*, vol. 1: *Prehistoric, Ancient, Oriental, Greece and Rome, Middle Ages* (1957; repr., New York: Vintage, 1985), 138. See also Alain Besançon, *The Forbidden Image: An Intellectual History of Iconoclasm*, trans. Jane Marie Todd (Chicago: University of Chicago Press, 2000).

52. Much of the literature focused solely on atrocity photography began to be published in the early 2000s. See Ariella Azoulay, *The Civil Contract of Photography*, trans. Rela Mazali and Ruvik Danieli (New York: Zone Books, 2008); Azoulay, *Civil Imagination: A Political Ontology of Photography*, trans. Louise Bethlehem (London: Verso, 2012); Ulrich Baer, *Spectral Evidence: The Photography of Trauma* (Cambridge, MA: MIT Press, 2002); Georges Didi-Huberman, *Images in Spite of All: Four Photographs from Auschwitz*, trans. Shane B. Lillis (Chicago: University of Chicago Press, 2007); Stephen F. Eisenmann, *The Abu Ghraib Effect* (London: Reaktion Books, 2007); Susie Linfield, *The Cruel Radiance: Photographs of Political Violence* (Chicago: University of Chicago Press, 2010); W.J.T. Mitchell, *Cloning Terror: The War of Images, 9/11 to the Present* (Chicago: University of Chicago Press, 2011); John Roberts, *Photography and Its Violations* (New York: Columbia University Press, 2014); Susan Sontag, *On Photography* (New York: Farrar, Straus and Giroux, 1980); Sontag, *Regarding the Pain of Others* (New York: Farrar, Straus and Giroux, 2003); Barbie Zelizer, *Remembering to Forget: Holocaust Memory through the Camera's Eye* (Chicago: University of Chicago Press, 1998); Zelizer, *About to Die: How News Images Move the Public* (Oxford: Oxford University Press, 2010). Other works are primarily collections of essays that cover multiple images and contexts and provide no synthetic argument but pose important questions. See Geoffrey Batchen, Mick Gidley, Nancy K. Miller, and Jay Prosser, eds., *Picturing Atrocity: Photography in Crisis* (London: Reaktion Books, 2012); and Di Bella and Elkins, *Representations of Pain*.

53. Didi-Huberman, *Images in Spite of All*.

questions, including how we determine when a photograph's overwhelming emotional resonance compromises its pedagogical function, or whether, when atrocity images are exhibited in a museum, they anesthetize viewers.[54] Critics turn spectators into faraway interpreters of events, weighing the benefits of photography's ostensibly transformative political function—to "bear witness," to ensure that there will "never again" be a Holocaust—against the often controversial display of violated human dignity. "Bearing witness" has become shorthand for the act of spectatorship associated with pictures of terrible suffering as well as a seemingly self-evident moral activity differentiated from the act of looking at other sorts of images.

In the late 1970s, drawing on photography's perilous and potentially transformative dimensions, Susan Sontag became the most prominent interpreter of these questions in a work that took up older themes about how the camera's mechanical reproduction of the world objectifies its subjects and traumatizes viewers; it extends the human eye, documenting abuse but also intruding into precarious lives.[55] Adopting these arguments, she denounced photography as a form of aggression against its objects, the product of an age of consumption and a cultural demand for "shocks." Photography's mechanically produced realism, she argued (digital photography was not yet on the horizon), always complicated if not compromised aesthetic accomplishment and could degenerate into voyeurism. "Photography," she wrote in 1977, "is the paradigm of an inherently equivocal connection between self and world—its version of the ideology of realism sometimes dictating an effacement of the self in relation to the world, sometimes authorizing an aggressive relation to the world which celebrates the self. One side or other of the connection is always being rediscovered and championed."[56]

---

54. When such images do have aesthetic properties, debates often ensue about the propriety of treating them as art. A good example is the images of Cambodians photographed before execution at Tuol Sleng prison that were exhibited in 1997 at the Museum of Modern Art in New York, known as the "*Photographs from S-21, 1975–1979.*"

55. In the nineteenth century, photographs generated mechanically reproducible images for passive consumption, advertising, technological surveillance, and political manipulation. Already by 1890 in the United States, the objectifying power of modern media led Samuel Warren and Louis Brandeis to assert a right to protect inviolate personhood against cameras and advertising. Warren and Brandeis, "The Right to Privacy," *Harvard Law Review* 4, no. 5 (December 15, 1890): 193–220. See also Walter Benjamin's "The Work of Art in the Age of Mechanical Reproduction," in *Illuminations*, ed. Hannah Arendt, trans. Harry Zohn (New York: Schocken Books, 1978), 222. Though he recognized the danger of the media spectacle and its capacity to distract, Benjamin hoped that the spectacular nature of photography and film might liberate us instead of transforming us into passive observers. For an ecstatic expression of the use of the camera in wartime see Ernst Jünger, *Storm of Steel*, trans. Michael Hofmann (New York: Penguin, 2004).

56. Sontag, *On Photography*, 123.

Sontag reiterated an old ambivalence about photographs, extending her argument specifically to "photographs of Agony" (the capital *A* an ironic reference to the tradition of expressive suffering) that "convey distress . . . by neutralizing it."[57] Photographs of agony represent a microcosm of the problem posed by photography because they turn agony into a spectacle to be consumed. Such images militate against a measured relation to the world and leave the self off balance, overly passive and effacing, or overly assertive and aggressive.

In *Regarding the Pain of Others* (1993), a revision of her previous views about the numbing effect of photos, Sontag was no longer willing to condemn such images and insisted on their power to haunt spectators, and even to move them. Yet her optimism about the potential impact of photos dissipates even as she insists on their importance.[58] She insists that the "vast repository" of atrocity images makes it hard for us to claim innocence and render those who do morally defective: "Let the images," she insists, "haunt us." She also extends her previous, less optimistic view that photographs of war and violence arouse rage but also numb viewers; "the image as shock and the image as cliché are two aspects of the same presence." But now this argument does not condemn photographs but rather mocks a "cliché" of "the cosmopolitan discussions of images of atrocity," which "assume[s] that they have little effect, and that there is something innately cynical about their diffusion."[59] Consumers are too distant to grasp the photographs' meaning, and the war-weary too proximate to violence not to feel exploited by them.

Michael Fried brings us closest to Sontag's 1993 work when he invokes her discussion of Jeff Wall's photograph of actors posing as slaughtered Russian soldiers in Afghanistan, *Dead Troops Talk*. (The whole artwork is formed by images taken at different times and later melded into one near life-size picture.) In the image, the dead troops of the title are enclosed in their own world—they look without seeing and speak without speaking. Sontag had used Wall's image to symbolize the insuperable gap between spectators and sufferers and to express solidarity with the victims who know the world has ceased to care. According to Fried,

---

57. Sontag, *On Photography*, 105. Most catalogs of war photography avoid discussion of these issues. See Jane Livingston, *The Indelible Image: Photographs of War, 1846 to the Present*, with a foreword by Frances Falin (New York: Abrams, 1982), and *Voir / ne pas voir la guerre: Histoire des représentations photographiques de la guerre* (Paris: Bibliothèque de documentation internationale contemporaine, 2001), 277.

58. Judith Butler notes that for Sontag, the photograph's haunting quality generates outrage but does not "show her how to transform that affect into effective political action." Butler, *Frames of War: When Is Life Grievable?* (New York: Verso, 2009), 98–99.

59. Sontag, *Regarding*, 114–15, 23, 111.

FIGURE 4.1 / Jeff Wall, *Dead Troops Talk (A Vision after an Ambush of a Red Army Patrol, near Moqor, Afghanistan, Winter 1986)*, 1992. Transparency in light box. 229 x 417 cm. Courtesy of the artist.

Wall's photograph illustrates "absorption"—the subjects don't care about those who behold them and have no interest in engaging their gazes.[60] By demonstrating how the image eliminates the beholder, he provides a sophisticated articulation of Sontag's reference to the soldiers who know that "we don't get it. We can't truly imagine what it was like."[61]

Sontag's resurrection of an old ethical ambivalence about atrocity photography's powers to haunt for better or worse has only intensified that ambivalence.[62] Dora Apel argues simply that "looking and seeing seem to implicate the viewer . . . in the acts that turned human beings into horribly shamed objects, as if viewing itself were a form of aggression."[63] When Susan Crane argues that the camera

60. Michael Fried, *Why Photography Matters as Art as Never Before* (New Haven, CT: Yale University Press, 2008), 30–35. Fried draws on the argument he first developed in *Absorption and Theatricality: Painting and Beholder in the Age of Diderot* (Chicago: University of Chicago Press, 1980).

61. Sontag, *Regarding*, 125. Clearly Fried has an investment in Sontag's general preference for aesthetic modernism.

62. Capturing this ambivalence without any investment in debates about photography, in 1960 Gerhard Schoenberner, who compiled a book of atrocity photographs for West German consumption, *The Yellow Star*, wrote that they "put [the viewers] into the role of the murderers," but also, that "the human dignity of the victims shines through." Gerhard Schoenberner quoted in Robert Sachett, "Pictures of Atrocity: Public Reception of *Der gelbe Stern* in 1960s West Germany," *German History* 24, no. 4 (2006): 529.

63. Dora Apel, *Imagery of Lynching: Black Men, White Women, and the Mob* (New Brunswick, NJ: Rutgers University Press, 2004), 9.

"redoubles" the "violence perpetrated on the victim," she intimates that making images constitutes violence against those pictured as if they were alive, claiming moreover that "the undignified deaths" will "forever be able to harm viewers."[64] Griselda Pollack writes that she does not reproduce particular images in her text because she wants to avoid "the risk [of] inflicting by exposure some [more] of that pain [already inflicted] upon those trapped under the documenting perpetrator's gaze."[65] The photograph's ability to bring dead and dying people to life only to wound them again is dark magic: there is no consolation, no rest for their weary subjects or viewers, only unremitting suffering and dying.[66] Viewers worry that looking at images desecrates the victims, or even that the images will punish them for looking.

This interpretative constraint emerges even in those works that most vehemently want looking at a photograph to affirm rather than abrogate the victim's dignity.[67] In the introduction to their recent compilation of essays, the editors of *Picturing Atrocity* argue that such photos might "have a function for us as citizens." Speaking of the "genre" of trophy photographs—those pictures taken as spoils of war—Jay Prosser asserts:

> The entanglement of photography in atrocity is one reason why photography is "in crisis." The photographing of atrocity always involves an ethical crisis of representation. . . . Does it bring more benefit or further harm? . . . On some level ethical questions about how we should respond affect whoever looks at atrocity photographs. . . . If the photograph asks us as viewers to witness, one characteristic of the atrocity photograph can be the inclusion of bystanders, those who simply watch, who can often show a disturbing lack of visible response to the event, and whose lack of response seems to increase its atrocity. The

---

64. Susan Crane, "Choosing Not to Look: Representation, Repatriation, and Holocaust Photography," *History and Theory* 47, no. 3 (2008): 318.

65. Griselda Pollack, "Dying, Seeing, Feeling: Transforming the Ethical Space of Feminist Aesthetics," in *The Life and Death of Images: Ethics and Aesthetics*, ed. Diarmuid Costello and Dominic Willsdon (Ithaca, NY: Cornell University Press, 2008), 221.

66. For a persuasive case that the photograph's magic, like Marcel Duchamp's "readymade(s)," may escape semiotic systems, see Martin Jay, "Magical Nominalism: Photography and the Reenchantment of the World," *Culture, Theory, and Critique* 50, no. 2–3 (2009): 165–83. W.J.T. Mitchell also discusses the "living" quality of images in *What Do Pictures Want? The Lives and Loves of Images* (Chicago: University of Chicago Press, 2005), 125–44; and Mitchell, *Cloning Terror*, 118. He also decries the use of atrocity photography: "What purpose, I want to know, is being served by putting these terrible, harrowing images of evil [photographs of lynching] on display for the voyeuristic gratification of the gallery-going public?" *What Do Pictures Want?*, 142.

67. See Sandra S. Phillips, ed., *Exposed: Voyeurism, Surveillance, and the Camera since 1870,* (New Haven, CT: Yale University Press, 2011), 11.

viewers *of* such a photograph will not want to replicate this failure of witnessing. But what else should we do?[68]

The spectator identifies with a potentially implicated bystander, becoming a witness to his own powerlessness to stop suffering in the world.

In *Civil Imagination*, Ariella Azoulay thoughtfully argues that photographs are an "encounter between citizens."[69] Their performative power might create a new "civil contract"; photographs create political relationships between people and are the product of those relations. Azoulay nonetheless feels compelled to add "a comment on the photographs" to justify her use of them that nicely sums up the dilemma I have discussed: "The question facing me again and again was whether or not to reprint photographs that show the photographed persons in situations so harsh as to entail humiliation or to cause injury to them."[70] Once each photograph is scrutinized and the conditions of its production thoroughly illuminated, she says,

> one should then make a careful attempt to assess the damage that the photograph might cause the person portrayed in it (damage that will compound the injury already caused to her or to him in the degrading situation itself and through previous dissemination of the photograph) and to gauge this possible damage against the photograph's potential contribution toward realizing the address of the photographed subject or of those who speak on their behalf. No less important is trying to assess the photograph's perception within the cultural milieu of the photographed subject. Also to be taken into account is the possibly weakened line of argument within this discussion, when it substitutes a verbal description for the photograph itself.[71]

The presumption here is that photographs that performatively constitute a civil contract might also violate that same contract. To avoid this outcome photographs must be meticulously curated, mediated by ethical concerns, and

---

68. Prosser's introduction to *Picturing Atrocity*, 9–10. Visual theorist John Roberts addresses this issue directly in the context of aesthetic theory about photography by asserting that the photograph is catachrestic: it is both indexical and figurative but not really either. In so doing he intervenes into debates about whether digital photography has finally eclipsed photography's indexical relation to the real with a nuanced "no." Ultimately, he is also interested in how the changing conditions of production (now, neoliberalism) impact how and whether we can tie photography to a larger project of political liberation. Roberts, *Photography and Its Violations*, 69–70.

69. Azoulay, *Civil Imagination*, 117

70. Azoulay, *Civil Contract*, 493.

71. Azoulay, *Civil Contract*, 493.

shielded from viewers' voyeurism. Even if they are curated and scrutinized exhaustively, as Azoulay suggests they must be, are these forms of evaluation not themselves interpretative processes that make it difficult to ascertain the actual political effects of images? It may not be possible to determine atrocity photographs' effects on viewers and on political action, because assertions about their haunting are interpretative and thus always speculative, linked to how an image comes to life, how it is curated, and by which route it circulates, and what kind of metaphorical displacement—what other, similar scenes an image can make us imagine—it is able to provoke.

Violent images often cannot be absorbed and paralyze viewers—such images are usually referred to as traumatic because they are too disturbing to build solidarity—and yet, as Sontag insisted, they also militate against amnesia.[72] In her discussion of Lee Miller's images of Dachau, Sharon Sliwinski writes, "The public bore witness in 1945, but they did not know what they had seen."[73] Such dramatic effects evoke different responses: Frances Guerin and Roger Hallas remind us that images of "historical trauma" require particular care because of the emotions they arouse;[74] for his part, Frank Möller suggests that the traumatic effects of photographs cannot be absorbed by spectators, and only art photography shot in the aftermath of genocide guarantees the critical distance required to "witness."[75]

Most worrisome of all, these same images may also become false idols. Cornelia Brink emphasizes the traumatic dimension of the photographs of dead and dying Jewish victims Americans forced German locals to look at after the war. She claims that Germans rejected the "moral appeal" of the horrible images they were forced to observe because the photos were traumatic—they provoked "terror and fear"—and demanded that someone be held accountable.[76] In order to explain how photographs that usually serve an evidentiary and moral purpose

72. Sontag, *Regarding*, 114.

73. Sharon Sliwinski, *Human Rights in the Camera's Eye* (Chicago: University of Chicago Press, 2011), 83.

74. Frances Guerin's and Roger Hallas's introduction to *The Image and the Witness: Trauma, Memory, and Visual Culture*, ed. Guerin and Hallas (New York: Wallflower, 2007), 14.

75. Frank Möller, "Rwanda Revisualized: Genocide, Photography, and the Era of the Witness," *Alternatives* 35, no. 2 (2010): 113–36. He writes, "Art photography, it is argued, may help transform viewers from consumer spectators into participant witnesses who self-critically reflect upon their own subject positions in relation to the conditions depicted in the image while simultaneously being aware that an adequate response to the image is not possible" (113).

76. Cornelia Brink, "Secular Icons: Looking at Photographs of Nazi Concentration Camps," *History and Memory* 12, no. 1 (2000): 146. Brink's invocation of the sublime in the terror and fear provoked by the images further underlines how German bystanders appropriated the trauma of others as their own by sacralizing it. Photographs could also be made into false idols if they are faked to

functioned instead as an alibi for German bystanders, she claims that the camp photographs taken by British and US journalists at liberation resemble Orthodox Christian religious icons. The pictures were "sacred" because the Allies rendered them iconic of human evil. The US general Dwight Eisenhower, when he was commander of the Allied Expeditionary Force, ordered that Germans witness the photographs as a moral lesson about the consequences of depravity and as punishment for having supported the regime responsible for victims' deaths.[77] In so doing, the Allies not only used the images to impose the victor's justice, but also turned them into fetishes. The images were no longer references to the specific evil with which German bystanders were said to have been complicit; instead, they functioned as a "protective layer" between German bystanders and victims.[78]

The promise of atrocity images to generate solidarity with the victims pictured is subsumed by anxiety about the effects of looking or soothes anxiety by making us feel better about ourselves. How do we look at such images when looking can further degrade a victim, or when images of victims make it possible merely to consume victims' pain rather than act to end it? If atrocity photographs reiterate the violence they are supposed to contest, are they doomed to undermine rather than generate our common bonds? The question is posed dramatically by Brink's claim that atrocity photos turned complicit German bystanders into innocents, and is also posed by the other critics who argue that such images make innocent bystanders complicit in crimes. If photographs that show extreme suffering paralyze, blind, or sap spectators of their rage, can they really mobilize movements on behalf of victims? From Sontag on, most critics express an explicit interpretative and an implicit cultural consensus that atrocity

---

incite a certain reaction. For a more affirming view of staged photos, see Linfield, *Cruel Radiance*, 175–202, on Robert Capa.

77. See the discussion in Zelizer, *Remembering to Forget*, 86–140.

78. Roberts also insists that images that might have called out injustice are potentially alibis now for humanitarians. An image can make spectators cringe and turn away, but it can also make them feel good about feeling bad. Atrocity images are potentially radical because they defy "a culture where the representations of direct violence are constantly being dissolved into humanist empathy and human tragedy." Like Brink, but also like critics of humanitarianism, Roberts wants to understand under what conditions the radical potential of the photograph—its demand that viewers do something—might be domesticated, and how it might provoke spectators to transform feeling empathy into acting responsibly. Roberts suggests a theoretical solution—"a third dialectical move" by which spectators "*return* to the image as a critical assimilation of the perceived suffering . . . as an act of *imaginative reconstruction*." But Roberts pushes any resolution into the future: such imaginative reconstruction cannot be accomplished under current regimes of imperialism and neoliberalism, which he argues makes viewers inevitably cringe or feel pity. Roberts, *Photography and Its Violations* (New York: Columbia University Press, 2014), 150, 163 (emphasis in the original).

photographs create conditions for a political will to dignity. Yet over and over, the spectator of atrocity photographs tries desperately to repair and stabilize a fraught relationship with the image, condemning or repeating the image's destabilizing effects without altering the terms of discussion. Is it good or bad? What should we do? Or "yes, but," as Sontag finally concluded.[79] Atrocity images transform spectators into witnesses who perpetrate violence they wish to stop, compromising spectators' integrity so powerfully that it is hard to say how images contribute to political or moral mobilization other than by the haunting effects Sontag denied could be transformative.[80]

Atrocity photography is one more cultural arena in which activists locate suffering victims to whose injuries we must attest and whose tormentors we wish to hold accountable; the vast circulation of atrocity images generates a symbolic victim on whose behalf activists combat human rights violations the world over. Yet the consensus that images of wounded or dead victims can be sources of moral authority and spurs to action also holds that they can be false idols. Spectators speak on behalf of victims but are also agents of victims' further (now symbolic) humiliation. Activists are self-consciously ambivalent, aware of their own potential to undermine the solidarity they aim to generate, but they also struggle to inhabit the images' revelations, to hear victims' voices, to bring them into being and defend them from becoming potential objects of others' pleasure or horror.[81]

I conclude this section by focusing on two very different accounts of Holocaust atrocity photos to reveal how, by addressing in an extended manner the relationship between the image and the spectator, each fashions a counterwitness as an antidote

79. Sontag, *Regarding*. Susie Linfield writes that looking at photographs of suffering can demonstrate "what happens to a society that loses sight of dignity as an organizing principle," and attributes the impact of images to the continued power of photographic realism over and against critics like Sontag. Linfield, *Cruel Radiance*, 102.

80. Some discussions address this issue by linking photographs and political recognition in a variety of ways. Robert Hariman and John Louis Lucaites, eds., *No Caption Needed: Iconic Photographs, Public Culture, and Liberal Democracy* (Chicago: University of Chicago Press, 2007) trace the instrumental methods by which Western media shape responses to distant others—making them recognizable to "us." Sliwinski, *Human Rights in the Camera's Eye*, argues that photographs make human rights claims by reference to a Kantian aesthetic tradition that calls on viewers' faculties of judgment. Their arguments rely on political instrumentality or philosophical concepts to link images and their effects.

81. Georges Didi-Huberman's criticism of Claude Lanzmann's iconoclasm suggests that we approach atrocity images "in spite of all" we know about their imperfection; they can never reveal all, but operate at once as veil and rupture, "fetish and fact," covering up and showing through a "tear" in the image that provokes new ways of seeing and knowing. Didi-Huberman, *Images in Spite of All*, 79–80, 85–88. He notes that Sontag interpreted her famous encounter with photographs of Holocaust atrocities as "a negative epiphany" (83–84).

to the spectator's passivity and voyeurism. The accounts are not identical, and yet they share similar features that suggest that one might tease broader cultural meanings out of the responses such images elicit. They do not try to ensure that images will not degrade their subjects or that the work of making suffering visible in some instances justifies the degradation. Instead, victims appear refashioned as counterwitness figures who refuse to let onlookers off easily or to appease their anxiety.

Documentary photographer Janina Struk's *Photographing the Holocaust* (2004) identifies locations and persons in anonymously taken snapshots of mass murder.[82] She is on guard against Holocaust deniers who exploit a belief in the evidentiary status of photographs to use errors of designation or editing to claim that the Holocaust has been exaggerated or did not happen.[83] Hers is a work of painstaking contextualization that embarks on a familiar and crucial mission to protect atrocity images from distortion by getting their provenance right.

The book begins with a detailed discussion of a devastating image of Jewish men and a boy about to be executed in Sniatyń, Poland, in May 1943. Struk expresses mixed feelings about the purpose of the picture and confesses to voyeurism in observing it. In her own eyes, she feels complicit with the photographer, whose angle of vision meant that he was among or known to the perpetrators. "But I was compelled to look," she states, "as if the more I looked, the more information I could gain."[84] As the book goes on and she gleans more information, she grows wearier of the voyeurism, complicity, and potential malleability of the images. At the very end, referring to a famous image of a woman and children walking to the gas chambers at Birkenau, posted for tourists on the path they once actually walked, she makes an iconoclastic plea that victims be left alone by the camera: "Whoever they were, they have been condemned to tread the path [into Birkenau] forever. Returning their image to Birkenau may be their final humiliation. They had no choice but to be photographed. Now they have no choice but to be viewed by posterity. Didn't they suffer enough the first time around?"[85]

---

82. Janina Struk, *Photographing the Holocaust: Interpretations of the Evidence* (London: I.B. Tauris, 2004).

83. For a powerful example of how minor mistakes can have an enormous impact on the willingness to believe, see the catalog of an exhibit that contested the myth of the German Wehrmacht as a "clean" army not complicit in crimes against Jews. The exhibit closed because of a few inaccurately designated photographs out of hundreds. See Hamburg Institute for Social Research, *Crimes of the German Wehrmacht: Dimensions of a War of Annihilation 1941–1944*, English edition by Paula Bradish (Hamburg: Hamburger Edition, 2004), 36.

84. Struk, *Photographing the Holocaust*, 3.

85. Struk, *Photographing the Holocaust*, 216. Sybil Milton shares this view in "The Camera as Weapon: Documentary Photography and the Holocaust," *Simon Wiesenthal Center Annual* 1 (1984): 49.

For Struk, such pictures perpetuate victims' suffering by mechanically reproducing their last moments or deaths. To make the point more salient, she argues that she sees little difference between one set of atrocity photographs and others of similar content, even if the photographers had different intentions in mind. She argues in frustration that pictures the Nazis took of dead Jews in the Warsaw ghetto, their bodies in piles awaiting burial, are barely discernible from those taken by the Allied troops who liberated Buchenwald and Dachau. The photo albums surreptitiously kept by German soldiers and SS, she claims, are similar to those kept by tourists taking pictures at Auschwitz-Birkenau. There is also little difference between the effects of photos of suffering taken for entertainment by Nazis and those provided for consumption on the Internet, accompanied by ads. Images conjure up and become indistinguishable from the violence of other images. "As visitors gasp with horror at the way victims were photographed, they photograph them again. Why photograph an atrocity photograph?"[86]

Struk notes that of course cameras put distance between photographer and subject, and that snapping pictures gives shape to the tourist's experience. The camera's distance makes picture taking bearable, but that distance, as critics of photographs' spectacular or kitschy effects argue, also turns subjects into sources of entertainment. Her argument for restricting photography to its evidentiary value thus ends up denouncing the instrument that provides the evidence. As one image flows into another image taken at another time often far removed, the camera not only records the doomed, but is also a harbinger of more doom, as if anyone taking pictures brings about one more version of the same catastrophe. Struk supplies historical information about specific images of people who died in the Holocaust to ensure their accuracy, but she also brings the dead to life, conveying the photographed people's (presumed) desire to be left alone. Her discussion, as so many discussions about atrocity photography, is finally about how to develop proper burial rites for those long dead.[87]

Why photograph an atrocity photograph? The relationship between Struk's principled motive for working with the images and the effects of the photographs is a spiral of ever-intensifying voyeurism, complicity, and violence that shatters the integrity she seeks desperately to preserve—her own and that of the image. Her unremittingly violent view of the camera's potential leads to iconoclastic

86. Struk, *Photographing the Holocaust*, 190.
87. In "Phantom Geographies: An Alternative History of Holocaust Consciousness" (PhD diss., Yale University, 2019), Kathryn L. Brackney analyzes Claude Lanzmann's *Shoah* as an elaborate and visually poetic metaphorical burial rite that was part of a broader cultural project of regulating proximity to victims and the remains of the past.

anger, for the victims pay the price for the information gleaned by their repeated symbolic degradation.

All Struk's efforts to bury the dead properly, identifying who they are and where they died, are also sabotaged by the living dead in the images; they compel her to look, they need the protection she could not have offered, and they are infinitely vulnerable. The person whose professional task it is to look at the photographs cannot bear the melancholy attachment to the dead the photographs sustain, and displaces her feelings about victims' helplessness onto an argument about how they should not be looked at. Her anxious iconoclasm is also a profound expression of hopelessness: we are too late.

Although Struk's wish to have protected and to protect victims from harm takes the form of a desire to shield them from prying eyes, she also reproduces images of victims, leaving readers to grapple with the paradoxical nature of her dilemma. Her iconoclasm is a symptom of an attachment to powerless victims who were never properly—literally or symbolically—buried. Refusing to look, she seems to suggest, is as problematic as a prurient spectator's gaze because it abandons the victims to their dreary fate. Indeed, the cover picture of the book, a photo of Jews in the Warsaw ghetto taken by a German photographer, shows a somewhat disheveled but upright man who stares directly into the camera. Behind him is a young and smooth-skinned older boy, perhaps his son, whose eyes are softer. The man's frontal gaze is haunting, "miles away from crying," and defies posterity to respond (figure 4.2).[88] By choosing this image for the cover Struk seems to be imploring readers to ask themselves how we should respond to the photograph that is likely all that is left of these men and those around them. More important, by placing so prominently the man's defiant, weary, inescapable despair—and thus the spectator's paralysis before a figure who knows he has been abandoned—Struk gives him the last word. In so doing, she also brings him back to life, perhaps because he proffers the illusion that he does not need to be spoken for.

In contrast to Struk, literary theorist Ulrich Baer denounces iconoclasm. But he builds an escape from the spectator's gaze into the very structure of the photograph. He analyzes photographs of everyday life in the Łódź ghetto taken by its resident SS accountant Walter Genewein between 1940 and 1944, as well as a 1998 documentary film about these photos, *The Photographer*, made by Polish filmmaker Dariusz Jabłoński. Historians, Baer argues, denounce photographs

88. This is Harry Mulisch's description of Ruzka Korshak, survivor of the Vilna ghetto uprising, in Mulisch, *Criminal Case 40/61: The Trial of Adolf Eichmann*, trans. Robert Naborn (Philadelphia: University of Pennsylvania Press, 2005), 40–41.

FIGURE 4.2 / A group of Jews on a street in the Warsaw ghetto doff their hats to the German photographer, 1941.

Photograph by Willy Georg. United States Holocaust Memorial Museum, courtesy of Rafael Scharf.

taken by perpetrators as implicitly reflecting Nazi perspectives on Jews. He claims instead that photographs resist spectators' all-encompassing gazes because they have a "structural affinity" with trauma. Images, that is, dissociate persons photographed from their conscious selves. Like trauma symptoms, which often emerge long after an event and whose causal relationship to that event is often difficult to discern, the photograph's subjects are inaccessible and unknowable no matter how present they seem to be.[89]

Baer dismisses anxieties about sharing the potential viewpoint of Nazis or the prurience of spectators as a form of "phobic repression" by people uncomfortable with images of suffering and pain, denouncing "the rush of moral indignation that often accompanies the encounter with graphic pictures of atrocities, [which] may be narcissistically satisfying, but . . . may also free us from the responsibility of placing our own experiences in relation to something that remains, finally, incomprehensible" (84). When spectators empathize with images, they appropriate and consume them. This empathic identification has an affinity, he claims, with the "Nazi gaze":

> If, however, that technical dimension records in these photographs something that might be saved from the Nazi gaze, it also undercuts our facile identification with the "humanity" portrayed in them. Such an identification can be achieved only at the risk of hitching the photograph's visual field onto a single viewpoint drenched in empathy. As we have seen . . . the empathic, identificatory perspective favored by some critics remains tied to the seductive myth of a viewer's self-aware, unified, and all-encompassing nonalienated gaze. The notion of such a gaze is itself part of the legacy of the Nazi worldview. (177)

In this passage Baer assimilates the empathic gaze to Nazism and conflates empathy with identification. The argument is obviously hyperbolic unless we are prepared to associate all contemporary humanitarianism with the legacy of Nazism and all moral feeling with narcissistic identification. But Baer's imaginative reading of how the victim evades the spectator's gaze is worth considering if we treat it less as a tenable analysis of the relationship between images and their audiences and more as a culturally salient response to the ethical dilemma images pose. In order to illustrate how the photograph is not merely traumatizing but structured

---

89. Ulrich Baer, *Spectral Evidence: The Photography of Trauma* (Cambridge, MA: MIT Press, 2005), 12. He speaks of the dissociative moment as contemporaneous with the camera's flash, presumably to conjure the image of a post-traumatic flashback. Further citations from this book appear in parentheses in the text.

by trauma, he examines Jabłoński's film, which focuses on a photograph of a Jewish man in a ghetto barbershop as he looks directly into the camera. The man is frozen, but the camera zooms in so that he fills the screen in a close-up shot that is dissolved, evading symbolic representation and the spectator's gaze. The dissolved face, Baer says, points to an unknowable beyond in which the viewer will be forced to reflect about this man without knowing who he was.[90] Most important, when the Jewish victim does appear, "the film does not invite viewers to identify with the Jew in the picture. . . . Instead they are made to feel addressed, and the right to appeal, to look back, to accuse or to denounce is restored to the Jew who was captured, framed, and labeled by the Nazi photographer" (156). Baer says that although "the Jews caught on film by the camera-wielding Nazi could rarely evade his probing lens, many of them did stare back" (169). In so doing a young boy in one instance "deflects his objectification and implicit subordination" (166).

The man living in the ghetto, Baer insists, defies spectators' gazes not only because he "looks back" but because he exceeds the camera's frame. For Baer, the photograph's referent is not the victim's trauma, but the belatedness of the traumatic wound. The image evades the spectator's objectification because it is both the photographic representation of a victim and a metaphor of what the image cannot show; the victim haunts, is present, and yet entirely inaccessible to the spectator. The victim does not show us his pain and we do not feel his pain except as our own failure to grasp it. Baer's effort to shield victims both from overexposure and "phobic repression" transforms the victim into a figure who stares back and always escapes the spectator's own look. The victim is cast as a defiant and yet fragile man immunized against both objectification and consumption.

These arguments constitute and recount a dilemma posed not only by photography, whose dual role as referent and simulacrum has caused havoc since its invention, but also by a historical and cultural moment in which photography turns all people potentially into witnesses—images are mobile, easily accessible, and circulate everywhere. The testimony of activists using photography—like that of lawyers or humanitarians—supplements victims' own testimony and transforms images into vehicles of human solidarity.[91] This time activists speak

---

90. The close-up exceeds the screen and thus defies the film's effort to maintain the illusion of narrative control. Baer does not comment on the difference between photography and film, and yet their effects are very different, particularly with regard to their relationship to time. Mary Ann Doane, "The Close-Up: Scale and Detail in the Cinema," *differences: A Journal of Feminist Cultural Studies* 14, no. 3 (2003): 89–111. See also Leo Bersani and Ulysee Dutoit, *Forms of Being: Cinema, Aesthetics, Subjectivity* (London: British Film Institute, 2004), 48–52.

91. Georges Didi-Huberman, *Sortir du noir* (Paris: Éditions de Minuit, 2015), 18, speaks of how images taken by *Sonderkommando* members at Auschwitz and scenes in the 2015 Hungarian film *Son of Saul* by László Nemes about a man working in a *Sonderkommando* offer "testimony of light"

on behalf of a symbolic victim, and their task is not to establish the truth, but somehow to curate, manage, and mobilize the shocking "truth" of the image on behalf of a more just present and future. Their supplementary testimonial role is thus to lay ground rules for looking that can best sustain the integrity of victims who will die "for eternity." Baer and Struk make no attempt to answer conclusively whether the images violate dignity or not, but pose instead a number of questions about how to protect and properly represent the once tormented and dead victims who continue to live on in images. The photograph's continuous time is not only a moment of eternal dying or grief or denial, but also, in Struk, a time of recognition, loss, and unfinished mourning, and in Baer, a time of eternal trauma to which victims are condemned to protect them from a "Nazi gaze": victims are inaccessible to spectators who are left anxious and unknowing. Baer has no interest in the victim's integrity in the usual sense because he—quite problematically—rejects healing or dignity as complicit with humanist forms of empathy, locating the victim's escape route from sentimentalism and prurience in the "missed encounter" between his image and the spectator.

Of course, these discussions are about symbolic, no longer living victims, but they are not merely curatorial, not only concerned with whether we should look or not. Such discussions invoke a victim whose own needs and desires are projections of the spectator's own, whether they are German bystanders, well-intentioned activists, or moved curators and critics. At other times, activists' melancholic habitation of the image calls into being a figure whose vulnerability they cast as an accusation or an angry demand for protection from those for whom it was already too late. People in the images plead, and they are also imagined to be defiant. The image of the man who stares back appears regardless of the critic's method: Struk and Baer in particular could not have more divergent approaches to images. This figure emerges as a symbol of a victim who was not saved and can no longer be saved, but who proclaims that he has been unjustly abandoned and expects no justice. Like Fassin, these critics too generate a counterwitness, one whose silence confronts onlookers but also conveys fragility, and who, despairing, challenges those spectators to live up to their promises.

All three discussions about the cultural preeminence of victims that I have reviewed suggest that victims no longer have the metaphorical armor of wisdom and restored dignity once attributed, albeit belatedly, to the Holocaust witness.

(*témoignage de la lumière*) emerging from darkness. I take this claim to be indubitable and most powerful when we know that victims took the pictures.

These few glimpses of the counterwitness suggest that we have exited one "era of the witness" and are entering another in which the Holocaust survivor's embodiment of unfathomable suffering and wisdom has given way to new perceptions of mass violence and its victims. The hope represented by the survivor's bearing witness is being replaced slowly by the conviction that hope is cheap and that appeals to "never again" and "bearing witness" are sentimental evocations that mask the reality of seemingly inevitable genocides and equally inevitable indifference to or feigned concern about their victims. Activist witnesses who struggle to aid or bring justice to victims, or to reform institutions to better respond to victims' needs, are now caught up in narratives of complicity with those who harm, no matter their intentions. Such claims of complicity may be exaggerated regarding humanitarians on the ground or lawyers in the court, as it may be necessary for activists to write off some cooperation with perpetrators and their allies as the cost of doing business, or to insist, with Sontag, that the struggle against political and moral amnesia may demand that we look at atrocity photographs. Yet the consensus that activists may do as much harm as good, if only as a recognition of political realities and an effort to reassess old and try new strategies, emphasizes the vulnerability of victims, the inevitability of further genocides, the glacial pace with which help will arrive, and the possibility that it never will.

This altered political and cultural landscape has provoked a radical change in the image of witnesses. The global victim is a haunting reminder of the pervasiveness and inevitability of genocide and represents the recognition conferred now on millions of victims. Unlike the Holocaust survivor, the global victim possesses no reference to a particular event, history, or people and represents our generic moral obligation to prevent further harm. The global victim also evokes the limits of that obligation; politicians denounce victims' demands as generated by excessive Western idealism, as if they were expressions of the lot of humanity rather than legitimate pleas related to specific circumstances, and as if help were a pie that can be sliced into only so many pieces.

The transition from the Holocaust witness to the global victim marks an important cultural recognition accorded to victims other than Holocaust survivors that has also arguably stripped them, paradoxically, of the authority of their experience. This diminution occurs not only because of inevitable institutional failures, important as they are to identify. From a Western perspective, the global victim symbolizes so many victims' woes and such varied projections about them that it embodies only a generic recognition that no one should be targeted for murder and the conviction that human rights violations are always undeserved; it cannot generate a cultural consensus that victims are worthy of recognition based on a particular narrative of what they have suffered and survived. The global victim no longer has any wisdom to dispense, something important to teach us, or, as Primo Levi put it, any "prophetic ability." In a twenty-first-century context, the global victim at least represents an obligation to do something. And yet the waning of the Holocaust witness's authority suggests that the moral witness has once again become a dismayed spectator aghast at violations of human conscience.

This analysis shows that moral witnesses emerge in tandem with the violence they explain and condemn. The appearance of the global victim is related to the perception of permanent catastrophe and the realities of providing care and dispensing justice. The counterwitness calls out broken promises and takes a defiant stand, yet has little hope that justice will be done. The appearance of this imaginary counterwitness, however dimly, suggests that a new era calls for another reckoning.

CONCLUSION

Nothing perhaps distinguishes modern masses as radically from those of previous centuries as the loss of faith in a Last Judgment: the worst have lost their fear and the best have lost their hope.

—Hannah Arendt, *The Origins of Totalitarianism* (1951)

Since the interwar period, moral witnesses have given victims of mass murder and genocide a symbolic form and meaning. They have shaped, altered, and defined the offense caused by mass atrocities and genocide since the naturalizing terms of barbarism and horror became inadequate to describe state-sponsored murder and the cultural destruction it has wrought. Moral witnesses expressed the public's initial horror of mass atrocities, its struggle to comprehend genocidal crimes, and, more recently, its obligation to care for victims of such violence. They figured innocence and honor and, in so doing, demonstrated how representations of whose particular suffering stands in for universal human suffering change over time, defining which victims are and are not worthy.

Since witnesses are symbolic, they are made and easily unmade; the unmaking of the Holocaust witness was part of a new politics of suffering that emerged during the 1990s, defining a novel way, to paraphrase Didier Fassin, of understanding the world, including perceptions that violence has increased when the opposite may be true.[1] In accord with the administrative and political expansion of courts, humanitarian organizations, and cultural institutions (museums, educational ventures, the press, Internet and social media coverage) devoted to combating crimes against humanity and genocide, second- and third-party

---

1. Didier Fassin, *Humanitarian Reason: A Moral History of the Present*, trans. Rachel Gomme (Berkeley: University of California Press, 2012), 6. There are debates about whether violence is increasing or not, the arguments of which depend on different historical data and interpretations of violent phenomena. See Steven Pinker, *The Better Angels of Our Nature: The Decline of Violence in History and Its Causes* (London: Penguin, 2012).

witnesses supplemented survivor witnesses' testimonial roles. Their supplementary role recasts the witness as a symbolic global victim whose suffering authorizes the work of institutions and people who bear witness within ethical, political, and ideological infrastructures that now constrain what actual victims say, how they say it, and whether or not they can be heard. Activists' concerns about the limits of humanitarian and human rights aims, their political skepticism and sense of failure, appear in their images of a counterwitness whose features symbolize victims' dignity, despair, and betrayal. The problem confronting victims and their allies now is the discrepancy between a global commitment to salve their wounds and the realities of global violence, often abetted by states that proclaim their commitments to victims most loudly. Activists discerning how to salvage the agency of victims most effectively from institutions and activities devoted to ending genocides have focused above all on this discrepancy and its consequences. The counterwitness symbolizes the actual victims whom the International Criminal Court, in the eyes of its most vociferous critics, no longer takes into account, as well as those made voiceless by humanitarian administrations, and dead and dying others whose photographic images have become a source of deep ambivalence.

This conclusion ends but does not terminate the book's argument, which future studies can track, deepen, and expand. I have sought to make a case for the importance of the long view when analyzing changing constructions of local and global moral obligations to alleviate the pain of others. Here I offer a chronological and conceptual outline defining the incarnations of the witness to mass atrocities and genocide as those incarnations have evolved over the past century. Some of the witnesses' features overlap because each one represents a branch in an emerging family tree. I identify three broad phases from the interwar period to today:

> **1919 to 1950:** The witness to mass atrocities and genocide challenged centuries-long evocations of "human conscience" by so-called civilized nations denouncing barbarism elsewhere, such as William Gladstone's 1876 British broadside against nineteenth-century Ottoman massacres of Bulgarian Christians and the 1899 and 1907 Hague Conventions' recognition of "laws of humanity" in the context of imperialism and national sovereignty. The dismay of the distant and shocked "civilized" spectator was slowly replaced by the victim's experience, injuries, and knowledge of human cruelty; the haunted witness more than the dismayed spectator became the symbolic locus of human conscience; and the witness to genocide eventually overshadowed the war veteran's testimony against the horrors of combat. These developments were shaped by the particular

historical positions of witness and spectator. Under certain circumstances, enduring presumptions about the naturalness of catastrophe in some regions or the foreignness of others were questioned if not overcome, as happened in the cases of Soghomon Tehlirian and Scholem Schwarzbard, whose humanity was defined by incorporating them into a restricted and imperial concept of civilization.

1950 to 1990: An old figure of protest against religious persecution and injustice, the witness now denounced genocide, becoming eventually an icon of universal human suffering. Witnesses to genocide came to symbolize a secular model of social solidarity based not only on appeals to sympathy for their plight, or on testimonies against war delivered by soldiers morally bound by comrades and country to expose war's brutalities. Survivors became a new type of victim by virtue of having survived genocide; their suffering was distinct from those who suffered and died in conventional wars, and their experience recast the meaning of survival itself. The witness to genocide urged publics to recognize an ostensibly new kind of crime, genocide, described by survivors who had undergone an unfathomable experience that included not only physical but also cultural death. By bringing their experience into being, survivors cast their suffering as a dramatic caesura between a familiar, naturalized world of death and dying and another world of planned and targeted murder in Soviet and especially Nazi camps; by bearing witness survivors testified to the destruction of the concept of humanity and redeemed it at once. The belated recognition of Holocaust witnesses was accomplished only by the redemption of Jewish victims and their incorporation into universal suffering humanity. By the 1970s, Jewish survivors no longer represented only a humanistic message about fighting tyranny of all sorts, but also became icons: they were figures of dark knowledge and stand-ins for all of human suffering.

1990 to the present: the Holocaust witness's moral authority was slowly recast in the image of a universal victim that accompanied new, global institutions for the protection of human rights. The global victim, an abstract, postcolonial, infinitely malleable image of victims everywhere whose needs and wants activists invoke, represents the perception of genocide as an intractable, constitutive feature of the political landscape whose violence knows no bounds. It unites the universalizing and particularizing poles of Holocaust remembrance—the genocide was a crime against humanity and also a crime against Jews—by making all people a potential target of violence and by authorizing the institutions that work for victims to be global humanity's representatives. The victim's testimonial role is now supplemented by activists who work as witnesses to ensure restorative justice and healing, as well as to create a future in which no suffering would occur.

In the wake of the challenges and failures of global governance, the counterwitness, the symbol of a global victim who testifies to institutional failure rather than success, is yet one more possible iteration of the witness to genocide. Its emergence is commensurate with the present historical and cultural moment and thus with current projections, anxieties, and concerns of those who advocate for victims. To the extent that there is finally a consensus about the wrongness of colonial crimes—though not, in the West, about more recent imperial adventures—it is embodied by the global victim, permeated by a Western perspective that either not enough or perhaps too much is being done for a seemingly endless number of victims.[2] That consensus is also compromised by the unevenness of geopolitical power manifest in the discrepancy between human rights rhetoric and the reality of institutional practices.

Each chapter in the book has explored in more detail the various figures of the witness that have populated the Western cultural landscape over the past hundred years:

The avengers (1921 to 1950): Europeans waged wars in defense of "civilization" against barbarism. Narratives of patriotic glory, heroism, and sacrifice renewed and repaired violations of national dignity. Witnesses represented specific mass atrocities elsewhere, particularly those committed against peoples outside of conventional or colonial warfare, not only as regrettable instances of barbarism but also as forms of injustice. A close reading of the trials of Soghomon Tehlirian (1921) and Scholem Schwarzbard (1927) demonstrates that to ensure acquittal, lawyers refashioned vigilante justice as a patriotic war in defense of civilization. When courts took the experience of the witnesses into account—the "unimaginable" and "shocking" violations to which they had been subjected—regrettable crimes against innocents demanded not only dismay about extreme violence elsewhere but also "humanitarian" justice.

The trials recast the defendants as righteous avengers and transfigured their crimes. The defense lawyers' strategies—the subject of Raphael

---

2. On the media's representation of nonwhite victims of catastrophe, see Jonathan Benthall, *Disasters, Relief and the Media* (London: I.B. Tauris, 1993), 187–216.

Lemkin's reference to ingenious lawyers—demonstrate the challenge posed by these initial efforts to make sense of and judge rather than only to naturalize and lament genocidal crimes and the behavior of their victims. Because the defendants were vigilantes, not soldiers, lawyers had to extend the mantle of civilization rhetorically to men whose people were "nations" in name only and whose persecution was unremarkable if regrettable because they were Armenians or (Ashkenazi) Jews, and of "Eastern" parentage. The challenge confronting the courts was how to define the specific kind of violation of humanity and human conscience at hand and how to adjudicate these crimes in the absence of an established legal framework to prosecute them.

The camp survivor (1950 to 1961): After World War Two, witnesses, though infused with patriotism, increasingly identified "humanity" outside of the framework of patriotic nationalism. This identification was also rooted deeply in visions of international social justice, not only through bonds uniting a fraternity of workers, soldiers, or supporters of democracy across national borders. This identification with universal humanity beyond the nation-state now also derived its particular expression from an experience of human degradation—Nazi and Soviet concentration camps—that linked witnesses both to the nation for which they fought, and also to an international brotherhood of other nationalities who had undergone a similar ordeal. The French writer David Rousset's recasting of Soviet and Nazi concentration camp survivors as moral witnesses vested them with special knowledge about human degradation. Victor Kravchenko's 1949 libel suit had paved the way for Rousset to make this witness come alive in his 1950–51 trial.

Camp survivors who became witnesses borrowed from the veteran whose combat experience was a revelation about the tragedy of war, but represented a concept of suffering humanity whose revelations came from another experience of extreme degradation and near annihilation. Survivors' testimonies were about the senselessness of war and persecution, but more, they articulated the special violation of humanity represented by the camps. Their knowledge emerged in the course of surviving persecution that gave them a cause to fight for, one that usurped previous commitments grand or small. Survivors lived to "bear witness." Rousset believed that they possessed a new and unique understanding of the most dramatic challenge confronting human existence.

The Holocaust witness (1961 to 1990): The 1961–62 Jerusalem trial of Adolf Eichmann rehumanized and repaired Jewish witnesses to genocide, restoring their human dignity by clarifying the circumstances of their suffering. The trial cast victims who were initially shamed for not having resisted persecution as innocent and without shame. But in order to describe survivors' burden and the torment to which they had been subjected, trial commentary also constituted an image of the survivor as a living witness to mass death not only literally but also symbolically: survivors dwelled in the world of the dead and were bound in life by their fealty to the dead. These witnesses, like Rousset's concentration camp survivors, had lived through an experience impossible to transmit, and their suffering was emotionally and conceptually distinct from the experience of combat. Unlike Rousset's camp survivors, however, Holocaust survivors' worthiness did not inhere in their past history as combatants who had struggled against injustice and therefore had special license to speak. In a radical reversal of received wisdom about victims whose mere survival had had no meaning, the Holocaust survivor's living death now conveyed a message not only about the necessity of resisting tyranny, but also about the life-long effects of extreme terror and vulnerability.

By the 1970s, as part of the legacy of the Eichmann trial, another narrative emerged in which survival conferred dark knowledge. The ghost-like appearance of life in death that made sense of and symbolized the burden of Jewish survival now conveyed the ubiquity of mass murder in the twentieth century. Surviving genocide alone was a source of revelation, and imbued the survivor with a wretched dignity commensurate with the knowledge that tragic heroism was irrelevant to the struggle against genocide. The moral authority of the witness not only gave pleas for compassion and justice their force, but also rendered bearing witness to genocide a prophetic, modern form of combat suited to our time. The experience of the Holocaust, and of Jews in particular, became paradigmatic; its exemplary status linked suffering humanity symbolically to genocide rather than to other forms of suffering and injustice.

The Holocaust witness became an object of moral consensus because there was general agreement that genocide represented violence that could not be justified under any circumstances. This consensus formed by the 1970s not only because of our current assumption that human rights violations are always undeserved, but also because Jewish victims were rendered blameless. The murdered victims facilitated Western soul-searching about the violence because they were people to whom Europeans felt accountable. The Holocaust witness became a projection of

Western self-regard, a reminder both of Western murderousness and Western willingness to take responsibility for crimes perpetrated in Europe. The witness to genocide became a symbol of Western moral conscience.

The global victim and the counterwitness (1990 to the present): The witness now represents a world of seemingly intractable violence and an ethical and political commitment to remedy the consequences. The witness to genocide has become a global victim whose symbolic power authorizes second- or third-party witnesses to supplement his or her testimony. The global victim sanctions activists who participate in the expanding infrastructure of global governance and who maintain the cultural pedagogy that is part and parcel of a sustained commitment to human rights. These developments—the emergence of the global victim and the work of activists—are entirely interdependent, related both to the perceived pervasiveness and increased unacceptability of mass violence and the expansion of institutions with missions to address victims' suffering. Like the Holocaust survivor witness whose symbolic incarnation was a composite of perceptions of survivors, the global victim stands in for victims of genocidal crimes but is no longer attached to specific victims and the experience they had undergone. The global victim is a rhetorical figure with no distinctive features, characterized by a generic helplessness.

The appearance of the global victim constitutes the point of departure for broad criticism of how legal, humanitarian, and cultural institutions treat actual victims, including assertions that all persons are now potential victims. For all of their differences, the critiques on which I have drawn offer a remarkably consistent account of the centrality of the global victim and his or her suffering in late twentieth- and early twenty-first-century Western culture. This criticism of what we might call institutional forms of witnessing interprets the global victim as a symbolic alibi. The global victim's indistinct features also suggest that the particular characteristics of colonial genocides—the murderous racism, exploitation, and destruction of peoples built into the expansion of imperial power—seem to have been erased as the price of their recognition.[3] Critics seek to make

---

3. In the absence of clear symbolic features, the global victim may even be a former perpetrator who now claims to be a victim of his own conscience, traumatized by his own actions. We might note in this regard, though it was not integral to my discussion because too far afield, that the global victim's pervasive presence also coincides with the increasingly invisible distinction between conventional warfare and the violence of counterinsurgency waged by Western powers against their perceived enemies. Indeed, the clarity of the boundary between perpetrators and victims was itself muddied as the clear symbolic distinction between legitimate combat and mass killing constituted

178 / CONCLUSION

victims more tangible, to avoid transforming them into objects of pity, and to protect them from additional trauma, whether real (after testifying in court or being denied the authority of their experience by humanitarians) or imaginary (as in atrocity photography). The counterwitness they generate calls out our inadequate care for victims, and the complicity of our institutions in their suffering. His or her silent reproach represents an institutional and a cultural overemphasis on victimization that takes the form of cheap sentimentality and new and fluid forms of state power. The counterwitness symbolizes a historically new moral obligation to fight genocide and mass violence that is global in reach but so hampered by moral and political dilemmas that activists' advocacy on victims' behalf is often in tension with the principles the activists pursue.

In the absence of a moral witness tied to a specific event or place, today the Holocaust witness remains the predominant reference and a point of comparison when genocidal violence is imagined and conveyed. It persists as an icon even as the Holocaust is known to be one among many other genocides. Its continued symbolic power indicates the power of the imaginary, historical, and institutional constraints that define the meaning of suffering and the traits of the sufferer, and suggests that Western moral conscience does not recognize itself as implicated in the global victim's suffering, for all of its purported rhetorical power. Indeed, the invocation of the Holocaust witness as often as the global victim to summon states and the international community to invest resources or to act boldly has turned the Holocaust into an explanation for the recognition of some crimes and the forgetting or marginalization of others, past and present. This rhetorical use of the Holocaust surely reflects the absence of a deep Western moral consensus about victims other than Holocaust survivors, whose experience ultimately embodied Western moral conscience.[4] After all, as one scholar has argued, how can it be that the death of nearly one million Rwandans is not enough to dislodge

---

by the witness to genocide eroded. This erosion may be as powerful an explanation of perpetrator trauma—that perpetrators suffer from war-induced PTSD—as the diffusion of the PTSD diagnosis itself.

4. In *Multidirectional Memory: Remembering the Holocaust in an Age of Globalization* (Stanford: Stanford University Press, 2009), Michael Rothberg nuances this view by insisting on the fluidity of Holocaust memory. Like Rothberg, I assume that Holocaust memory is a fluid, historical construct. Unlike him, I am interested in how its universality was constituted as such.

the invocation of Auschwitz to describe the genocide in Rwanda?[5] The global victim is less an embodiment of moral conscience in the West than it is a symbol of an entirely new responsibility for victims that cannot live up to its own promises and is still embedded in colonial and postcolonial frameworks.

The righteous avenger, the concentration camp survivor, the Holocaust witness, and the global victim and counterwitness emerged and changed commensurate with perceptions of genocide and its affront to humanity in the course of the last hundred years. Perhaps the counterwitness will soon represent victims of failed global justice. Or perhaps another witness will emerge entirely, one who will generate a universal moral consensus around crimes that have never been fully recognized or which have not yet been imagined.

---

5. Małgorzata Wosińska, "Murami Is Not Auschwitz: The Holocaust in Representations of the Rwandan Genocide," in *Replicating Atonement: Foreign Models in Commemoration of Atrocities*, ed. Mischa Gabowitsch (New York: Palgrave Macmillan, 2017), 187–208. Wosińska also argues that invoking the Holocaust may serve to distance Rwandans from the genocide that still marks the nation's politics and landscape.

ACKNOWLEDGMENTS

This book has been a work in progress for a long while. I thank various audiences—in the US, at Amherst College, the City College of New York, Cornell University, Dartmouth College, the New School, the Shelby Cullom Davis Center at Princeton University, Rutgers University–New Brunswick, the University of Massachusetts Amherst, the University of Minnesota, Wesleyan University, and those colleagues who participated in Yale's Modern European History Colloquium. Abroad, thanks go to audiences at the American University of Paris, Birkbeck College, the Institute of Literary Research of the Polish Academy of Science, Linnaeus University, the Vienna Wiesenthal Institute for Holocaust Studies, the University of Basel, and the University of Vienna. Thanks especially to Philip Nord and Hendrick Hartog for indispensable feedback at an early stage of the project.

Other interlocutors have been essential at different stages. Martin Jay's probing questions made me go back to the drawing board. Dominick LaCapra applied his usual rigor to the text and was unfailingly generous. Samuel Moyn read the manuscript carefully and provided incisive feedback, as did an anonymous reader for the press. Sam is also the source of many references for the last chapter. Laurie Bernstein generously took on the task of editing the work and forced me to clarify my thoughts. For other readings, insights, invitations, references, and friendship, not necessarily in that order, I thank Peter Becker, Kathy Brown, Rosie Bsheer, Cathy Caruth, Bruno Chaouat, Rohit De, Federico Finchelstein, Amrita Ghosh, Amos Goldberg, Peter Gordon, Johan Höglund, Lynn Hunt, Alice Kaplan, Andreas Killen, Ethan Kleinberg, Éva Kovacs, Lawrence Kritzman, Emma Kuby, Sabina Loriga, Hannah Pollin-Galay, Bélá Rasky, Camille Robcis, Sophia Rosenfeld, Michael Roth, Joanne Rudoff, Maurice Samuels, Austin Sarat, Brian Schiff, Gary Shaw, Miranda Spieler, Adam Stern, Ron Suny, Judith Surkis, Khachig Tölölyan, and Kari Weil.

At the press, Liz Anker generously took the book on, Diane Berrett Brown helped with all the various stages until the end, including formulating a title, and Jennifer Dana Savran Kelly and Sheila Marie Flaherty managed the rest. Yale graduate students, including Kathryn Brackney, Heather Horn, Charlotte

Kiechel, and Margaret Traylor, have been essential fellow travelers, readers, and research assistants. Kathyrn Brackney also edited a first draft of the manuscript. I have relied on their creativity and resources for ideas, references, critical readings, intellectual energy, and fun. I also want to thank family and friends in Italy and France, especially Isabelle Lauze and Claire Lissalde. A special thank you to Cathy Caruth, Ellen Rooney, Kach Tölölyan, Laurie Bernstein, and Bob Weinberg.

For all other things vital to life, intellectual and not, thanks to Francesca Trivellato. This book is for her and in memory of Harriet Katzman Dean.

INDEX

Note: Page numbers in *italics* indicate illustrations.

www.ingramcontent.com/pod-product-compliance
Lightning Source LLC
Chambersburg PA
CBHW030332270326
41926CB00010B/1588